Essential ColdFusion 4.5 for Web Professionals

ISBN 0-13-040646-5

The Prentice Hall Essential Web Professionals Series

- *Essential ColdFusion 4.5 for Web Professionals*
  Micah Brown and Mike Fredrick

- *Essential Design for Web Professionals*
  Charles Lyons

- *Essential Flash™ 5 for Web Professionals*
  Lynn Kyle

- *Essential Flash™ 4 for Web Professionals*
  Lynn Kyle

- *Essential ASP for Web Professionals*
  Elijah Lovejoy

- *Essential PHP for Web Professionals*
  Christopher Cosentino

- *Essential CSS & DHTML for Web Professionals*
  Dan Livingston and Micah Brown

- *Essential JavaScript™ for Web Professionals*
  Dan Barrett, Dan Livingston, and Micah Brown

- *Essential Perl 5 for Web Professionals*
  Micah Brown, Chris Bellow, and Dan Livingston

- *Essential Photoshop® 5 for Web Professionals*
  Brad Eigen, Dan Livingston, and Micah Brown

Essential ColdFusion 4.5 for Web Professionals

Micah Brown
Mike Fredrick

Prentice Hall PTR
Upper Saddle River, NJ 07458
www.phptr.com

Library of Congress Cataloging-in-Publication Data

CIP Data available

Editorial/Production Supervision: Mary Sudul
Acquisitions Editor: Karen McLean
Marketing Manager: Kate Hargett
Manufacturing Manager: Alexis Heydt
Cover Design: Design Source
Interior Design Director: Gail Cocker-Bogusz
Series Design: Patti Guerrieri

© 2001 Prentice Hall PTR
Prentice-Hall, Inc.
Upper Saddle River, NJ 07458

Prentice Hall books are widely used by corporations and government agencies for training, marketing, and resale.

The publisher offers discounts on this book when ordered in bulk quantities. For more information, contact: Corporate Sales Department, Phone: 800-382-3419; Fax: 201-236-7141; E-mail: corpsales@prenhall.com; or write: Prentice Hall PTR, Corp. Sales Dept., One Lake Street, Upper Saddle River, NJ 07458.

All rights reserved. No part of this book may be reproduced, in any form or by any means, without permission in writing from the publisher.

Phone.com and UP.SDK are trademarks of Phone.com, Inc.
Palm OS is a registered trademark, and Palm is a trademark of Palm Inc.

Printed in the United States of America

10 9 8 7 6 5 4 3 2 1

ISBN 0-13-040646-5

Prentice-Hall International (UK) Limited, *London*
Prentice-Hall of Australia Pty. Limited, *Sydney*
Prentice-Hall Canada Inc., *Toronto*
Prentice-Hall Hispanoamericana, S.A., *Mexico*
Prentice-Hall of India Private Limited, *New Delhi*
Prentice-Hall of Japan, Inc., *Tokyo*
Prentice Hall (Singapore) P.T.E., Ltd.
Editora Prentice-Hall do Brasil, Ltda., *Rio de Janeiro*

Contents

Introduction xi

Chapter 1 Database Basics 1
    A Look at Relational Databases 2
    Introduction to SQL 5
    To Quote or Not to Quote? 7
    Project I: Creating an Access Database File 8
    Setting Up an ODBC Connection 10
        Windows Control Panel 10
        ColdFusion Administrator 12
    Project II: Retrieving Data 16
    SQL Builder 21
    Recap 23

Chapter 2 ColdFusion Basics 25
    Commenting Your Code 26
    Using Quotes 26
        <CFPARAM> 27
    Passing Variables 28

VARIABLES 29
URL 30
FORM 30
COOKIE 30
ATTRIBUTES 30
SESSION 31
CGI 31
APPLICATION 31
CLIENT 31
SERVER 31

Scope 31

Project I: Passing Variables Between Pages 32
<CFIF></CFIF> 35
<CFELSE> 37
<CFELSEIF> 39
Now Function 39
Date Functions 40
DateFormat 40
TimeFormat 42

Project II: Display Days Left Until a User-Defined Date 43
DateDiff 43
IsDefined 43
Replace 44

Project III: Using <CFLOOP> 46

Recap 49

Advanced Project 50

Chapter 3 Global Templates 51

Defining the Application File (application.cfm) 52
<CFAPPLICATION> 53
<CFERROR> 55

Project I: Setting Global Values for Your Site 57

Project II: Defining Header and Footer Files 58
<CFINCLUDE> 58

Recap 63

Advanced Project 63

Chapter 4   Building an Online Catalog   65
   Building an Administration Screen   66
   Setting Up the Administration Screen   67
   Project I: Viewing Items in Your Database   68
      DollarFormat Function   69
      CurrentRow   70
      MOD   71
      IIF   72
      RecordCount   74
   Project II: Uploading Files to Your Site   75
      <CFFILE>   75
      <CFDIRECTORY>   79
   Project III: Adding Records to Your Database   82
   Project IV: Editing an Existing Record in Your Database   86
   Project V: Processing the Information   90
      Adding a Record   91
      <CFINSERT>   91
      Updating a Record   93
      <CFUPDATE>   93
      Deleting a Record   95
   Project VI: User Pages   96
   Recap   103
   Advanced Project   103

Chapter 5   Sending Email   105
   <CFMAIL>   106
   <CFFORM>   109
   <CFINPUT>   110
      <CFSWITCH> <CFCASE> and <CFDEFAULTCASE> Tags   111
   Project I: Sign Up!   112
   <CFPOP>   117
   Project II: Retrieving Your Email from a POP Server   118
   Recap   121
   Advanced Project   121

Chapter 6	Searching the Site 123	
	PreserveSingleQuotes 124	
	<CFTABLE> and <CFCOL> 124	
	<CFTABLE> 125	
	<CFCOL> 125	
	Project I: Search Engines 'R' Us 126	
	Using Verity with ColdFusion 130	
	<CFCOLLECTION> 130	
	<CFINDEX> 131	
	<CFSELECT> 133	
	Project II: Collection Management 134	
	Project III: Searching with Verity 137	
	<CFSEARCH> 138	
	Recap 142	
	Advanced Project 142	
Chapter 7	Knowing Who's Who 143	
	Security Basics 143	
	Project I: Protect Your Management Templates 144	
	Adding a Table to the shelleyCatalog Database 144	
	C Is for Cookie 148	
	Project II: Enhanced Functionality with <CFCOOKIE> 149	
	Recap 151	
	Advanced Project 151	
Chapter 8	Using Custom Tags 153	
	Introduction to Custom Tags 154	
	The Ins and Outs of Custom Tags 154	
	Where Can I Use Custom Tags? 155	
	Project I: Counting Your Hits 157	
	SCRIPT_NAME Variable 157	
	Adding the Hits Table to the shelleyCatalog Database 157	
	Project II: Creating a Random Product Custom Tag 159	
	ListLen Function 159	

ListAppend Function   160
ListGetAt Function   160

Other Functions Used in this Project   160
RandRange Function   160
Option 1—Code Every Page   162
Option 2—Make Use of the Developer's Friend, the application.cfm File   162

Recap   163

Advanced Project   163

Chapter 9   ColdFusion and Wireless   165

What Is WAP and How Is It Useful?   165
Limitations   166

MIME Types   167
Internet Information Server 4 and 5   168
Personal Web Site (PWS)   169
<CFCONTENT>   169

Project I: WAP-Enabled Product List   170

Wireless Palm™ Series of Handhelds   174
Limitations   175
Palm Query Application   175

Project II: Palm™-Enabled Product List   175
META Tags   177

Building and Installing the Palm™ Query Application   183

Recap   184

Advanced Project   184

Appendix A   An Introduction to Forms   185
GET   185
POST   186

Buttons   187
Two Types of Buttons   188

Single-Line Text Box   188

Scrolling Text Box   190

Menus   192

Check Boxes   195

Radio Buttons 196
Putting It All Together 197

Appendix B ColdFusion Reference 201

Index 203

Introduction

In the beginning, creating websites using static pages was enough until people started to realize that updating content on their sites was a tedious chore. People also realized they had huge amounts of information they wanted to list on their constantly-changing websites, as well as in their databases.

Also needed was the ability to add logic to the websites, allowing the users to search through their products, buy their products online, or perform a number of other functions, turning it into one giant web application or a series of small ones. If a user comes to the website and performs a search, or navigates a certain way through the site, it would be nice to have pages dynamically built for them to accommodate where they are in the site. Suddenly several languages popped up that allowed the web developer to do all of these things and more. Each language had strengths and weaknesses such as learning curves and cost, but for the most part, many of these languages allowed you to create the same types of applications.

♦ Languages Used for Web Application Development

There are several types of languages used for web development with new ones popping up all the time. Here are a few examples of some of the better-known ones being used today:

ColdFusion	ASP—Active Server Pages
PHP	C++
Drumbeat	Lasso
JSP—Java Server Pages (Servlets)	Perl
PHP	Tango
Tcl	

♦ How Does ColdFusion Work?

ColdFusion doesn't require a high level of knowledge in programming or server-side scripting to get started in developing some pretty powerful applications. Written in a way that resembles HTML syntax, ColdFusion Markup Language (CFML) consists of tags and attributes that transform a static web page into a truly dynamic and customizable experience for each and every user. CFML consists of a series of tags and formatting options that perform different functions:

Syntax:
```
<CFOUTPUT>
Today's date is: #DateFormat(Now(), "DDDD, MMMM DD, YYYY")#
</CFOUTPUT>
```

Output:
```
Today's date is: Saturday, November 25, 2000
```

The ColdFusion application server runs behind your existing web server and parses the .cfm file (.cfm is the extension all ColdFusion pages are saved with) that was passed and converts it into plain HTML, which is then presented to the viewer. The user never sees the actual CFML coding which took place.

◆ About ColdFusion

ColdFusion Application Server

REQUIREMENTS

With the introduction of ColdFusion 4.5, ColdFusion Application Server now runs on several operating systems including Windows 95/98/2000/NT, Solaris, and Linux. The recommended minimum requirements are:

Enterprise Server
ColdFusion 4.5 for Windows
- Windows NT, with service pack 4 or above
- 150-MB hard drive
- 128 MB of RAM

ColdFusion 4.5 for Linux
- Red Hat Linux 6.0 or above
- 150-MB hard drive
- 128 MB of RAM

ColdFusion 4.5 for Solaris
- SPARC Solaris 2.5, 2.6, or 7 with patch 103582-1B or above
- 200-MB hard drive
- 128 MB of RAM

Professional Server
ColdFusion 4.5 for Windows
- Windows 95, 98, NT, or 2000
- 50-MB hard drive
- 32 MB of RAM

(Windows 2000 systems should have a minimum 96 MB of RAM)

ColdFusion 4.5 for Linux
- Red Hat Linux 6.0 or above
- 100-MB hard drive
- 64 MB of RAM

NOTE
There have been some problems using the tag <CFCONTENT> (introduced in chapter 9) with service pack 6 for NT 4.0. If you are currently using this you should upgrade to service pack 6a to fix this problem.

Download ColdFusion 4.5

You can download a full-featured 30-day trial version of ColdFusion from Allaire's website (http://www.allaire.com) to install on your machine. You can also grab a copy of another version of ColdFusion called ColdFusion Express, that you can run as long as you would like absolutely free. The catch, you ask? It doesn't have all the functionality, nor can it handle all the tags the full version offers.

What's the Difference?

As mentioned before, ColdFusion comes in three versions. Express is considered the development platform for many newcomers to ColdFusion.

This leaves Professional and Enterprise editions to tangle with. For all intents and purposes these versions are identical. They will process your ColdFusion code exactly the same. The benefit to having ColdFusion Enterprise is its ability to use and administer a clustered ColdFusion server environment to deal with failover (one system receiving too many requests and a second system (or more) assisting in handling the traffic). It also has native support for more database solutions such as Oracle and Sybase.

Differences Between Express and the Full Version

Yep, the other shoe has dropped. Express is a great product to get your feet wet with ColdFusion. Since its creation its intent was to feed you and allow you to learn ColdFusion for free and fall in love. Then once you're hooked, you'll have to pony up for the Enterprise or Professional versions of the product.

Rather than telling you what won't work, we'll list the tags that will work in ColdFusion Express. Most of these tags will be covered in this book along with some of the other full-version tags.

Tags in this book that are supported by ColdFusion Express

<CFABORT>
<CFAPPLICATION>
<CFBREAK>
<CFCOOKIE>

> Tags in this book that are supported by ColdFusion Express
> <CFIF> <CFELSEIF> <CFELSE>
> <CFINCLUDE>
> <CFINSERT>
> <CFLOCATION>
> <CFLOOP>
> <CFOUTPUT>
> <CFPARAM>
> <CFQUERY>
> <CFSET>
> <CFSETTING>
> <CFSWITCH> <CFCASE> <CFDEFAULTCASE>
> <CFUPDATE>

Now if these aren't enough tags to work with, you have another option! Allaire provides free 30-day evaluations of most of their products, including ColdFusion. I would get very comfortable with the tags above while using Express and then give the evaluation full version a shot to do some test development. But make sure to do it quickly; 30 days really flies when you're having fun!

ColdFusion Studio

Although ColdFusion Studio is not required to create ColdFusion pages, it will make your life a little easier with all the wizards and built-in tools it has to offer, which will aid you in creating your pages quicker than if you were to do this in a regular text editor.

Cold Fusion Studio 4.5 has the following minimum requirements:
- Windows 95, 98, 2000, or NT
- 35 MB of disk space
- 32 MB of RAM

(Windows 2000 systems should have a minimum of 96 MB of RAM)

◆ Who This Book Is Written for and What Is Assumed

This book is written for anyone wanting to learn how to build dynamically driven database sites. You should already know how to use HTML and have an understanding of HTML forms. If you are unfamiliar with HTML forms or need a quick tutorial, check out Appendix A.

You should also have an understanding of Microsoft Access and the Structured Query Language (SQL). All of the Access databases we use in this book as well as the code and images will be on the companion website (www.phptr.com/essential/coldfusion45). In chapter 1 we will also go over creating the *shelleyCatalog* Access database which you will use in a few of these chapters.

Find Online Support and Documentation

There are several sites on the web that have communities of Cold-Fusion programmers who openly share their knowledge and expertise. One of the best places is the Allaire website itself where there is support for all of Allaire's products:

http://www.allaire.com/developer

You will also want to check out the Allaire Knowledge Base from time to time to find answers to frequently asked questions:

http://www.allaire.com/Support/KnowledgeBase/SearchForm.cfm

ColdFusion 4.5 server also comes with online documentation that was installed on your hard drive during the installation process. This can be found at:

http://127.0.0.1/CFDOCS/dochome.htm

NOTE
127.0.0.1 is used throughout this book to refer to your local machine. This is the loopback IP address used for your local machine. The name *localhost* will work as well, or if your machine has been assigned its own IP address you can use it.

During installation you can choose to install the example applications that come with ColdFusion server. This is good for poking around and learning some already functional applications. Additional references are listed in Appendix B.

Sites Using ColdFusion

Here are a few sites now using ColdFusion:

Ablecommerce	http://www.ablecommerce.com
Autobytel	http://www.autobytel.com
PolarisMan.com	http://www.polarisman.com
OnVia	http://www.onvia.com
E-ThePeople	http://www.e-thepeople.com
Computer Acquisition Guide	http://computer.pwgsc.gc.ca
Wireless Advisor	http://www.wirelessadvisor.com

How This Book Is Laid Out

In order to demonstrate a wide range of functionality and practicality, a fictitious company "Shelley Biotechnologies" will be used to showcase its product line.

As we build this site we will teach you the components that go into creating different types of applications with ColdFusion.

The projects in each chapter are designed to build on the new functionality you are learning and apply it toward an application you would use in a real-life situation. At the end of each chapter you will be asked to complete a more advanced project based on what you have just done. The answer or possible solution is on the companion website.

While we teach you how to use ColdFusion using some of the most widely used tags and functions in the language, there are still plenty of other tags and functions that this book does not cover. These can be found in the documentation that comes with ColdFusion.

Acknowledgments

◆ Micah Brown

I would like to thank my wife, Dawn, for all the help and encouragement she gives me in everything I do. And a special thanks to our daughter, Ashley, who constantly shows us that we sometimes take ourselves to seriously and we shouldn't forget the simple pleasures in life. And of course to my parents who have helped me so much in life and have encouraged me every step of the way. Finally thanks to my co-author Mike for making this such a fun project to work on.

◆ Mike Fredrick

Wow. What a ride this has been! I have a few important people I would like to acknowledge. My co-author, Micah, has been nothing short of fantastic! I can say I was shocked to be the selection of such an accomplished author, being that I have not done anything like this before. Everything went so smoothly and it's a tribute to Micah's skills and dedication. Thanks a million, it's simply awesome!

I would also like to thank my parents who have always stood behind me in whatever I do. I am really glad I can make them proud of what I say, do, and promise to do in the future. Your support has been immeasurable and will always be grateful for everything you have done and will do in the future.

Last but certainly not least I would like to thank the love of my life! Misty, you have been standing by me for what seems like forever now and I can't say how much I love you. Your support through this book and through life in general has been tremendous and I can honestly say I don't know where I would be without you. Someday, I promise, we will make our lives much happier as a couple, and I can't wait.

We would both like to thank Karen McLean for helping us put this book on the shelves. And thanks to Shaun St Louis and Aaron Gorsky for reviewing this book and making sure we knew what we were talking about. And finally thanks to Allaire for putting out such a great product.

chapter 1
Database Basics

IN THIS CHAPTER:

- A Look at Relational Databases
- Introduction to SQL
- To Quote or Not to Quote?
- Project I: Creating an Access Database File
- Setting Up an ODBC Connection
- Project II: Retrieving Data
- SQL Builder
- New Functions
  - SELECT
  - FROM
  - INSERT
  - ORDER BY
  - WHERE
  - DISTINCT
  - INNER JOIN
  - ASC/DESC
  - <CFOUTPUT>
  - <CFSET>
  - <CFQUERY>
- Recap

Let's face it . . . nowadays, just about every major site is using some sort of database on the backend to power their site in one way or another. Even smaller sites have started incorporating databases into their websites due to the amazing flexibility it offers. Not to mention the somewhat short learning curve involved in understanding the basics of what is involved in actually using them. Today, with applications such as ColdFusion, ASP, PHP, and countless others, integrating database functionality into a website is becoming increasingly easier.

But in order to effectively work with databases you need to have some sort of idea of how they actually work. And with a chapter called "Database Basics" I'm sure you are counting on learning exactly that.

There are several types of database applications out on the market, ranging in price from under a hundred dollars to tens of thousands of dollars. The application that most people have available to them—or that doesn't cost an arm and a leg—is Microsoft's Access. Others that you can use if you are going to be doing some heavy-duty database work that needs to span multiple servers are Microsoft SQL server, Oracle, or Sybase. While these cost much more than Access, they offer a lot more in functionality, scalability, and security. They are also designed to handle a lot more simultaneous requests than Microsoft Access.

For the examples in this book we will be using Microsoft Access. You will find the data sources (also known as DSNs which we will be explaining in the next few pages) and all the examples from this book on the *Essential ColdFusion 4.5 for Web Professionals* accompanying website which is located at www.phptr.com/essential/coldfusion45/.

If you do not have a copy of Microsoft Access you can still use the data files to run with ColdFusion and do all the fun stuff like adding, deleting, and editing your data.

◆ A Look at Relational Databases

What is a relational database? In simplest of terms it can be defined as a series of tables that have common fields linking related information. It's a way to relate different information that has a common bond. For instance, a simple online store application may have three tables:

- **Customer table**
  Where all the personal information about the customers is stored.
- **Products table**
  Lists information about the products.
- **Category table**
  Contains the various categories the products will fall under.

The **Customer** table will be a stand-alone table meaning that it will not relate to the other two tables. Only the **Products** and **Category** tables will be related. The relationship between these two tables could look something like this:

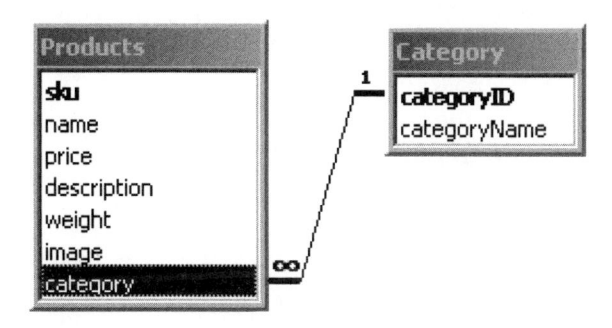

FIGURE 1-1 Relationship of the *category* field to the **Category** table

You'll notice the **Products** and **Category** tables have primary keys (shown in bold) associated with them. A primary key is used to uniquely identify a row in a table. For a relational database to function properly, primary keys cannot be duplicated. The relationship shown above demonstrated a "one to one" relationship. In the **Products** table the **sku** field is the primary key, which has the data type of *AutoNumber*. This means that every time you add a new product into the **Products** table the **sku** will *AutoNumber* itself in increments of one.

TABLE 1-1 Common Data Types Found in Access

Text	Holds text up to 255 characters.
Memo	Holds text up to 65,535 characters.
Number	Holds numerical characters only. Good to use for mathematical calculations.

TABLE 1-1 Common Data Types Found in Access *(continued)*

Date/Time	Holds date and time values.
Currency	Holds currency (numeric) values.
Autonumber	Incremented value by 1 when a new record is added. Can also be set to randomly autoincrement.
Yes/No	Contains a value of 0 or 1. Used for 'NO/YES', 'OFF/ON', 'TRUE/FALSE'.

The *categoryID* field in the **Category** table is the primary key for that table. The *category* field in the **Products** table holds the value of the *categoryID* in the **Category** table and therefore uses the *categoryID* in the **Category** table. This might sound a little confusing at first, so take a look at Figure 1-2 and you'll see how this is working.

sku	name	price	category
6	Floro-Flubulator	$12.99	1
7	Bio Hazard Gloves	$39.00	1
8	Beaker 15oz	$9.99	2
9	Beaker 20oz	$15.99	2
10	Beaker 30ox	$25.99	2

		categoryID	categoryName
▶	+	1	Main Products
	+	2	Accessories

FIGURE 1-2 The values of the *category* field of the **Products** table are related to the values of the *categoryID* field in the **Category** table.

Through the use of SQL you can now interact with the data in your tables.

◆ Introduction to SQL

The Structured Query Language, known as SQL, is the language used to talk to most databases. All the previously mentioned databases understand this language, which allows you to talk to them. SQL is a very powerful language and can be a little complicated the further you dive into it. But for now you need to know only a few frequently used commands.

TABLE 1–2 SQL Basics

Keyword	Definition and Usage
SELECT	Used to select data from the database **Usage** SELECT * FROM table Note: The (*) selects all fields in the specified table.
INSERT	Used to insert new information into the database **Usage** INSERT INTO table (field1,field2) Values ('Micah','Mike')

DELETE	Used to delete data from a database
	Usage
	    DELETE FROM table
	    WHERE name = 'Mike'

UPDATE	Used to update data in the database
	Usage
	    UPDATE table
	    SET Name1 = 'Mike', Name2 = 'Micah'

TABLE 1–3 SQL Basics—Attributes

Keyword	Definition and Usage

WHERE	Used to select a certain record
	Usage
	    SELECT *
	    FROM table
	    WHERE name = 'Micah'

ASC	Used to sort results in ascending order
	Usage
	    SELECT *
	    FROM table
	    WHERE name = 'Micah' ASC

TABLE 1-3 SQL Basics—Attributes *(continued)*

DESC	Used to sort results in descending order
	Usage
	  SELECT *
	  FROM table
	  WHERE name = 'Mike' DESC

ORDER BY	Used to sort results by a field name
	Usage
	  SELECT *
	  FROM table
	  ORDER BY name

DISTINCT	Used to list distinct field names. If multiple names appear in a field column only one is returned
	Usage
	  SELECT DISTINCT category
	  FROM table

LIKE	Used to search a field for certain text
	Usage
	  SELECT *
	  FROM table
	  WHERE name LIKE '%Mike%'
	
	Note: The '%' is a wildcard character which will return any record that has the string 'Mike' in it.

AND	Condition used to ensure two or more fields of information hold true
	Usage
	  SELECT *
	  FROM table
	  WHERE fName = 'Mike' AND lName = 'Fredrick'

OR	Condition used to ensure that any of the two or more fields of information holds true
	Usage
	  SELECT *
	  FROM table
	  WHERE fName = 'Mike' OR fName = 'Micah'

BETWEEN	Condition used to return a result within a certain range
	Usage
	  SELECT *
	  FROM table
	  WHERE birthDate BETWEEN '01' AND '10'

TABLE 1-3 SQL Basics—Attributes *(continued)*

IN	Condition used to return any specified results in a field **Usage** SELECT * FROM table WHERE birthDate IN ('01','10','23')
=	Equal to operator, used to find exact matches. Mostly used with WHERE clause
<>	Not equal to operator, used to return results that do not equal. Again used in the WHERE clause
>	Greater than operator
>=	Greater than or equal to operator
<	Less than operator
<=	Less than or equal to operator

◆ To Quote or Not to Quote?

This is by far the largest issue when dealing with SQL. Depending on what datatype you are dealing with (such as a number or character string) you have to interface the database differently. Don't worry for now if you don't understand the ColdFusion tags we're mentioning here, they will be explained a later in this chapter.

Let's say you have two fields in a table called *userID* and *Password*. *userID* is numeric and *Password* is a character string. Consider the following code.

```
<CFSET userID = 12345>
<CFSET password = "myPass">
<CFQUERY NAME="record">
    UPDATE users
    SET userID = #userID#, password = '#password#'
</CFQUERY>
```

Pay close attention to the quotes when setting new variables. *userID* is defined as numeric so the value does not need to be quoted. However, since the *Password* field is a character string (like text or memo in Microsoft Access) it must be enclosed in single quotes. Date formats must also be enclosed in quotes to be inserted or updated in a table.

◆ Project I: Creating an Access Database File

For several of the projects throughout the rest of the book we will be using a database file that you will create in Microsoft Access for the Shelley Biotechnologies website. This is a database containing the three tables we discussed earlier: **Customer**, **Products**, and **Categories**.

While Microsoft Access is great for setting up databases quickly or for smaller database-driven websites, you might want to consider using something like Microsoft SQL server or Oracle to handle the larger-scale websites. These types of databases are designed to handle a large number of simultaneous requests whereas Microsoft Access is not and response times will suffer as a result.

Use the following information to set up your tables:

Customer Table

Field Name	Data Type
customerID	AutoNumber—**Primary Key**
firstName	Text
lastName	Text
address	Text
city	Text
state	Text
zip	Text
country	Text
phone	Text
email	Text
mailingList	Text

Products Table

Field Name	Data Type
sku	AutoNumber—**Primary Key**
name	Text
price	Currency
description	Text
weight	Text
image	Text
category	Number

Project I: Creating an Access Database File

Category Table

Field Name	Data Type
categoryID	AutoNumber—**Primary Key**
categoryName	Text

Below is the content we will be using throughout the examples in the following chapters. Some fields were left blank intentionally.

The database file (*shelleyCatalog.mdb*) is also available from our website under chapter 1.

Customer : Table

customerID	firstName	lastName	address	city	state	zip	country	phone	email	mailingList
1	Micah	Brown	1234 Main Street	West Hills	CA	91304	USA	818-555-9988	micah.brown@shelleybiotechn	☐
2	Mike	Fredrick	5678 Elm Street	Minneapolis	MN	55110	USA	555-555-3210	mike.fredrick@shelleybiotechn	☐
3	Fredrick	Kruger	3234 Elm Street	Killroy	MA	38372	USA	223-555-6940	fredrick.kruger@shelleybiotech	☐
4	Michelle	Rhoads	1243 Cantara Lane	Burbank	CA	91203	USA	818-555-4039	michelle.rhoads@shelleybiotec	☐
5	Willy	Tutone	19222 Falken Ave	Santa Barbara	CA	93111	USA	805-555-6811	willy.tutone@shelleybiotechno	☐
6	Dawn	Brown	1234 Main Street	West Hills	CA	91304	USA	818-555-9988	dawn.brown@shelleybiotechnc	☐
7	Ashley	Nova	10010 Nova Lane	Santa Clarita	CA	91310	USA	805-555-3200	ashley.nova@shelleybiotechnc	☐
8	Max	Parker	981 Homer Way	West Hills	CA	91304	USA	818-555-5509	max.parker@shelleybiotechno	☐
9	Peter	Pumpernickle			MN	55110			peter.pumpernickle@shelleybi	☐
10	Penelope	Snodgrass		Roswell	NM	88201	USA		penelope.snodgrass@shelleyb	☐
(AutoNumber)										☐

FIGURE 1–3 *Customer* table.

Products : Table

sku	name	price	description	weight	image	category
1	DNA Duplicator	$595.99	Looking for an easy way to clone DNA? Here's your answer at a very affordable price.	22		1
3	Retina Scanner 6000	$3,200.00	Retina scanner with storage device for storing up to 100 retina scans.	15		1
5	Microscope	$99.99	10000 time zoom!	12		1
6	Floro-Flubulator	$12.99	A Flubulator like no other! Be the envy of everyone on your block.	5		1
7	Bio Hazard Gloves	$39.00	Working with dangerous material? These gloves make life a lot simpler by keeping your hands from dissolving.	2		1
8	Beaker 15oz	$9.99	Clear beaker made of authentic clear pyrex. Will hold 15 ounces.	1		2
9	Beaker 20oz	$15.99	Clear beaker made of authentic clear pyrex. Will hold 20 ounces.	1		2
10	Beaker 30oz	$25.99	Clear beaker made of authentic clear pyrex. Will hold 30 ounces.	2		2
11	Test Tube	$2.99	Clear test tube made of authentic clear pyrex.	1		2
12	Test Tubes (4)	$9.99	Clear test tubes (4) made of authentic clear pyrex.	1		2
13	Test Tubes (10)	$19.99	Clear test tubes (4) made of authentic clear pyrex.	1		2
14	Dropper Bottle 30mL	$19.99	Glass bottle made of borosilicate glass with rubber tip.	1		2
15	CryoBox	$14.99	Great for holding your precious enzymes and other types of samples. Holds 25 2mL Microtubes.	2		1
(ber)		$0.00				0

FIGURE 1–4 *Products* table.

Category : Table

categoryID	categoryName
1	Main Products
2	Accessories
(AutoNumber)	

FIGURE 1–5 *Category* table.

Obviously this was just a brief overview of what can be done with databases. We suggest you pick up a book specifically on databases if you plan on doing more sophisticated database designs.

◆ Setting Up an ODBC Connection

In order for your applications, which you will be building soon, to know where the database file is and how to talk to it, you will use open database connectivity also known as ODBC. ODBC usually comes with several database drivers already installed such as Access, SQL Server, dBase, Excel, FoxPro, Oracle, and text. Each of these drivers knows the characteristics of their respective data type and communicates your SQL commands to it. This way you don't have to know exactly how to talk to each individual data type. This is the beauty of SQL!

Once you have a data file saved to an appropriate spot on your machine or on a shared drive on your network, you need to set up the ODBC connection. There are a couple of ways in which to do this.

Windows Control Panel

First open the **control panel** from your **settings** menu and choose the **ODBC** control panel. There are several tabs you can choose from but we will only be paying attention to the tab **System DSN** (Data Source Name).

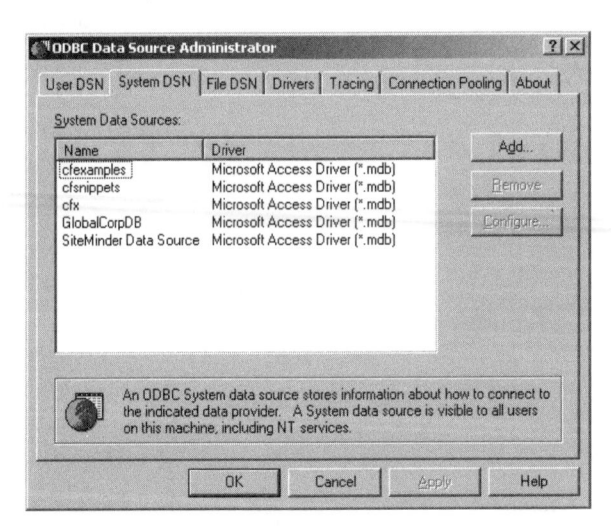

FIGURE 1-6 ODBC Control Panel—System DSN.

Now you need to locate the data file and establish an ODBC connection by clicking the **Add** button, which will bring you to a list of several types of database drivers to choose from. Select the **Microsoft Access Driver**. Once you have done this click **Finish**.

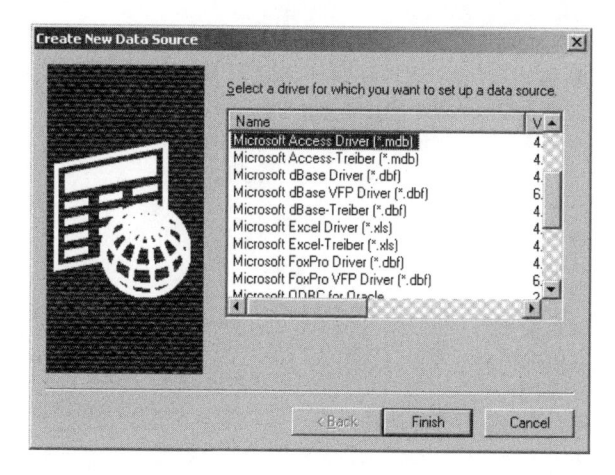

FIGURE 1-7 ODBC control panel—select the Microsoft Access driver.

Now you will tell the system the location of the Access database by clicking the **Select** button and locating the file. Next give the file a name. For our example we will name it shelleyCatalog. Don't use spaces for the name. You can use underscores (such as shelley_catalog) for the sake of clarity if needed. Now hit OK.

FIGURE 1-8 ODBC control panel—naming the ODBC connection and defining the location of the data source.

Now you have successfully set up your ODBC connection to the *shelleyCatalog.mdb* file which you will start working with later in this book.

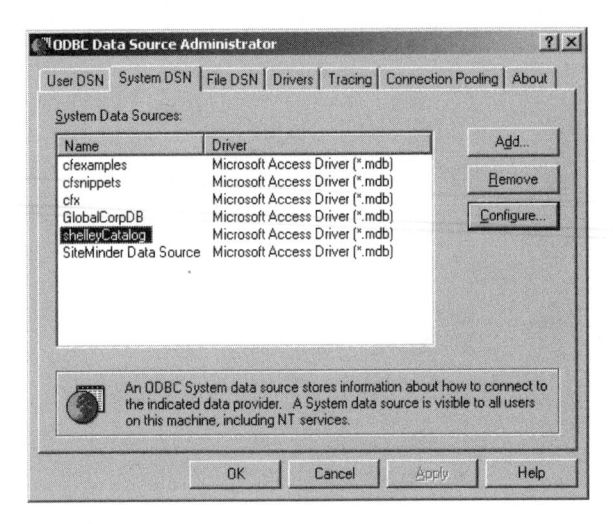

FIGURE 1-9 ODBC control panel—ODBC connection is now set up.

ColdFusion Administrator

The better and far easier way to set up an ODBC connection is through the ColdFusion server's built-in administration screen. Again, if you are going through an ISP that is hosting your website, chances are you cannot use this. The ISP will have to set it up for you.

The ColdFusion server has a built-in administration interface that allows you to control many features of your server either locally or remotely. The server's URL is:

http://127.0.0.1/CFIDE/Administrator/index.cfm

You will be asked to enter a password to log into it. This is the password you entered when you originally set up the ColdFusion server.

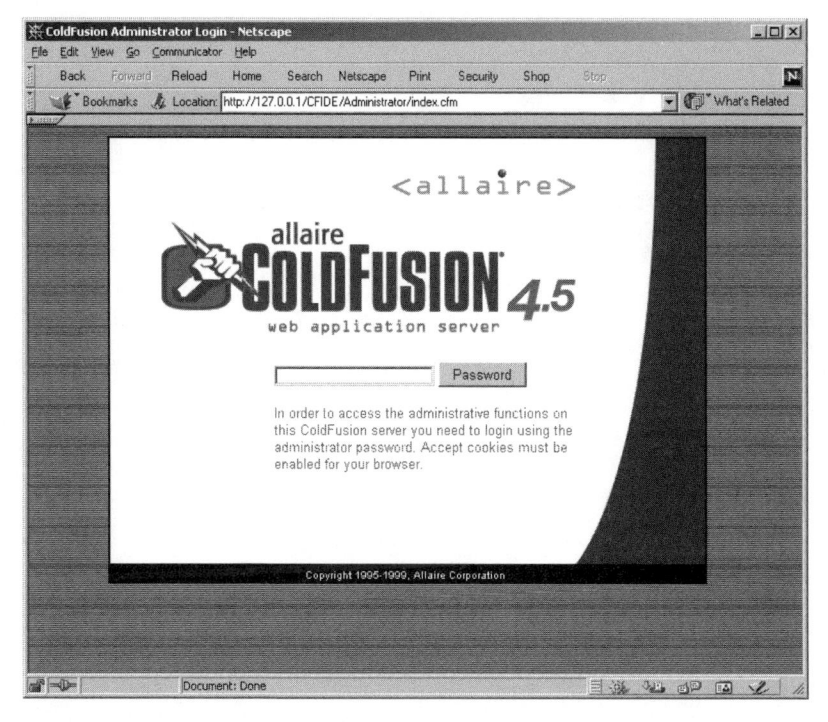

FIGURE 1-10 ColdFusion server administrator.

Under the **Data Sources** heading select **ODBC**. This will list all the ODBC connections currently running on this machine. It tells you the name of the file and the ODBC driver it is using and verifies the connection. If you have made a change to a file and want to make sure the DSN connection is still intact, click the **Verify** link to have the application check it for you. Alternatively you can select the **Verify All** button at the top to have all of your DSNs verified.

Now you want to set up your ODBC connection (assuming you haven't already done so using the Windows ODBC control method). Once you select ODBC under the **Data Sources** heading you will see the list of your current ODBC connections. Select the **ADD** button with the appropriate database type selected in the drop-down menu. Here is where you will add the database name and the location of the database you will be using.

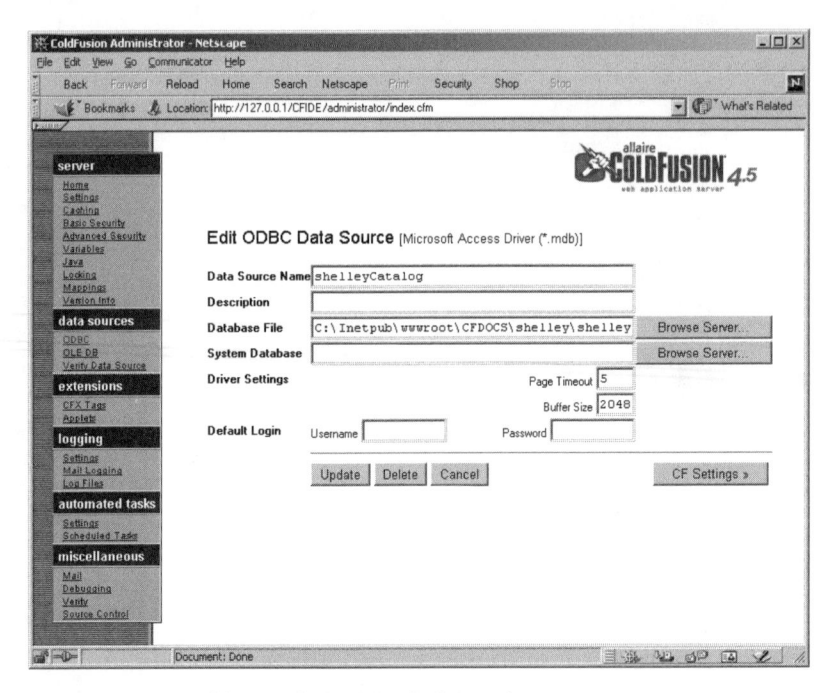

FIGURE 1–11 ColdFusion's ODBC administration screen.

Different database drivers ask for different types of information. All of them ask for three common pieces of information:

- **Database name**—This doesn't necessarily have to be the name of the database file but it is the name you will be using for that connection down the road.
- **Description**—Only used for reference. When you get to the point of running several types or different versions of a database this is a good way to remember which is which.
- **Database File** or **Server**—Using the *Browse Server* button you can locate the file on your hard drive or network. Using SQL server you must type in the location of the machine on your network. If this database file is on the same machine just type in (**local**) and enter the database name in the **Database** field next to **Login Info**.

NOTE

The Browse Server is a Java class application that under Netscape operates fine. However, under Internet Explorer (all versions) it may ask you to connect to the Microsoft site to download the necessary Java class files.

If you have set any password restrictions on a database be sure to enter that in this area. If you are using SQL server connections, select the **CF Settings** to enter this information.

After you have created the ODBC connection, go back to your list of ODBC connections and your new connection will be listed. You are now ready to start learning ColdFusion commands.

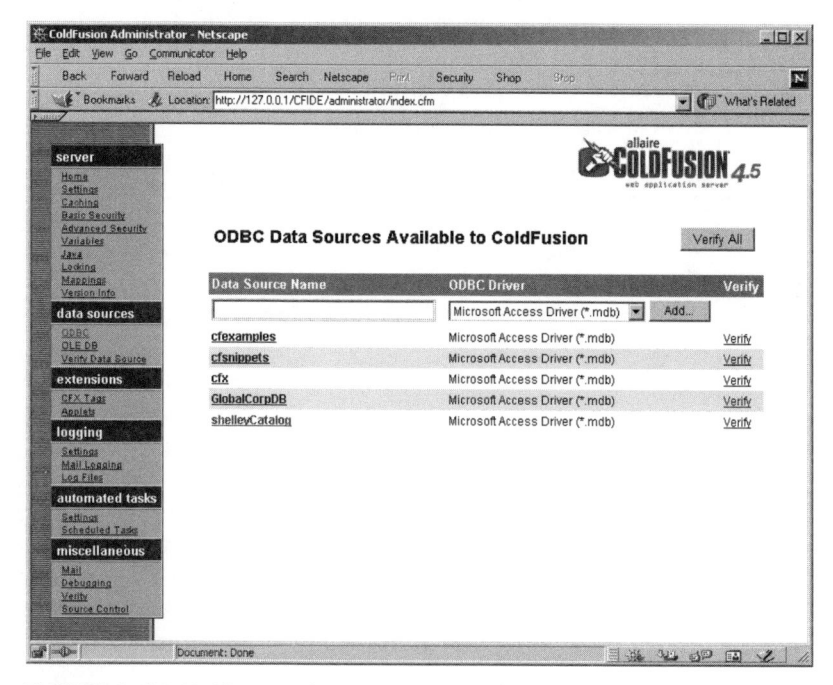

FIGURE 1-12 Verification that the ODBC connection was set up correctly.

◆ Project II: Retrieving Data

Now that you have your database set up, it's time to pull some data from those tables. Here are a few basic elements of ColdFusion you need to know in order to make this happen. These will help you understand how ColdFusion works and give you some hands-on experience right up front.

<CFSET>

The `<CFSET>` tag allows you to set a value to a ColdFusion variable. For example:

```
<CFSET firstName = "Mike">
<CFSET lastName = "Fredrick">
```

Now that you have set the variables *firstName* and *lastName*, you can reference them anywhere in the ColdFusion template and they will hold these values. You will learn other ways you can use this as you are introduced to more functions.

CONCATENATING VARIABLES

You can also very easily concatenate variables by assigning a variable to equal the value of two or more variables:

```
<CFSET firstName="Mike">
<CFSET lastName="Fredrick">
<CFSET wholeName="#firstName# #lastName#">
```

Now the variable *wholeName* will be: **Mike Fredrick**

<CFOUTPUT>

```
<CFOUTPUT
    QUERY="name of the query"              Optional
    GROUP="query column"                   Optional
    GROUPCASESENSITIVE="yes | no"          Optional
    STARTROW="row of query to start from"  Optional
    MAXROWS="maximum number of rows to return"  Optional
</CFOUTPUT >
```

The `<CFOUTPUT>` tag will allow you to output ColdFusion content requests to your browser, such as the variables that were set above.

TABLE 1-4 <CFOUTPUT> Attributes

Attribute	Description
QUERY	The name set in the CFQUERY in which you are querying the database from.
GROUP	Defines the column in the query to use when sets of records are grouped.
GROUPCASESENSITIVE	Defines whether to group by case sensitivity. Default value is set to YES.
STARTROW	Defines the row of the recordset to start the output from.
MAXROWS	Defines the number of rows from the recordset you want returned.

#—THE POUND (#) SIGN

Whenever you are going to be displaying a variable to the browser you must enclose the variable within pound characters. This lets the ColdFusion server know at runtime that this is not just ordinary text but it is a variable that must be processed before being displayed to the user's browser.

For example:
`<CFOUTPUT>Welcome back firstName lastName!</CFOUTPUT>`

Will output to the screen:
`Welcome back firstName lastName!`

If you wrap pound (#) signs around the variables **FirstName** and **LastName**, then ColdFusion will know to process these since they are not just ordinary characters.

For example:
`<CFOUTPUT> Welcome back #firstName# #lastName#!</CFOUTPUT>`

Will output to the screen:
`Welcome back Mike Fredrick!`

Keeping these basics in mind, we can now grab data from the **Customer** and **Products** table from the Shelley Catalog we built earlier in this chapter.

<CFQUERY>

```
<CFQUERY
      NAME="name of query"                          Required
      DATASOURCE="datasource name"                  Required
      DBTYPE="database type"                        Optional
      DBSERVER="database server"                    Optional
      DBNAME="database name"                        Optional
      USERNAME="username"                           Optional
      PASSWORD="password"                           Optional
      MAXROWS="maximum number of rows"              Optional
      BLOCKFACTOR="block-size"                      Optional
      TIMEOUT="time in milliseconds"                Optional
      CACHEDAFTER="date"                            Optional
      CACHEDWITHIN="time-span"                      Optional
      PROVIDER="COM provider"                       Optional
      PROVIDERDSN="datasource name"                 Optional
      DEBUG="Yes | No"                              Optional
</CFQUERY>
```

TABLE 1-5 <CFQUERY> Attributes

Attribute	Description
NAME	Defines what you would like to name the query.
DATASOURCE	Defines the name of the data source you set up in your ODBC connection.
DBTYPE	Defines the database driver type. By default, ODBC is set which is perfectly fine for most cases. If using other types of connections like DB2, Informix, OLEDB, Oracle, or Sybase use the following accordingly: - DB2 - Informix73 - OLEDB - Oracle73 - Oracle80 - Sybase11
DBSERVER	Used with native drivers to specify the database server machine.
DBNAME	SQLOLEDB and Sybase drivers specific; specifies the name of the database.
USERNAME	Defines the username set on the data source.
PASSWORD	Defines the password set on the data source.

TABLE 1-5 <CFQUERY> Attributes *(continued)*

Attribute	Description
MAXROWS	Defines the maximum number of rows to return from the recordset.
BLOCKFACTOR	Used to set a maximum number of records an Oracle or ODBC driver will return from a query.
TIMEOUT	Defines the time in milliseconds to timeout from query.
CACHEDAFTER	Returns cached data from the same query that was executed previously. SQL statement and data source must be the same as the original to retrieve cached data.
CACHEDWITHIN	Retrieves the cached data if the query was run within the parameter supplied here. Use the ColdFusion function CreateTimeSpan to create a valid entry.
PROVIDER	Defines the COM provider and is used for OLE-DB only.
PROVIDERDSN	Defines the name of the COM provider and is used for OLE-DB only.
DEBUG	Used for debugging queries.

The <CFQUERY> tag is the method of communication to the ColdFusion application server, which allows you to retrieve data from a data source. <CFQUERY> uses SQL to extract the data you are looking for. For example, let's start the application with a statement to retrieve all the customers.

1. <CFQUERY NAME="getCustomers" DATASOURCE="shelleyCatalog">
2. SELECT *
3. FROM Customer
4. </CFQUERY>

HOW THIS WORKS

1. NAME defines the name used to reference this query statement. DATASOURCE is the name of the data source you set up in your ODBC connection. In this case we are using *shelleyCatalog*.
2. Using the SQL statement SELECT you will select ALL the fields using the * wildcard character.

3. Using the SQL statement FROM you will SELECT * FROM the Customer table.
4. Close the <CFQUERY> statement with </CFQUERY>.

Now that you have made your request to the database for the information, you can display it to the browser with <CFOUTPUT>.

The <CFOUTPUT> now has the QUERY attribute attached to it and the name of the query that you specified with <CFQUERY> as the NAME attribute. <CFOUTPUT> will now loop through all the records pulled from the <CFQUERY> and display them. We will throw this into a table to produce a nicely formatted output.

Script 1-1
firstQuery.cfm

```
<!DOCTYPE HTML PUBLIC "-//W3C//DTD HTML 4.0 Transitional//EN">
<HTML>
<HEAD>
<TITLE>My First QUERY!</TITLE>
</HEAD>
<BODY>

<CFQUERY NAME="getCustomers" DATASOURCE="shelleyCatalog">
SELECT *
FROM Customer
</CFQUERY>

<H2>Customers of Shelley Biotechnologies, Inc.</H2>
<TABLE BORDER="0">
<CFOUTPUT QUERY="getCustomers">
<TR>
        <TD>#customerID#</TD>
        <TD>#firstName#</TD>
        <TD>#lastName#</TD>
        <TD>#address#</TD>
        <TD>#city#</TD>
        <TD>#state#</TD>
        <TD>#zip#</TD>
        <TD>#country#</TD>
        <TD>#phone#</TD>
        <TD>#email#</TD>
        </TD>
</TR>
</CFOUTPUT>
</TABLE>
</BODY>
</HTML>
```

SQL Builder

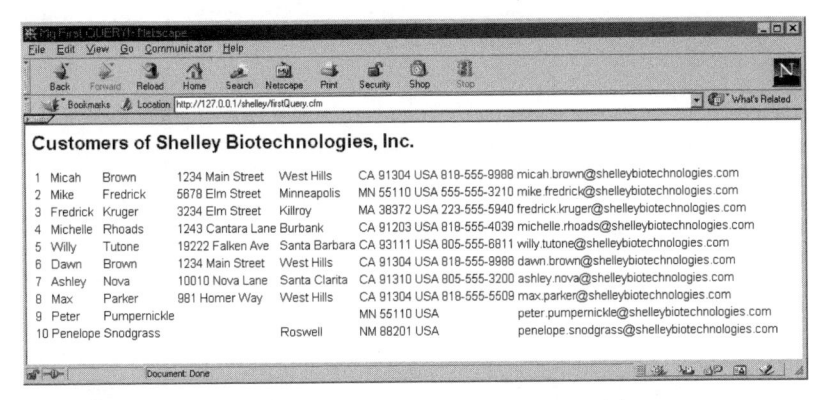

FIGURE 1-13 Output of all the fields in the *Customer* table.

◆ SQL Builder

A useful built-in feature of ColdFusion Studio is the **SQL Builder** which allows you to view the table layouts and make queries on the fly.

To do this click on **Tools > SQL Builder**

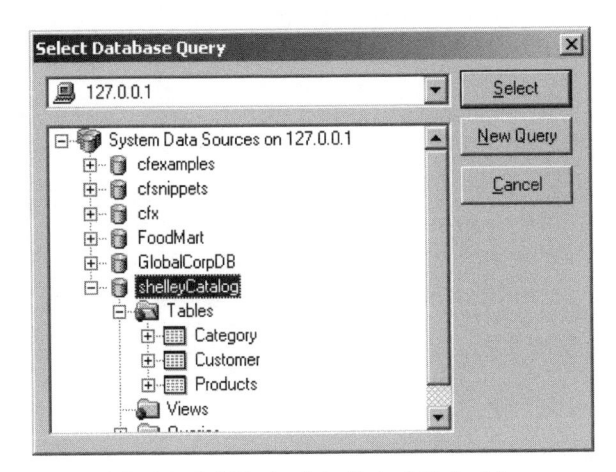

FIGURE 1-14 ColdFusion's built-in SQL builder.

When you see this screen you'll have to have an RDS connection to the source you will be working with. If you are going to be using a data source on your own machine make sure you have

RDS services running. (Check in your ColdFusion Server folder and run the "ColdFusion RDS Services.") Drill into the **Customer** table and click on **New Query**.

Choose the *shelleyCatalog* data source and select **New Query**. Now you will be able to choose which table from the *shelleyCatalog* you would like to use. If you would like to use another when building a query, right-click and choose **Add Table** where you will be able to select from a list of all the other tables available from the data source you are working in. For this example we will just be using the **Customer** table.

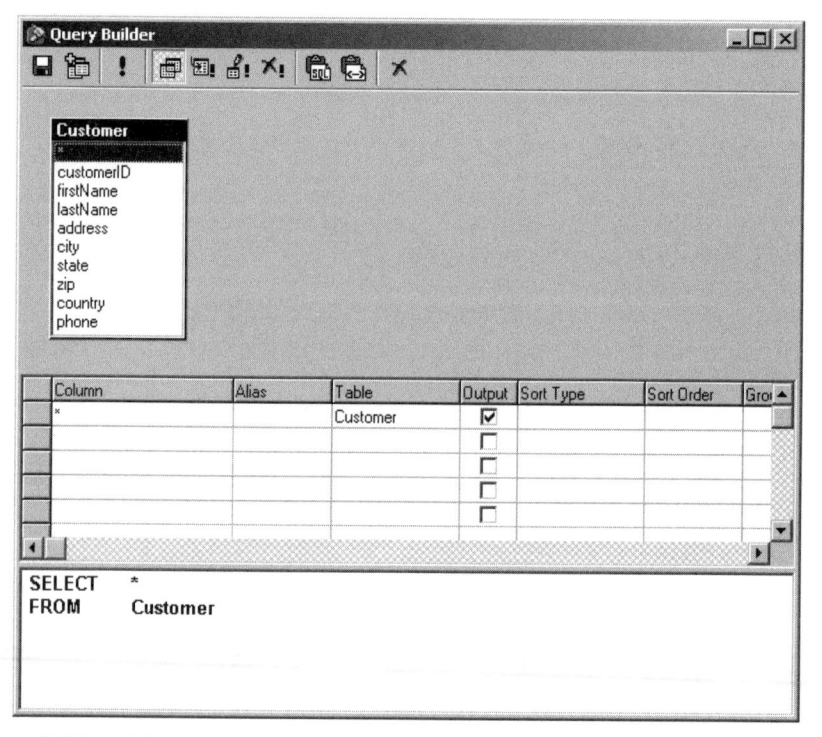

FIGURE 1-15 As you choose your fields, the query statement is automatically built for you.

By double clicking on the wildcard * you will choose all fields in the table. As you will notice in the bottom window, the SQL statement is built for you. Once the query statement is built, select the **RUN Query !** button and the query will execute. This is used to validate the query.

customerID	firstName	lastName	address	city	state	zip	country	phone	email	mailingList
1	Micah	Brown	1234 Main Street	West Hills	CA	91304	USA	818-555-9988	micah.brown@shelleybiotechnologies.com	0
2	Mike	Fredrick	5678 Elm Street	Minneapolis	MN	55110	USA	555-555-3210	mike.fredrick@shelleybiotechnologies.com	0
3	Fredrick	Kruger	3234 Elm Street	Killroy	MA	38372	USA	223-555-5940	fredrick.kruger@shelleybiotechnologies.com	0
4	Michelle	Rhoads	1243 Cantara Lane	Burbank	CA	91203	USA	818-555-4039	michelle.rhoads@shelleybiotechnologies.com	0
5	Willy	Tutone	19222 Falken Ave	Santa Barbara	CA	93111	USA	805-555-6811	willy.tutone@shelleybiotechnologies.com	0
6	Dawn	Brown	1234 Main Street	West Hills	CA	91304	USA	818-555-9988	dawn.brown@shelleybiotechnologies.com	0
7	Ashley	Nova	10010 Nova Lane	Santa Clarita	CA	91310	USA	805-555-3200	ashley.nova@shelleybiotechnologies.com	0
8	Max	Parker	981 Homer Way	West Hills	CA	91304	USA	818-555-5509	max.parker@shelleybiotechnologies.com	0
9	Peter	Pumpernickle	NULL	NULL	MN	55110	USA	NULL	peter.pumpernickle@shelleybiotechnologies.com	0
10	Penelope	Snodgrass	NULL	Roswell	NM	88201	USA	NULL	penelope.snodgrass@shelleybiotechnologies.com	0

FIGURE 1-16 The results from running the SQL builder.

This can also be helpful when working with several tables at once. With a little investigation, it can really save you some time!

◆ Recap

A lot has been covered in this first chapter. By now we're sure you can see some of the possibilities ColdFusion offers. It's very simple to pull data from a database and believe it or not, it's not much harder to add or change data in the database as well. We've only introduced you to some of the basics of SQL and more will be covered in the book as we move along. There is a tremendous amount of flexibility that SQL offers that is good to know when you continue to learn more about web and database development. There are plenty of good SQL books on the market, and if you plan on working with databases you should pick up a copy to learn more.

chapter 2
ColdFusion Basics

In This Chapter:

- Commenting Your Code
- Using Quotes
- Passing Variables
- Scope
- Project I: Passing Variables Between Pages
- Project II: Display Days Left Until a User-Defined Date
- Project III: Using <CFLOOP>
- New Functions
    - <CFPARAM>
    - <CFIF>
    - <CFELSE>
    - <CFELSEIF>
    - DateFormat
    - TimeFormat
    - DateDiff
    - IsDefined
    - Replace
    - <CFLOOP>
- Recap
- Advanced Project

◆ Commenting Your Code

There are many bad habits a programmer can get into. But one good habit to get into (and keep) is commenting your code. In most cases, your boss is paying you to write code and not comments but they can save you time and your boss money! To comment your ColdFusion code you have a couple of options.

```
<!-- These comments can be seen in the source code -->
```

The above comment is the standard HTML comment syntax. This comment will show up in the source code of your application. Notice it uses two dashes (--) to denote that it's a comment block. If you wish to comment your code, but not reveal it in your source code you must use three dashes:

```
<!--- These comments are processed by the ColdFusion Server --->
<!--- and are not visible in your source code --->
```

Generally it's a good idea to comment as often as possible. In many situations you'll have multiple developers working on the same project, so it makes it easier for everybody to be on the same page from the outset.

Areas you will want to comment include any individual functions within a page. I usually start each page with a header block that will explain the purpose of the template. It's also a good idea to comment the variables that are passed into the page as well as any that are going out, such as form or session variables. When it comes to commenting, you can never have enough (as long as the comments are about code and not your boss).

◆ Using Quotes

Using quotes in ColdFusion can be a hit-or-miss type of operation. In some cases, you can use quotes or not use quotes and get the same result. However, this is not the case in all situations. It's still best to know the basic rules of the quote!

```
<CFSET myName="Mike">
```

The above statement does just what you're thinking, sets myName equal to "Mike." Now consider the following statement.

```
<CFSET myName=Mike>
```

Looks pretty much the same, but without the quotes. The quotes define "Mike" as a string that myName was equal to in the first example. But here in the second, "Mike" is now a variable name that ColdFusion is trying to set myName equal to. This results in a typical ColdFusion error:

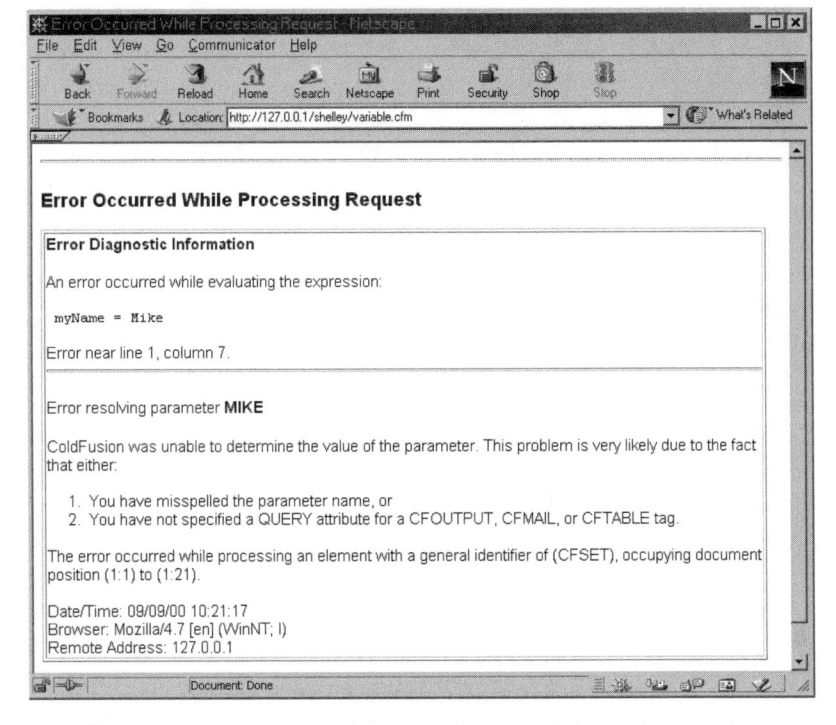

FIGURE 2-1 ColdFusion error message. Gives you information on where the error occurred and possible reasons.

One remedy for the missing variable is to set a default value with the `<CFPARAM>` tag.

<CFPARAM>

```
<CFPARAM
    NAME="name of query"                        Required
    DEFAULT="default value">                    Optional
```

TABLE 2–1 <CFPARAM> Attributes

Attribute	Description
NAME	Defines the name of the parameter.
DEFAULT	Defines the default value set if nothing is defined.

The `<CFPARAM>` tag allows you to define default values for ColdFusion variables. `<CFPARAM>` has two attributes, Name and Default. Name is required where Default is used only if you wish to specify a default value. This is a useful tag to use to "trap" any possible errors that could occur due to absent variables. Your pages will not cause an error, but may have inconsistent results when using default values.

Let's try this code using the `<CFPARAM>` tag:

```
<CFPARAM NAME="myName" DEFAULT="Mike">
<CFOUTPUT>
    #myName#
</CFOUTPUT>
```

This code will successfully display the variable "myName" even though we did not set the value to anything. Its value will be "Mike".

```
<CFPARAM NAME="myName" DEFAULT="Mike">
<CFSET myName="Micah">
<CFOUTPUT>
    #myName#
</CFOUTPUT>
```

Now since we set the variable, its value will be "Micah" instead of the default of "Mike." There are many tricky situations that you will have using quotes, but for the most part ColdFusion will let you know when you misuse them. But special attention needs to be paid when using the `<CFPARAM>` tag with variables as it can "hide" the existence of a variable you thought you had!

◆ Passing Variables

One of the core operations used in ColdFusion is the passing of variables from one page to the next. There are many different types of variables that are available in ColdFusion. Below are the types of variables you can use and a short explanation of how to use them.

TABLE 2-2 Common ColdFusion Variable Types

VARIABLES.fieldname	ColdFusion variables
URL.fieldname	Parameters passed to a URL
FORM.fieldname	Variables passed via FORMs
COOKIE.fieldname	Variables passed via client side cookies
ATTRIBUTES.fieldname	Attributes passed to custom tags
SESSION.fieldname	Variables passed via session variables
CGI.fieldname	Variables passed via CGI
APPLICATION.fieldName	Variables passed via the application scope
CLIENT.fieldname	Variables passed via client
SERVER.fieldname	Variables passed via the server scope

VARIABLES

Normal ColdFusion variables can be set inside the <CFOUTPUT> tags. They will be available only on the current template, unless passed via some method mentioned above.

EXAMPLE 2-1 To set a local variable that can be used within the current page

```
<CFSET Homepage.UserName="Mike">
<CFSET Homepage.Password="Polaris">
```

NOTE

You can set a local variable without giving it a prefix like "homepage." Applying scope to local variables is considered good programming practice however.

URL

URL variables are passed on the URL of a page. These can be useful to pass parameters between multiple pages in an application. The URL prefix is used to identify URL parameters.

EXAMPLE 2-2 You can interpret a URL parameter using a **URL** prefix.

```
<CFSET myVar=#URL.myVar#>
```

FORM

Form variables are one of the most commonly used ColdFusion variables. They are variables that are inputted from an HTML form in your applications.

EXAMPLE 2-3 This works the same way as URL variables except with the form prefix.

```
<CFSET myVar=#FORM.myVar#>
```

COOKIE

Cookies are used to store personalized information about your website. They are stored on your client's computer for use by your applications. The Cookie prefix is used to reference these types of variables.

EXAMPLE 2-4 This will set a cookie and create a local variable.

```
<CFSET LocalCookie=#Cookie.myCookie#>
```

ATTRIBUTES

These variables are for use with custom tags. Custom tags are used to encapsulate functions of a website. The custom tags can receive parameters, and the attributes preface is used to reference those parameters within the custom tags.

EXAMPLE 2-5 Name is an attribute passed into a custom tag. Use the Attributes prefix to reference it within the custom tag.

```
<CF_MyCustomTag name="Mike">
<CFSET LocalName=#Attributes.name#>
```

SESSION

Session variables are invisible to the user and are stored in memory. They are very useful if you have a value that needs to be used on many pages. The session variable can be used as long as the user's browser session is active.

CGI

Common Gateway Interface variables can be displayed with the CGI preface.

APPLICATION

These variables are to be used within the scope of your application. They are usually set in the application.cfm file. (See chapter 3 for details on how to use the *application.cfm* file.) These are prefaced with the **Application** prefix.

CLIENT

These variables are used to maintain a record of a particular client. This record is stored in the web server's registry, but can also exist in a database or cookie. These variables are accessed via the **Client** prefix.

SERVER

A server variable can be used to hold values of variables that all your ColdFusion applications can use. They will persist on the ColdFusion applications server until the services are restarted. These variables are accessed via the **Server** prefix.

◆ Scope

No, not the mouthwash. We are talking about the life of a variable here! Scope in this context basically defines where and when you can use variables within your application. Consider the following statements:

```
<CFSET LocalVariable="Yes">
```

The above variable is only available for use in the *current template*. Once processing moves to another page, this variable is lost and will need to be reset.

```
<CFSET Session.GlobalVariable="Maybe">
```

The session variable can be considered a global variable of sorts. It can be set in any place throughout your application for use by any other page. Once your session times out, however, your variable will be destroyed. Timeout can occur by an elapsed period of inactive browsing or by shutting down your browser window. Refer to chapter 3 on how to control your timeouts.

```
<CFSET Application.GlobalVariable="You Betcha!">
```

The application preface to this variable defines it as an application level variable. This signals that the variable is created in the application.cfm file (refer to chapter 3 for usage of the application.cfm file).

The application.cfm file executes every time you request a page in your application. Therefore, the value of "Application.GlobalVariable" will be available to every page in your application.

◆ Project I: Passing Variables Between Pages

For our first project on passing variables we will be using HTML FORMs. If you need a quick tutorial on using HTML forms, refer to Appendix B for more explanation.

Script 2-1
myInfo.cfm

```
<!DOCTYPE HTML PUBLIC "-//W3C//DTD HTML 4.0 Transitional//EN">
<HTML>
<HEAD>
<TITLE>Contact Information</TITLE>
</HEAD>
<BODY>

<FORM ACTION="myInfo2.cfm" METHOD="post">

<FONT FACE="Arial, Helvetica" SIZE="3">
<H3>Please enter some information about yourself</H3>
```

```
First Name:
<INPUT TYPE="text" NAME="firstName" SIZE="10"><BR>
Last Name:
<INPUT TYPE="text" NAME="lastName" SIZE="10"><BR>
Phone Number:
<INPUT TYPE="text" NAME="phoneNumber" SIZE="10"><BR>
Age:
<INPUT TYPE="text" NAME="age" SIZE="3"><BR>
<INPUT TYPE="submit" VALUE="Submit">
</FONT>
</FORM>

</BODY>
</HTML>
```

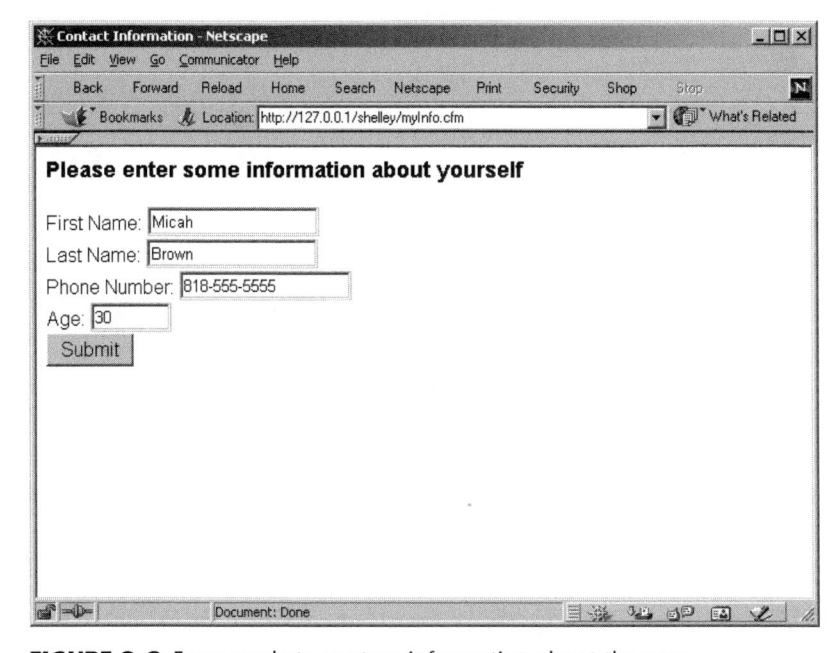

FIGURE 2-2 Form ready to capture information about the user.

Script 2-2
myInfo2.cfm

```
<!DOCTYPE HTML PUBLIC "-//W3C//DTD HTML 4.0 Transitional//EN">
<HTML>
<HEAD>
<CFOUTPUT>
<TITLE>#FORM.firstName#'s Contact Information</TITLE>
</CFOUTPUT>
</HEAD>
<BODY>

<CFOUTPUT>
<FONT FACE="Arial, Helvetica" SIZE="3">
<H3>Here is the information you submitted</H3>
First Name: #FORM.firstName#<BR>
Last Name: #FORM.lastName#<BR>
Phone Number: #FORM.phoneNumber#<BR>
Age: #FORM.age#
</FONT>
</CFOUTPUT>

</BODY>
</HTML>
```

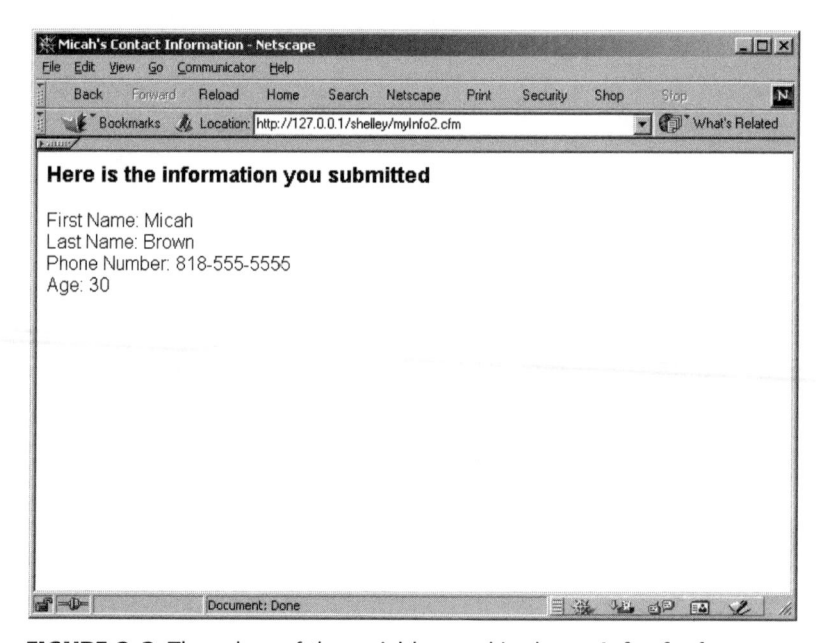

FIGURE 2-3 The values of the variables used in the **myInfo.cfm** form are displayed back to the user.

<CFIF></CFIF>

The `<CFIF>` tag is a very flexible tag to use in your applications. There are several ways which it can evaluate a condition between two pieces of information.

IS, EQUAL (EQ)

These two operators accomplish the same thing. They allow you to check to see if argument A IS argument B or A is EQUAL to B.

    <CFIF A EQ B>

IS NOT, NOT EQUAL (NEQ)

These operators allow you to reverse any logic you may want to test for.

    <CFIF A NEQ B>

CONTAINS, DOES NOT CONTAIN

Contains works similarly to the IN operator of SQL. It allows you to evaluate any number of values.

    <CFIF "12345,23645,46597" CONTAINS #B# >

If "B" is equal to any of those three numbers then the <CFIF> will evaluate to true.

GREATER THAN (GT), LESS THAN (LT), GREATER THAN OR EQUAL (GTE), LESS THAN OR EQUAL (LTE)

These operators will test different states of the variables in question. They can be used in their long-winded format listed first (not recommended!) or the shorter, concise abbreviations.

    <CFIF A GT B>

NOT, OR, AND

Standard Booleans can be used to test multiple variables in one `<CFIF>` statement.

    <CFIF #SessionID# GT 1 AND #SessionID# LT 100>

What happens if a user does not type in a phone number? When the **myInfo.cfm** page is submitted the **myInfo2.cfm** page will display the values but the *phoneNumber* field will be left blank. If you are not going to make this a mandatory field (more about this in Chapter 5) then you probably shouldn't have the entire line appear at all. You will use the `<CFIF></CFIF>` tags to do error checking on the data to make certain actions happen if certain criteria is met or ignore it if it's not. This is called **Conditional Logic**.

1. `<CFIF FORM.phoneNumber IS NOT "">`
    `Phone Number: #FORM.phoneNumber#`
2. `</CFIF>`

HOW THIS WORKS

1. If the variable *phoneNumber* IS NOT empty, meaning that it contains at least something, process the next line.
2. If the IF statement is not met, the phone number line will not be displayed and the rest of the page will continue to be processed.

Try replacing the above code from **myInfo2.cfm** to include your newfound knowledge of the `<CFIF>` tag with everything between the `<CFOUTPUT></CFOUTPUT>` tags with this:

```
<CFOUTPUT>
<FONT FACE="Arial, Helvetica" SIZE="3">
<H3>Here is the information you submitted</H3>
First name: #FORM.firstName#<BR>
Last Name: #FORM.lastName#<BR>
<CFIF FORM.phoneNumber IS NOT "">
Phone Number: #FORM.phoneNumber#<BR>
</CFIF>
Age: #FORM.age#
</FONT>
</CFOUTPUT>
```

When you pass **myInfo.cfm** again without a phone number, the page will process the `<CFIF>` tags and ignore the **Phone Number** line.

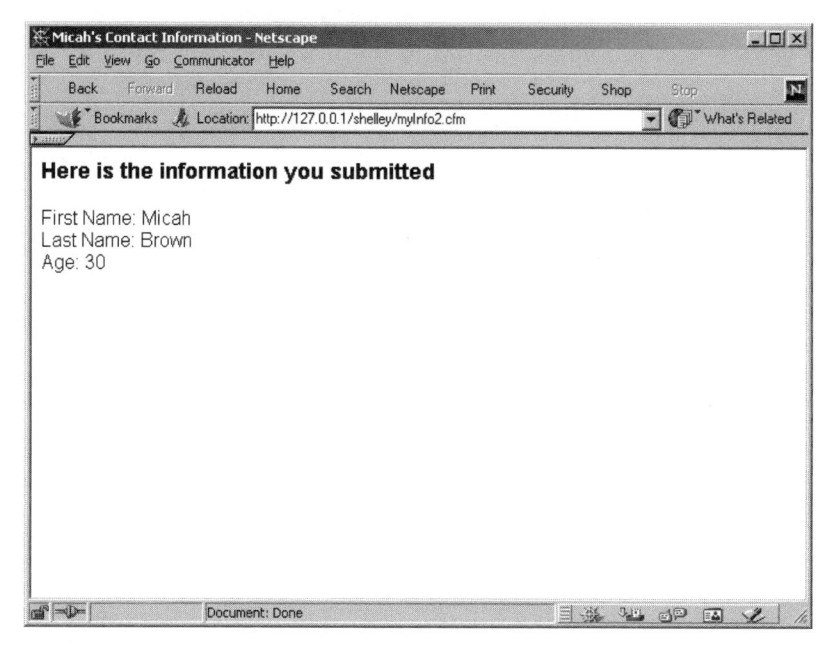

FIGURE 2-4 The values of the variables used in the **myInfo.cfm** form are displayed back to the user without the *phoneNumber* field filled in.

<CFELSE>

Taking the above code from **myInfo.cfm** we will need to modify it to make certain lines appear if the appropriate field contains data and not appear if the field is empty.

1. `<CFIF FORM.phoneNumber IS NOT "">`
   `Phone Number: #FORM.phoneNumber#<BR>`
2. `<CFELSE>`
   `<FONT COLOR="red">`
   `Please go back and enter a phone number!<BR>`
   `</FONT>`
3. `</CFIF>`

HOW THIS WORKS

1. If the variable *phoneNumber* IS NOT empty, process the next line. At this point the condition will be met and the rest of the testing up to and including the `</CFIF>` will be ignored.

2. If line 1 fails because the variable *phoneNumber* is empty then we get to the `<CFELSE>` and the rest of the lines up to the close of the `<CFIF>` tag are processed.

Try replacing this code in the **myInfo2.cfm** page you just created.

```
<CFOUTPUT>
<FONT FACE="Arial, Helvetica" SIZE="3">
<H3>Here is the information you submitted</H3>
First Name: #FORM.firstName#<BR>
Last Name: #FORM.lastName#<BR>
<CFIF FORM.phoneNumber IS NOT "">
Phone Number: #FORM.phoneNumber#<BR>
<CFELSE>
    <FONT COLOR="red">
    Please go back and enter a phone number!<BR>
    </FONT>
</CFIF>
Age: #FORM.age#
</FONT>
</CFOUTPUT>
```

Here is the information you submitted

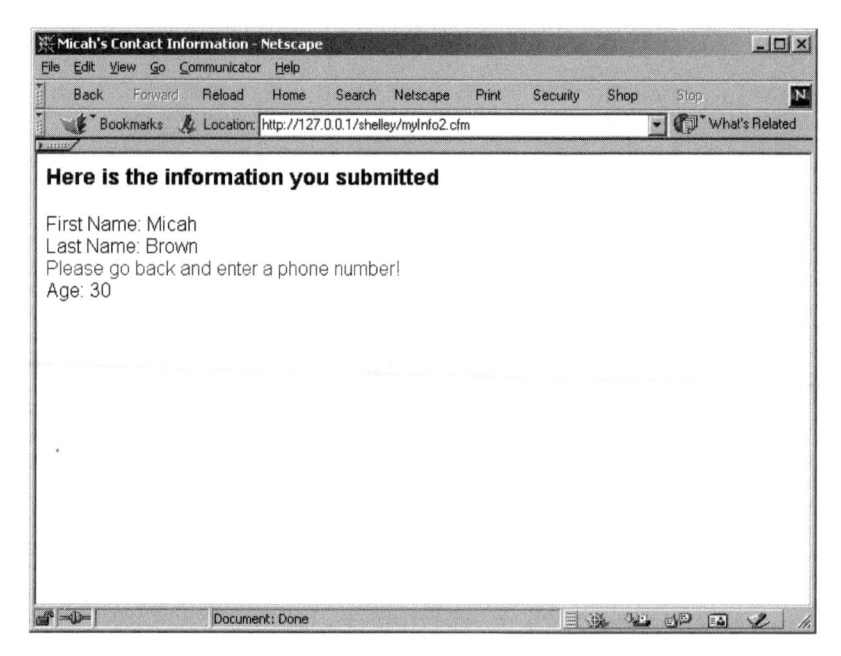

First Name: Micah
Last Name: Brown
Please go back and enter a phone number!
Age: 30

FIGURE 2–5 A message is displayed if the variable *phoneNumber* is left empty.

<CFELSEIF>

If you have more than two types of actions that could happen while testing, you will want to use the <CFELSEIF> tag to structure the list of the possible outcomes. You can nest as many <CFELSEIF> tags as you would like to have a wide range of things happen. For our next example we will test the value of the person's age and display different messages if they enter 16, 18, or 35 for their ages:

1. `<CFIF FORM.age IS "16">`
   `You're legal to drive!`
2. `<CFELSEIF FORM.age IS "18">`
   `You're legal to vote!`
3. `<CFELSEIF FORM.age IS "35">`
   `You're legal to register to run as president!`
4. `<CFELSE>`
   `Age: # FORM.age#`
   `</CFIF>`

HOW THIS WORKS

1. If the variable FORM.age has the value of 16, the message *"You're legal to drive!"* is displayed. If the value of FORM.age is not equal, the next line is tested.
2. If the value of FORM.age has the value of 18, the message *"You're legal to vote!"* will be displayed. If the value of FORM.age still isn't met, the next line is tested.
3. If the value of FORM.age has the value of 35, the message *"You're legal to register to run as president!"* will be displayed. If the value of FORM.age still isn't met, the next line is tested. This could go on for quite awhile, as you can imagine.
4. Finally we must display something if none of the conditions were met using the <CFELSE> tag. Then finally close the <CFIF> statement.

Now Function

The Now() object is used to display the time and date in raw format. Using other types of functions, which are discussed right after this, you can dress the Now() object up to format the time and date several different ways.

Example:
```
Today's date is #Now()#
```
Display:
```
Today's date is {ts '2000-12-31 10:45:09'}
```

Without any type of formatting, the `Now()` object doesn't look terribly useful. Using the following functions with `Now()` you will see how to use it to display the time and date along with the various formatting rules.

Date Functions

Displaying the current time and date at the top of your company's website page doesn't really serve much of a practical purposes in most cases—unless you have viewers like me who, nine times out of ten, are usually off a day or two and it serves as a good reminder.

Time and date functions serve several different purposes not only for display purposes but also for backend functionality. You can use them for such cases as:

- Time/date stamping actions in your database such as when transactions occur
- Comparing lengths in times
- Sorting items by date
- Setting beginning and ending times for actions to start and end

NOTE
Remember that since the following ColdFusion tags are going to be processed by the ColdFusion server they must be enclosed within the `<CFOUTPUT></CFOUTPUT>` tags or ColdFusion will treat them as ordinary characters and you will not get the desired results.

DateFormat

```
DateFormat(Now())
```

The `DateFormat` function is very flexible in that you can set different types of formatting to have it display the date in a number of ways. Here's an example without setting any specific type of formatting and letting ColdFusion format the date for you.

Example:

Today's date is `#DateFormat(Now())#`

Display:

Today's date is 09-Oct-00

That's fine, but setting different types of formatting attributes allows you to specify how you want this to look, whether you would like the date to appear after the month, add characters such as hyphens between the elements, or simply spell the month out instead of abbreviating it. These are called *MASKS*.

Take a look at the table below and the different types of masks you can use to format the *day*, *month*, and *year*.

TABLE 2-3 Types of Masks to Format Day, Month, and Year

Mask	Displays
DATE	
D	1 – Displays day of month as single digit unless it's a double digit
DD	01 – Displays day of month as double digit
DDD	Sun – Displays the day of week as a three letter abbreviation
DDDD	Sunday – Displays the day of week spelled out
MONTH	
M	1 – Displays month in single digit numeric form unless it's a double digit
MM	01 – Displays month in two digit numeric form
MMM	Jan – Displays abbreviated month
MMMM	January – Displays entire month name
YEAR	
Y	0 – Displays last two digits of year or last single digit for years under 10
YY	00 – Displays last two digits of year
YYYY	2000 – Displays all four digits of a year

DateFormat with formatting

#DateFormat(Now(), "MM DD, YY")#	01 01, 01
#DateFormat(Now(), "MMMM D, YYYY")#	January 1, 2001
#DateFormat(Now(), "MMMM DD, YYYY")#	January 01, 2001
#DateFormat(Now(), "DDDD - MMMM - YYYY")#	Monday - January - 2001

TimeFormat

```
TimeFormat(Now())
```

The `TimeFormat` function, like the DateFormat we just discussed, can also have different types of formatting set to have it display the time several different ways. Here's an example without setting any specific type of formatting and letting ColdFusion format the time for you.

Example:

The time is `#TimeFormat(Now())#`

Display:

The time is 06:04 PM

TABLE 2-4 Types of Masks to Format **Time**

Mask	Displays
h	**1** – Displays single digit hour unless double digit is called for (12 hour clock)
hh	**01** – Displays double digit hour (12 hour clock)
H	**13** – Displays single digit hour unless double digit is called for (24 hour clock)
HH	**13** – Displays double digit hour (24 hour clock)
m	**1** – Displays single digit minute unless double digit is called for
mm	**01** – Displays double digit minute
s	**1** – Displays single digit second unless double digit is called for
ss	**01** – Displays double digit second
t	**A** – Displays **A** or **P** for AM or PM time markers
tt	**AM** – Displays **AM** or **PM** time markers

TimeFormat with formatting	
#TimeFormat(Now(), "HH:mm:ss")#	18:04:07
#TimeFormat(Now(), "HH:mm:ss tt")#	18:04:07 PM
#TimeFormat(Now(), "hh:mm:ss tt")#	06:04:07 PM
#TimeFormat(Now(), "HH m s t")#	18 4 7 P

◆ Project II: Display Days Left Until a User-Defined Date

Now that you know how to pass variables from page to page we can try using some of ColdFusion's functions to manipulate that input! Countdown will return the number of days that are left from the date you input on a form. In Project I we used two templates to handle form input. Here is an easy way to accomplish the same result with one less template. This will allow you to keep all the functionality of an application on a minimal amount of pages.

DateDiff

```
DateDiff("d", firstDate,secondDate)
```

This function will allow you to determine how much time has elapsed between two variables. The first parameter ("d" above) represents the time period you wish to determine. "d" would mean that you want to find out the number of days between the two variables (check Appendix A for a complete listing of the masks available with the DateDiff function). The second and third parameters (firstDate and secondDate above) represent the two dates you wish to compare. You need to be careful that your firstDate is smaller then your secondDate. Even though it's legal to do, it will return a negative value if they are reversed.

IsDefined

```
IsDefined("URL.countdown")
```

The IsDefined function will let ColdFusion know if a certain variable exists within a template. In the case above, IsDefined is testing for the URL parameter called countdown. That variable would be in the URL of your template. IsDefined is almost always used in conjunction with the <CFIF> tag to determine what block of code is executed next.

Replace

```
Replace(myString, "A", "B", "ALL")
```

The replace function will allow you to search any string and replace a value with another. In the above example, I am looking for the character "A" in myString. Once the character is found, it's replaced with the letter "B." The fourth parameter is an optional parameter telling the function how many of the occurrences to replace. "ALL" is the default.

Script 2-3
countdown.cfm

```
<!DOCTYPE HTML PUBLIC "-//W3C//DTD HTML 4.0 Transitional//EN">
<HTML>
<HEAD>
<TITLE>Project II: Countdown</TITLE>
</HEAD>

<BODY>
```
1. `<FORM ACTION="countdown.cfm?countdown=yes" METHOD="post">Enter A Date <INPUT TYPE="Text" NAME="TheDate"> (mm/dd/yy)<BR>`
2. `<INPUT TYPE="Submit" VALUE=" Begin Countdown! ">`
3. `</FORM>`
   `<BR>`
4. `<CFIF IsDefined("URL.countdown")>`
5. `    <CFSET DaysLeft=DateDiff("d", Now(), FORM.theDate)>`
   `    <CFOUTPUT>`
6. `    <CFIF daysLeft LT 0>`
7. `    <CFSET daysLeft=Replace(daysLeft,"-","")>`
8. `    Whoops! #DateFormat(Form.theDate,"mmmm d yyyy")# was #daysLeft# day<CFIF daysLeft GT 1>s</CFIF> ago!`
9. `    <CFELSE>`
   `    There are <FONT COLOR="red">#daysLeft#</FONT> Day`
   `    <CFIF daysLeft GT 1>s</CFIF> until`
   `    #DateFormat(FORM.theDate,"mmmm d yyyy")#`
   `    </CFIF>`
   `    </CFOUTPUT>`
   `</CFIF>`
   `</BODY>`
   `</HTML>`

HOW THIS WORKS

1-3. This section is the form that will allow you to input your date to compute the remaining days from today's date. Notice the action of the form has a variable attached to the template. *countdown=Yes* is a variable that is passed back to this same page telling ColdFusion that we are ready to start the countdown.

4. Notice the *URL.countdown* inside the IsDefined function. Remember that *countdown* is the URL parameter we specified above in the form's action parameter. ColdFusion will look for any variable called *countdown*; it's a good habit to preface the type of variable like I have above. Since this is a URL parameter we would use *URL.countdown*.

5. Using the DateDiff function we can compute how many days are left until the specified date.

6. This `<CFIF>` statement evaluates the number of days that are left. If it's less than 0 days, then we execute one series of code, otherwise we execute another.

7. If there are less than 0 days left, meaning you entered a day in the past in the form box, we need to remove the minus (-) sign from the value of *daysLeft*. Using the replace function we can replace the minus with a blank.

8. A message will appear notifying you that the date was in the past. If *daysLeft* was more then one day in the past, then the proper tense was added with the `<CFIF>` statement.

9. The `<CFELSE>` statement belongs to the first `<CFIF>` statement evaluating the *daysLeft* variable. At this point, the *daysLeft* variable represents a positive number so the *daysLeft* are just displayed along with the date you entered in the form before.

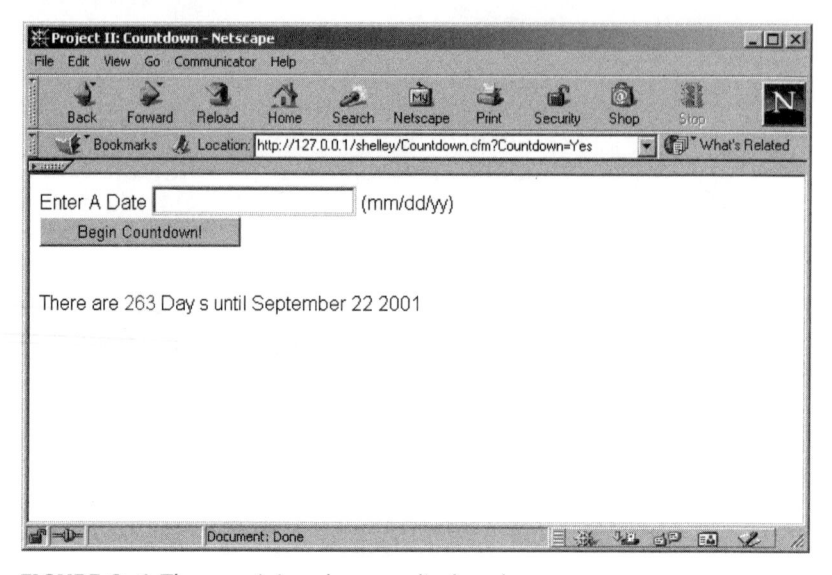

FIGURE 2-6 The remaining days are displayed.

◆ Project III: Using <CFLOOP>

Index Loops
    INDEX="*name of parameter*"   Required
    FROM="*start value*"   Required
    TO="*end value*"   Required
    STEP="*increment value*"   Optional

Conditional Loops
    CONDITION="*condition*"   Required

Query Loops
    QUERY="*query name*"   Required
    STARTROW="*start value*"   Optional
    ENDROW="*end value*"   Optional

List Loops
    LIST="*list*"   Required
    INDEX="*name of parameter*"   Required
    DELIMETERS="*delimiter*"   Optional

Collection or Structure Loops
    COLLECTION="*COM collection or structure*"   Required
    ITEM="*current item*"   Required

TABLE 2–5 <CFLOOP> Attributes

Attribute	Description
INDEX	Defines the name of the loop.
FROM	Defines the value you wish to start from.
TO	Defines the value you wish to end with.
STEP	Defines the increment value you wish to use while processing the loop. The default value is set to '1'.
CONDITION	Defines the condition you wish to loop until evaluated TRUE. Ex: <CFLOOP CONDITION="MyVar LTE 5">
LIST	Defines the list you want to loop through.
QUERY	Defines the name of the query you wish to loop through.
STARTROW	Defines the row you wish to start on when looping through a query.
ENDROW	Defines the row you wish to stop on when looping through a query.
DELIMITERS	When looping through a list, specifies how the items are delimited. Typically a comma.
COLLECTION	Name of a COM Collection or Structure you wish to loop through.
ITEM	Used in a Collection loop to identify the current item.

One of the most useful kinds of operation is a loop. A loop allows you to do many things a certain number of times. ColdFusion gives you this functionality with the <CFLOOP> tag. Loops can be confusing (and even intimidating) at times but <CFLOOP> makes if easy for the developer to understand and use.

To illustrate the simplicity of <CFLOOP> we'll create a simple looping application that will create a drop-down list box with today's date. Then we'll populate it with seven prior days to that date.

Here is the code to do just that!

Script 2-4
cfLoop.cfm

```
<!DOCTYPE HTML PUBLIC "-//W3C//DTD HTML 4.0 Transitional//EN">

<HTML>
<HEAD>
<TITLE>Using CFLOOP</TITLE>
</HEAD>
<H3>A Simple CFLOOP!</H3><BR>
<BODY>
```
1. `<FORM ACTION="cfLoop.cfm" METHOD="post">`
2. `<SELECT NAME="myListBox">`
3. `<CFOUTPUT><OPTION SELECTED>#DateFormat(Now(),"mmmm d, yyyy")#</OPTION></CFOUTPUT>`
4. `<CFLOOP INDEX="myIndex" FROM="1" TO="7">`
    `<CFOUTPUT>`
5. `<CFSET getDate="-" & myIndex>`
6. `<OPTION>#DateFormat(DateAdd("d",getDate,Now()),"mmmm d, yyyy")#</OPTION>`
    `</CFOUTPUT>`
```
</CFLOOP>
</SELECT>
</FORM>
</BODY>
</HTML>
```

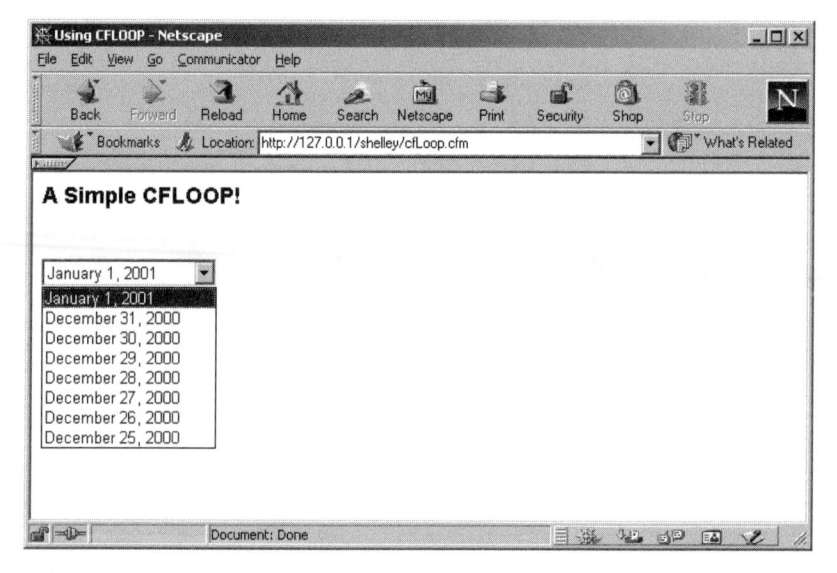

FIGURE 2–7 `<CFLOOP>` in action.

The first thing you need to understand about `<CFLOOP>` is that you will need an index to reference by. An index is just any string you wish to use and it's treated like a variable. I am using `MyIndex` as the index in this example. Once you set your index, you must supply FROM and TO parameters. These are just what they sound like; they provide a starting and ending point for your loop to execute. In this case I am choosing to start at one and end up on seven, meaning the loop will execute seven times.

HOW THIS WORKS

1-3. The first three lines define the list box we are going to use and also a default value of today's date for the first value in the list.
4. Line 4 sets the `<CFLOOP>` with the required parameters. Remember any code placed within `<CFLOOP></CFLOOP>` tags will execute the number of times you have in your TO and FROM attributes; in this case it's seven.
5. The first time the loop is executed `myIndex` will have a value of one. A "-" (minus) sign is added to the beginning to give us the result of "-1".
6. The `getDate` variable is used to tell the `DateAdd` function how many days to add to the current date. In this case, the `DateAdd` function is used to subtract days from the current date.

This simple looping application will pave the way for you to dynamically create content on your websites. `<CFLOOP>` can be used with many different types of data including queries. You can take any query and loop through the results to create dynamic content. A word of caution though, an infinite loop is easy to accomplish if you're not careful!

◆ Recap

Well, those are the ColdFusion basics. Granted this chapter doesn't cover all the basic things you need to know about ColdFusion but it should give you a good foundation to build on. Part of learning a new language is trial and error and figuring out how to fix the code when it doesn't work. In the coming chapters we'll introduce you to additional features of ColdFusion but will most definately refer to techniques in this chapter as we move forward.

◆ Advanced Project

This project will use skills you learned in projects II and III. Set up an application that will allow the user to enter a date into a form field. Based on what was entered, display a list of dates starting with what was entered and the following 10 days.

3 Global Templates

IN THIS CHAPTER:

- Defining the Application File (*application.cfm*)
- Project I: Setting Global Values for Your Site
- Project II: Defining Header and Footer Files
- New Functions
  - <CFAPPLICATION>
  - <CFERROR>
  - <CFINCLUDE>
- Recap
- Advanced Project

In this chapter we are going to show you how to make life much easier by using some simple techniques to set up global functionality throughout your application.

With these techniques you with be able to set variables globally in the *application.cfm* file or set up templates, such as a file for site navigation, and use that template throughout several pages with the `<CFINCLUDE>` tag.

◆ Defining the Application File (application.cfm)

The *application.cfm* file is an auto included file. This infers that ColdFusion will automatically launch this file *IF* it exists. Typically it is created in the root directory of your web server so all parts of your application can access it. The *application.cfm* file will be executed first every time a client requests a ColdFusion page as it looks for global variables that might be set. This can be said for every file at or below the level of the file within your file tree. This may sound confusing at first, but consider the following directory structure.

We have two directories in this application, an *index.cfm* file, which is in the root directory, and a *products.cfm* file, which is in the Products directory. If I were to request the *index.cfm* or the *products.cfm* file the *application.cfm* file would execute from the root.

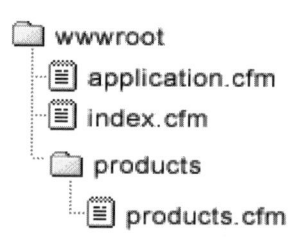

```
wwwroot
├── application.cfm
├── index.cfm
└── products
    └── products.cfm
```

FIGURE 3-1

However, if we add an *application.cfm* file into the products directory, the *application.cfm* file in the Products directory would execute since it is local to that directory.

```
wwwroot
├── application.cfm
├── index.cfm
└── products
    ├── application.cfm
    └── products.cfm
```

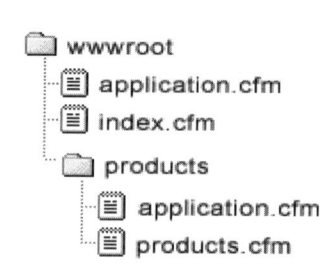

FIGURE 3-2

The types of variables to set inside the *application.cfm* file are up to you. Think about some basic variables you will be using throughout your templates that will remain consistent. Usually data source names are a good thing to store in there as well as username or a password you might have set on the data source. That way in the future if you need to change any of these (the password is good to change from time to time) you simply update it in the *application.cfm* file and it's globally changed! Then you don't have to go through all your files to change the names for these. It is also useful for setting page titles, fonts, etc.

Defining the Application File (application.cfm)

```
<CFSET dataSource="shelleyCatalog">
<CFSET userName="shelley">
<CFSET password="mypassword">
<CFSET title="Shelley Biotechnologies">
```

Now that we know when the application file is executed, let's learn a bit more about what can be in it to make your life much easier!

<CFAPPLICATION>

```
<CFAPPLICATION
    NAME="application name"                              Required
    APPLICATIONTIMEOUT="#CreateTimeSpan(0,1,0,0)#"       Optional
    CLIENTMANAGEMENT="yes or no"                         Optional
    CLIENTSTORAGE="storage type"                         Optional
    SESSIONMANAGEMENT="yes or no"                        Optional
    SESSIONTIMEOUT="#CreateTimeSpan(0,1,0,0)#"           Optional
    SETCLIENTCOOKIES="yes or no">                        Optional
```

The <CFAPPLICATION> tag only has one relevant file location, and that is to be placed in the *application.cfm* file. It tells the ColdFusion server how to control each of your applications and what features to use (such as session management). The complete list of attributes for the <CFAPPLICATION> tag:

TABLE 3–1 <CFAPPLICATION> Attributes

Attribute	Description
Name	Required: The name of your application.
ApplicationTimeout	Defines the period of time application variables exist; defaults to the values set in the ColdFusion administrator. #CreateTimeSpan(days, hours, minutes, seconds)# Default is two days.
ClientManagement	Enables or disables client variables; defaults to NO.
ClientStorage	Sets device for storage of client variables. Defaults to *registry* but can be stored as *cookie* or any ODBC data source.
SessionManagement	Enables or disables session variables; defaults to NO.

TABLE 3–1 <CFAPPLICATION> Attributes *(continued)*

Attribute	Description
SessionTimeout	Defines a period of time session variables exist; defaults to values set in the ColdFusion administrator. #CreateTimeSpan(days, hours, minutes, seconds)# Default is 20 minutes.
SetClientCookies	Enables or disables the use of client cookies; defaults to YES. (Remember, not everyone accepts cookies.)

A typical <CFAPPLICATION> tag would look like:

```
<CFAPPLICATION NAME="shelleyBio" SESSIONMANAGEMENT="yes">
```

This names the application we are working with ("shelleyBio") and allows the use of session variables within the application. By default, the session timeout value would be set in the ColdFusion administrator. This is fine if you are allowed to administer it, but in the case of using an ISP you most likely will not be able to. If you wish to have different timeout values than specified by your ISP you may set them with the SessionTimeout attribute of the <CFAPPLICATION> tag.

To set the timeout on session and application variables you must use the CreateTimeSpan function. Its usage is very simple to understand. Take a look at the following example.

```
<CFSET timeout=CreateTimeSpan(0,1,0,0)>
```

The CreateTimeSpan function has four parameters that must be supplied. They are, in order from left to right: days, hours, minutes, and seconds. The value of Timeout set above would be one hour from when the statement was executed. Now that you have a valid timeout, you can plug it into your <CFAPPLICATION> tag.

```
<CFAPPLICATION NAME="shelleyBio" SESSIONMANAGEMENT="yes"
SESSIONTIMEOUT="#timeout#">
```

Or you could just nest the function into the tag like:

```
<CFAPPLICATION NAME="shelleyBio" SESSIONMANAGEMENT="yes"
SESSIONTIMEOUT="#CreateTimeSpan(0,1,0,0)#">
```

<CFERROR>

Sometimes for unexpected reasons, your site will crash (and don't think it won't, it's a matter of when, not if). That's when ColdFusion can really help you out. Using the <CFERROR> tag, you can build a custom template that will allow your users to submit any errors they encounter to the Webmaster.

You will place the <CFERROR> function in your *application.cfm* file so that if any page encounters an error the <CFERROR> tag will be triggered.

For Example:

```
<CFERROR TEMPLATE="cferror.cfm" TYPE="request"
MAILTO="webmaster@shelleybiotechnologies.com">
```

When an error occurs, the contents of the *cferror.cfm* page will be displayed to the user. This will allow you to customize the look of your error page and hide the ugly (and sometimes downright scary) web server error pages.

There are two types of <CFERROR> variables available, validation and request. The validation variables are available to you when a user is trying to use a form and errors occur. Request variables are available to you under the most common circumstances, when a user requests a page that has an error on it. The most common use for <CFERROR> is to create a form and use these variables to allow your users to report them back to you. This makes nice use of <CFMAIL>, which will be explained in the chapters ahead.

The variables that are available for use with the <CFERROR> tag are:

TABLE 3-2 <CFERROR> Variables

Type	Field	Description
Validation	#Error.InvalidFields#	Lists the invalid form fields.
Validation	#Error.ValidationFooter#	Instructions to be included in the footer of the error message.
Validation	#Error.ValidationHeader#	Instructions to be included in the header of the error message.
Request	#Error.Template#	The template that has caused the error.

TABLE 3-2 <CFERROR> Variables *(continued)*

Type	Field	Description
Request	#Error.QueryString#	The query string variables that are associated with the template.
Request	#Error.MailTo#	Email address of the webmaster.
Request	#Error.HTTPReferer#	The page that referred the error template.
Request	#Error.Diagnostics#	The error diagnostics message that ColdFusion supplies.
Request	#Error.DateTime#	The date/time when the error occurred.
Request	#Error.Browser#	The browser of the user that accessed the template.
Request	#Error.RemoteAddress#	The user's IP address.

Now we will set up the *cfError.cfm* page that will be displayed when an error occurs. This will be used by the *application.cfm* file that immediately follows this template.

Script 3-1
cferror.cfm

```
<!DOCTYPE HTML PUBLIC "-//W3C//DTD HTML 4.0 Transitional//EN">

<HTML>
<HEAD>
      <TITLE>Whoops...!</TITLE>
</HEAD>

<BODY>
<H2>We're sorry, but this page has encountered an error.<BR>
Please try again later.</H2>
<H3>Thank you for visiting Shelley Biotechnologies</H3>

</BODY>
</HTML>
```

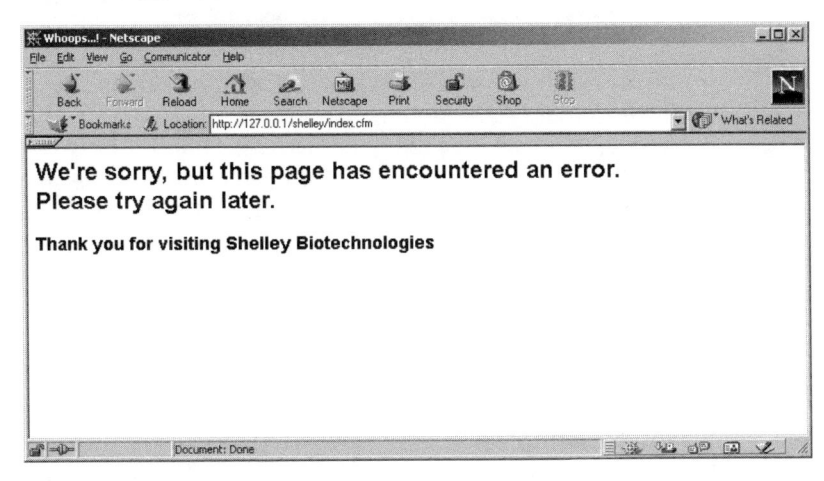

FIGURE 3-3 The contents of the `<CFERROR>` page are displayed to the user when an error occurs.

◆ Project I: Setting Global Values for Your Site

The *application.cfm* file can really help you organize your website by consolidating tasks that are shared by several applications. The *application.cfm* file *cannot* be displayed in your browser window; rather it's used as an invisible global file where you can stash any important information about your applications. Before we go into coding a project, we'll give a short introduction to the functions used with this project.

Now you can set your global variables like so:

Script 3-2
application.cfm

```
<CFAPPLICATION NAME="shelleyBio" SESSIONMANAGEMENT="Yes"
SESSIONTIMEOUT=#CreateTimeSpan(0,1,0,0)#
APPLICATIONTIMEOUT="#CreateTimeSpan(2,0,0,0)#">

<CFSET Application.dataSource="shelleyCatalog">
<CFSET Application.userName="shelley">
<CFSET Application.password="mypassword">
<CFSET title="Shelley Biotechnologies">
<CFERROR TEMPLATE="cferror.cfm" TYPE="Request" MAILTO=
"webmaster@shelleybiotechnologies.com">
```

> **NOTE**
>
> In this situation we are creating APPLICATION variables to store our global information. By setting APPLICATIONTIMEOUT with the CreateTimeSpan function to two days we can limit the time the variables hang around in memory before they are reset. We also set the SESSIONMANAGEMENT equal to YES to allow us to use session variables within our application. We also set a timeout of one hour with the SESSIONTIMEOUT attribute.

Choosing the correct type of variables to use in an application is very important. Application variables can be convenient but can remain in memory if not properly controlled. This can hinder the performance of your web server. Session variables, however, are much more controllable and can be destroyed when a user is done using them within your applications. This also provides for a better level of security when dealing with sensitive information.

We are not going to dive into application and security variables since that is beyond the scope of this book. The Allaire manual that comes with ColdFusion Studio talks in-depth about these issues.

◆ Project II: Defining Header and Footer Files

<CFINCLUDE>

Using global templates on your website can be critical in controlling the amount of development time you invest. I like to use the common phrase: "Why reinvent the wheel?" If I can get away with doing less work and gaining more flexibility then I am all for it! One of the most common things you can do is to use common headers and footers in your application. Through the help of the <CFINCLUDE> tag you can make your site as dynamic as you wish, but still retain total control within only a few templates.

This is especially useful if you plan on changing one of these files from time to time. You just change it once and every page will be updated since they are including that one particular file.

Example:

```
<CFINCLUDE TEMPLATE="_fileName">
```

Now let's build our _header.cfm and _footer.cfm files and view them in a new page by using our newly learned tag.

NOTE
We are only using the underline (_) at the beginning of the filename to make it easier to differentiate which files are being used as include files. You can name them whatever you would like as long as it follows typical file naming conventions.

Script 3-3
_header.cfm

```
<TABLE BORDER="0" CELLPADDING="0" CELLSPACING="0" WIDTH="600">
<TR>
   <TD COLSPAN="5">
   <IMG SRC="images/shelleyHeader.gif" WIDTH="" HEIGHT=""
ALT="Shelley Biotechnologies">
   </TD>
</TR>
<TR>
   <TD COLSPAN="5" VALIGN="top">
   <FONT FACE="Arial, Helvetica" SIZE="2">
   <CFOUTPUT><B>#DateFormat(Now(), ("DDDD MMMM D,
YYYY"))#</B></CFOUTPUT></FONT>
   </TD>
</TR>
<TR>
   <TD VALIGN="top">
   <A HREF="">
   <IMG SRC="images/shelleyNews.gif" ALT="News" BORDER="0"></A>
   </TD>
   <TD VALIGN="top">
   <A HREF="">
   <IMG SRC="images/shelleyProducts.gif" ALT="Products"
BORDER="0"></A>
   </TD>
   <TD VALIGN="top">
   <A HREF="">
   <IMG SRC="images/shelleyContactUs.gif" ALT="Contact Us"
BORDER="0"></A>
```

```
        </TD>
        <TD VALIGN="top">
        <A HREF="">
        <IMG SRC="images/shelleyAboutShelley.gif" ALT="About Us"
BORDER="0"></A>
        </TD>
        <TD VALIGN="top">
        <A HREF="">
        <IMG SRC="images/shelleySearch.gif" ALT="Search" BORDER="0"></A>
        </TD>
    </TR>
    <TR>
        <TD COLSPAN="5" VALIGN="top">
        <HR WITDH="100%" SIZE="1">
        </TD>
    </TR>
</TABLE>
```

> **NOTE**
>
> When using include files be sure not to have duplicate tags running such as HTML, HEAD, TITLE, or BODY. Otherwise your users might experience undesirable results.

Script 3-4
_footer.cfm

```
<TABLE BORDER="0" CELLPADDING="0" CELLSPACING="0" WIDTH="600">
<TR>
    <TD VALIGN="bottom">
    <HR WITDH="100%" SIZE="1">
    </TD>
</TR>
<TR>
    <TD VALIGN="top">
    <CENTER>
    <FONT FACE="Arial, Helvetica" SIZE="2">
    <A HREF="mailto:jobs@shelleybiotechnologies.com">
<B>Jobs@shelleybiotechnologies.com</B></A>
    <BR>
    <BR>
    <B>Copyright 2000 - Shelley Biotechnologies, Inc.</B>
    </CENTER>
    </TD>
</TR>
</TABLE>
```

Now that we've built our header and footer files, let's build our *index.cfm* page and include these.

Script 3-5
index.cfm

```
<!DOCTYPE HTML PUBLIC "-//W3C//DTD HTML 4.0 Transitional//EN">

<HTML>
<HEAD>
   <TITLE>Shelley Biotechnologies</TITLE>
</HEAD>
<BODY>

<CFINCLUDE TEMPLATE="_header.cfm">
<BR>
<BR>
<BR>
<TABLE BORDER="0" CELLPADDING="0" CELLSPACING="0" WIDTH="600">
<TR>
   <TD VALIGN="top">
   Body content goes here...
   </TD>
</TR>
</TABLE>
<BR>
<BR>
<BR>
<CFINCLUDE TEMPLATE="_footer.cfm">

</BODY>
</HTML>
```

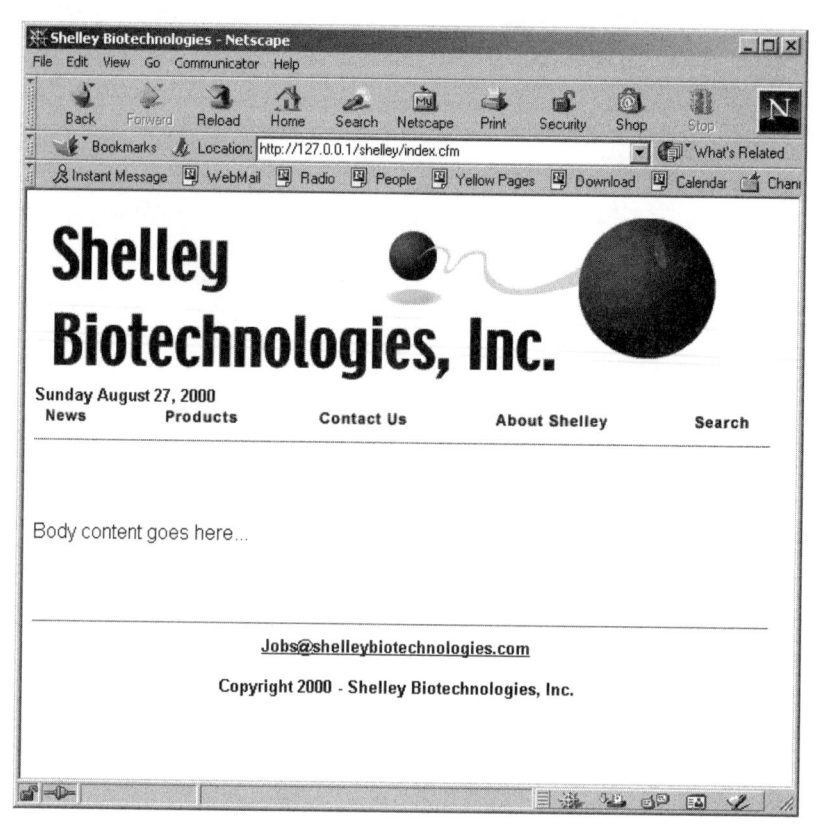

FIGURE 3-4 `<CFINCLUDE>` Tag.

HOW THIS WORKS

The *index.cfm* page is including the header and footer files we will use throughout the site with the use of the `<CFINCLUDE>` command at the top and bottom of the *index.cfm* page. You can use this as a template for all of your pages and simply add the page-specific contents between them. Now when we go back and link up some of the graphics in the *_header.cfm* file, all the pages using this will be updated as well. View the source on the *index.cfm* file and you will see that all the code for the three files are there.

◆ Recap

As you have seen, the *application.cfm* file can be a very useful tool to aid your development. You can do many of the repetitive things in this one tidy area. However, you must keep in mind that this file will get executed every time that you execute a page. If you get too dependent on the use of the *application.cfm* file it can hinder the performance of your web site. Like anything, moderation is always key to having a manageable application file.

◆ Advanced Project

Error handling in your applications is a very important piece of programming. Your code is going to go belly-up sometime, whether it's a programming error or gremlins residing on your server, so be ready! The more information you receive as a developer, the better you can debug your applications. Allaire has made debugging ColdFusion very easy through the **Debugging** category under the **Miscellaneous** section on the ColdFusion server administrator.

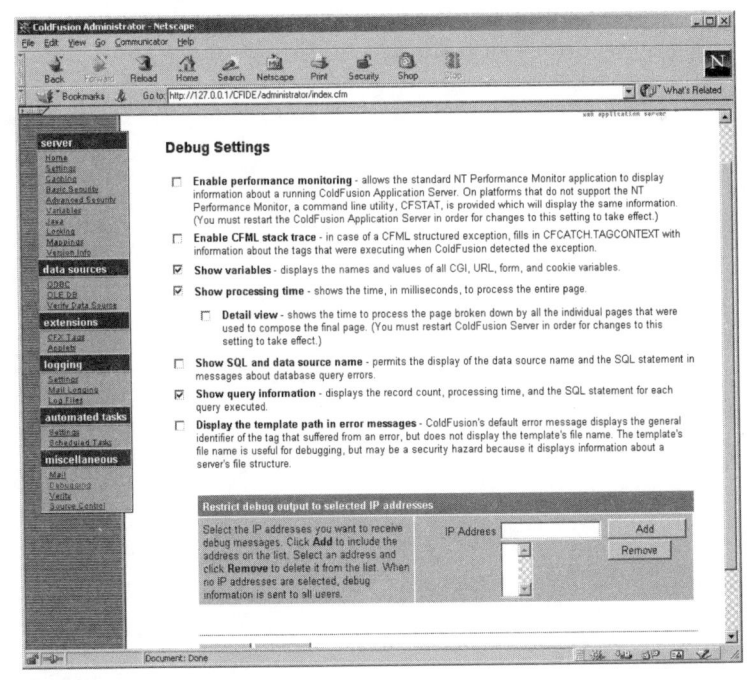

FIGURE 3-5 Debugging window in the ColdFusion Server Administrator.

Here you can choose from several options to easily debug your pages. The ones that will help you out the most are:

Show variables

Displays the values in the form, CGI, URL, and cookie variables.

Show processing time

Displays the time to process the page in milliseconds.

Show query information

Displays all the SQL statements on the page as well as the record count at processing time for each query.

Turning on any of these will give you some great debugging information but it lets everyone else see this as well, which will look like garbage to them. The solution: Toward the bottom there is a section called **Restrict debug output to selected IP addresses**. This lets you restrict the debugging output to only the IP addresses you tell it and only those machines will see it. If nothing is in there, as is the default, then everyone can see it.

chapter 4
Building an Online Catalog

IN THIS CHAPTER

- Building an Administration Screen
- Setting Up the Administration Screen
- Project I: Viewing Items in Your Database
- Project II: Uploading Files to Your Site
- Project III: Adding Records to Your Database
- Project IV: Editing an Existing Record in Your Database
- Project V: Processing the Information
- Project VI: User Pages
- New Functions
  - <CFDIRECTORY>
  - <CFFILE>
  - <CFINSERT>
  - <CFDELETE>
  - <CFUPDATE>
  - DollarFormat
  - URLEncodedFormat
  - CurrentRow
  - MOD
  - IIF
  - RecordCount
- Recap
- Advanced Project

Now that you have some ColdFusion basics under your belt you feel like you're ready to tackle some real world examples to put to use in your own site. Your boss tells you he/she and the rest of the board members are ready to move from being just a mail order catalog to being an online catalog. Not a big deal . . . after all, you have this book to guide you.

For the projects in this chapter we will be using the Microsoft Access database (*shelleyCatalog.mdb*) we built together in Chapter 1. At this point you should have your ODBC connection already set up using *shelleyCatalog* as the DSN and verified through the ColdFusion administrator that it is running. If you are using a hosting company you will not have access to the ColdFusion administrator and you will have to trust that the hosting company's administrator has set you up correctly.

◆ Building an Administration Screen

Having a web-based administration screen is useful for several reasons. It:

- Gives access to others to manage content on the website
- Lets you access it from anywhere to update at anytime
- Lets you dynamically change the content, add files such as word documents, images, or PDF files, and have them instantly updated on the web site

Of course with these advantages there are also some disadvantages. As we have all learned by now, nothing is as easy as it seems. By taking a few precautionary steps, you can minimize many of the security risks involved from using web-based administration.

- Store your datafile in a location outside the web directory. Otherwise, if a potential hacker knew the location and name of the datafile and it was located inside the web directory, the hacker could easily download it.
- Use a username and password on your datafile (this was mentioned in the last chapter).
- Store all your web-based administration templates in a secure directory with a hard to guess directory name. Using a name like /admin/ or /administration/ is generally always a bad idea. Kind of like using *password* as your password.

- Set up HTTP authentication for this directory. If you are using a hosting provider ask them to do so and they most likely will.

Simple steps like this will usually make the bad-evil hacker-person angry and go away to hack another.

◆ Setting Up the Administration Screen

First we need to decide what is required to completely administer the catalog.

- View the items that are currently in the catalog as well as edit and delete them
- Add new items to the catalog
- Create new categories for the products to fall under when necessary
- Upload images to the website to include with the products

Script 4-1
_navBar.cfm

```
<LI> <A HREF="viewItems.cfm">View items in inventory</A></LI>
<LI> <A HREF="itemManager.cfm?method=Add">Add items to inventory</A></LI>
<LI> <A HREF="createCategory.cfm">Create a new category</A></LI>
<LI> <A HREF="uploadImage.cfm">Upload an image</A></LI>
```

Script 4-2
index.cfm

```
<!DOCTYPE HTML PUBLIC "-//W3C//DTD HTML 4.0 Transitional//EN">
<HTML>
<HEAD>
   <TITLE>Shelley Biotech - Administration Screen</TITLE>
</HEAD>
<BODY>

<CFINCLUDE TEMPLATE="_navBar.cfm">

</BODY>
</HTML>
```

By using the `<CFINCLUDE>` function to call the **_navBar.cfm** template, we include the navigation into the *index.cfm* template. We will be using this on all the other templates in this section.

◆ Project I: Viewing Items in Your Database

Script 4-3
viewItems.cfm

```
1.  <CFQUERY NAME="listItems" DATASOURCE="shelleyCatalog"
    DBTYPE="ODBC">
2.  SELECT sku, name, price, description
3.  FROM   Products
4.  </CFQUERY>

    <!DOCTYPE HTML PUBLIC "-//W3C//DTD HTML 4.0 Transitional//EN">
    <HTML>
    <HEAD>
        <TITLE>Shelley Biotech - Administration Screen</TITLE>
    </HEAD>
    <BODY>

    <CFINCLUDE TEMPLATE="_navBar.cfm">
    <H3>Items in your inventory:</H3>
5.  <TABLE BORDER="0" CELLPADDING="2" CELLSPACING="0">
6.  <CFOUTPUT QUERY="listItems">
7.  <TR>
8.      <TD VALIGN="top"><FONT SIZE="1">SKU: #sku#</FONT></TD>
9.      <TD VALIGN="top"><B>#listItems.name#</B></TD>
10.     <TD VALIGN="top">#listItems.price#</TD>
11. </TR>
12. <TR>
13.     <TD VALIGN="top"> </TD>
14.     <TD VALIGN="top" COLSPAN="2">#listItems.description#</TD>
15. </TR>
16. </CFOUTPUT>
17. </TABLE>

    </BODY>
    </HTML>
```

HOW THIS WORKS

1-4. `<CFQUERY>` sets up a query with the data source *shelleyCatalog* and selects the fields *sku, name, price,* and *description* from the **Products** table.

5-17. Set up a table to display the four fields we are pulling from the table. First you will set up the shell of the table and use the `<CFINCLUDE>` before the table row tags since the `<CFQUERY>` will loop the results.

Now when you select the **View items in inventory** link (*view-Items.cfm*) you will display a page with all your items and the four fields associated with them.

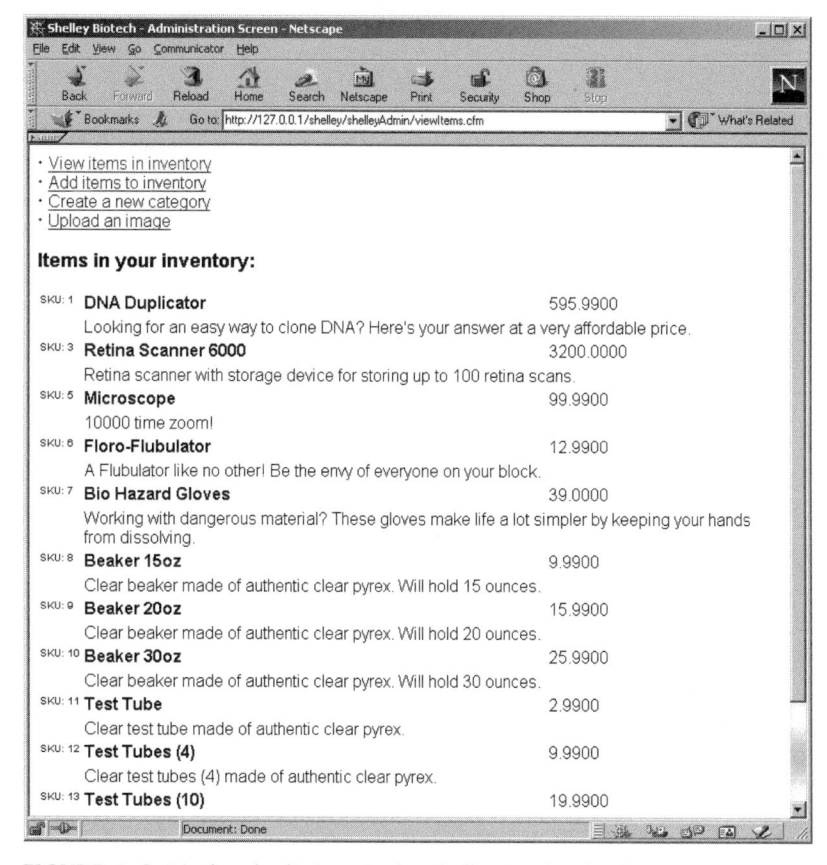

FIGURE 4–1 Display the listings in the *shelleyCatalog* database.

First thing you might notice is, "Why are the prices showing up with four characters after the period?" As with dates numbers can be formatted as well.

DollarFormat Function

The `DollarFormat` function allows you to easily format any number into U.S. currency format.

```
<CFSET myDollarFormat=DollarFormat(1.34)>
```

The value of myDollarFormat will be $1.34.

```
<TABLE BORDER="0" CELLPADDING="2" CELLSPACING="0">
<CFOUTPUT QUERY="listItems">
<TR>
   <TD VALIGN="top"><FONT SIZE="1">SKU: #sku#</FONT></TD>
   <TD VALIGN="top"><B>#listItems.name#</B></TD>
   <TD VALIGN="top">#DollarFormat(listItems.price)#</TD>
</TR>
<TR>
   <TD VALIGN="top"> </TD>
   <TD VALIGN="top" COLSPAN="2">#listItems.description#</TD>
</TR>
</CFOUTPUT>
</TABLE>
```

CurrentRow

Another thing we can do here to make this listing a little easier on the eyes is to alternate the background color of the rows. The CurrentRow function does exactly what it says, it displays the current row that is being returned. You can use this function at the beginning of each table row to list the items numerically, which is helpful in a particularly long listing of information.

```
<TABLE BORDER="0" CELLPADDING="2" CELLSPACING="0">
<CFOUTPUT QUERY="listItems">
<TR>
   <TD VALIGN="top"><B><FONT SIZE="1">Record:
   #CurrentRow#</FONT></B></TD>
   <TD VALIGN="top"><FONT SIZE="1">SKU: #listItems.sku#</FONT></TD>
   <TD VALIGN="top"><B>#listItems.name#</B></TD>
   <TD VALIGN="top">#DollarFormat(listItems.price)#</TD>
</TR>
<TR>
   <TD VALIGN="top" COLSPAN="2"> </TD>
   <TD VALIGN="top" COLSPAN="2">#listItems.description#</TD>
</TR>
</CFOUTPUT>
</TABLE>
```

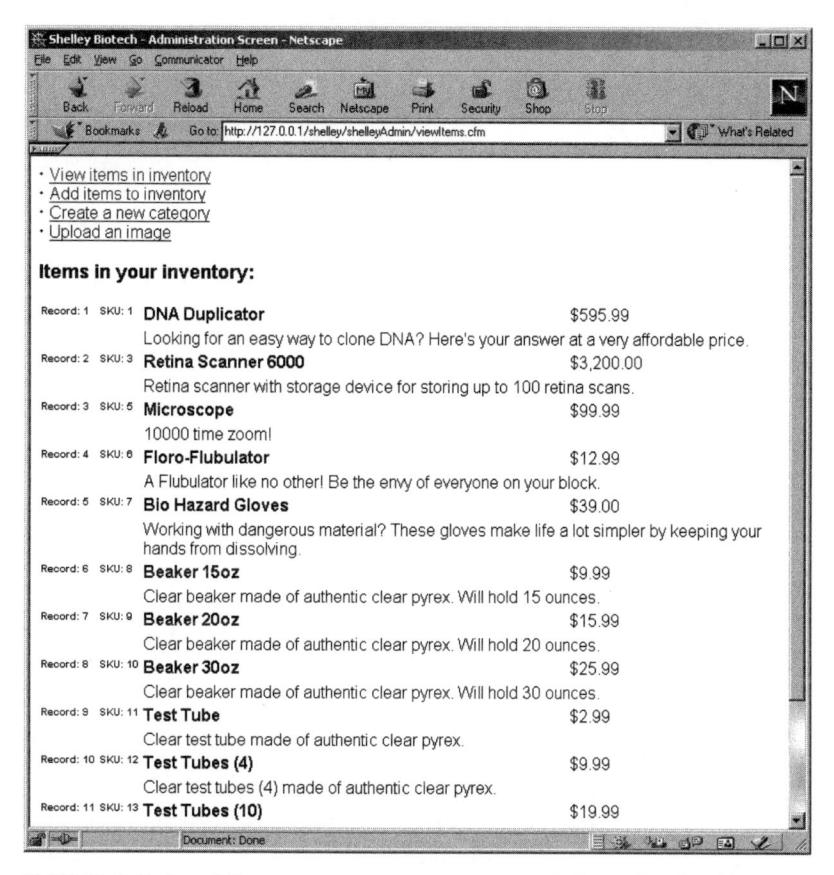

FIGURE 4-2 By adding `CurrentRow` you can count through a list. Use the `DollarFormat()` function to format the price.

MOD

Going back to alternating the background color for each record in the list you will use the MOD function. In case you don't remember the MOD function from math class, it is the remainder after a division has occurred.

9 divided by 2 is 4 with a remainder of 1

10 MOD 3 = 1

Now we will test the `CurrentRow` against 2 since we want to alternate every 2 rows. If the `CurrentRow` is an odd number divided by 2 then the MOD will be 1.

```
<CFIF (CurrentRow MOD 2) IS 1>
    ...do one thing
<CFELSE>
    ...do another thing
</CFIF>
```

IIF

We could create two separate blocks of code to alternate our backgrounds using the MOD function explained above. However, there is a more suitable solution than repeating the same code. We can use the `IIF` function to evaluate the results of the MOD operation. Let's use the classical example to show the functionality of `IIF`:

Example:

```
#IIF(1+1=2, DE("Today is a good day"), DE("Better go home!"))#
```

`IIF` has three parameters. The first is the expression you wish to evaluate. The second contains the output you wish to produce when the condition in position 1 is evaluated `TRUE`. The third position contains the output when the condition is evaluated to `FALSE`.

Notice there is one more piece here. `DE` is a function that stands for *delayed evaluation*. Normally, the conditions in positions one and two are evaluated before they are displayed. In this case we want to delay evaluation and output the actual string contained in this function.

Now let's apply this to the table we have used for the last two examples and test the `CurrentRow` and a background color to the table cell if the `MOD` is 1. Also while we're at it we are going to set up an `EDIT` and `DELETE` link from each record to use in the upcoming examples. Each of these links will pass the distinct `sku` number associated with the record along with a method: `EDIT` or `DELETE`.

Script 4-4
viewItems.cfm

```
<TABLE BORDER="0" CELLPADDING="2" CELLSPACING="0">
<CFOUTPUT QUERY="listItems">
<TR BGCOLOR=#IIF(listItems.currentrow MOD 2, DE ('FFFFFF'), DE ('EBEBEB'))#>
    <TD VALIGN="top"><B><FONT SIZE="1">Record: #CurrentRow#</FONT></B></TD>
```

Project I: Viewing Items in Your Database 73

```
    <TD VALIGN="top"><FONT SIZE="1">SKU: #sku#</FONT></TD>
    <TD VALIGN="top"><B>#listItems.name#</B></TD>
    <TD VALIGN="top">#DollarFormat(listItems.price)#</TD>
</TR>
<TR BGCOLOR=#IIF(listItems.currentrow MOD 2, DE ('FFFFFF'), DE
('EBEBEB'))#>
    <TD VALIGN="top">
    <FONT SIZE="1">
<A HREF="itemManager.cfm?sku=#listItems.sku#&method=Edit">EDIT</A>
    </FONT></TD>
    <TD VALIGN="top">
    <FONT SIZE="1">
<A HREF="itemManagerProcess.cfm?sku=#listItems.sku#&method=Delete">
DELETE</A>
    </FONT></TD>
    <TD VALIGN="top" COLSPAN="2">#listItems.description#</TD>
</TR>
</CFOUTPUT>
</TABLE>
```

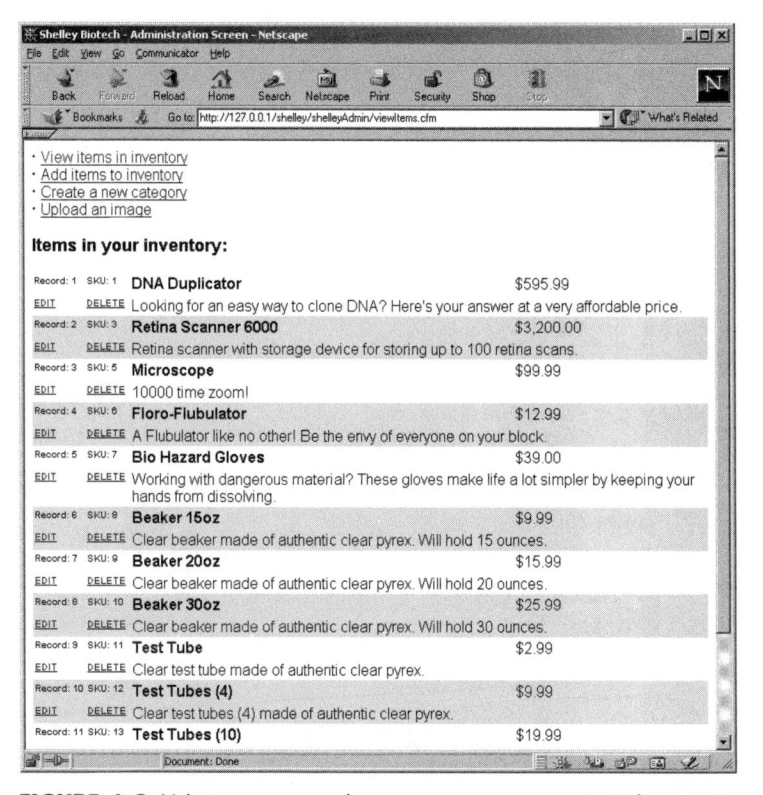

FIGURE 4–3 Using <CFIF> and CurrentRow you can test the MOD to alternate background colors for table rows.

RecordCount

`RecordCount` allows you to numerically list the number of records that are returned from a query. To view the number of records that are being returned from the query `listItems` add the following function before the `<CFOUTPUT QUERY="listItems">` and before the `<TABLE>`. Since we are not already inside an existing query there is no way ColdFusion knows for which query this `RecordCount` is to be used. So we will append the query name to the beginning of `RecordCount`.

```
<CFOUTPUT>
<FONT COLOR="red">#listItems.RecordCount#</FONT> items
exist in the database
</CFOUTPUT>
```

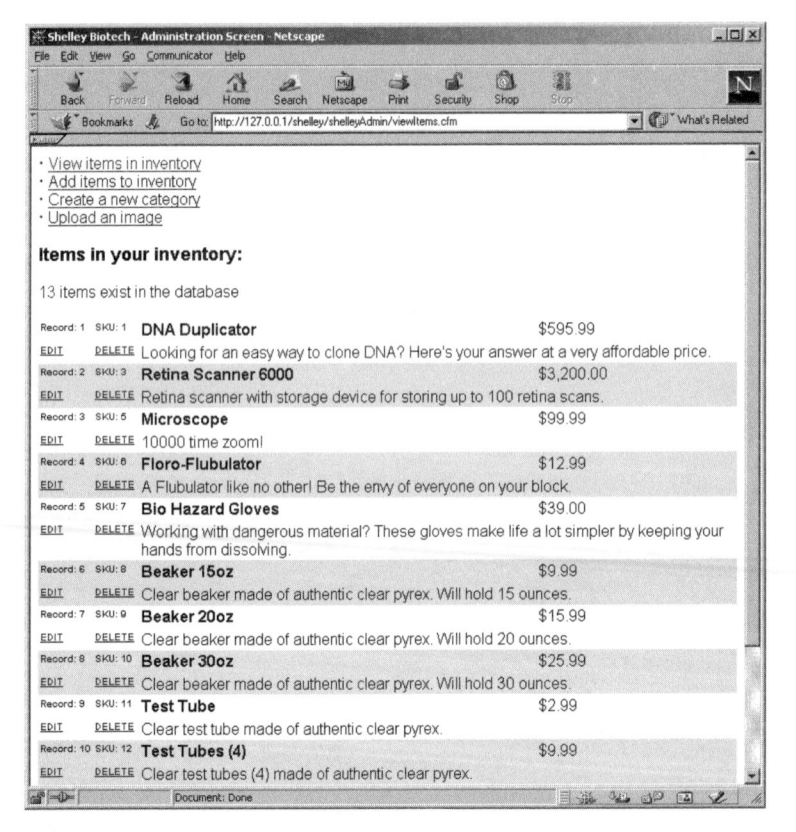

FIGURE 4-4 Using the `RecordCount` function with a query will give you the number of records that are being returned.

◆ Project II: Uploading Files to Your Site

<CFFILE>

Used with ACTION="Upload"

```
<CFFILE
ACTION="action attribute. See list below"     Required
FILEFIELD="form field"                         Required
DESTINATION="path"                             Required
NAMECONFLICT="name conflict behavior"          Optional
ACCEPT="MIME type"                             Optional
MODE="permission - UNIX only"                  Optional
ATTRIBUTES="file attributes">                  Optional
```

In order to use CFFILE, you must turn it on in the ColdFusion administrator under the **Basic Settings** screen. If you are using an ISP this might be turned off due to security reasons. If files can be uploaded there's always the chance that a malicious file such as a virus could be uploaded as well.

CFFILE has several different types of attributes used depending on the type of ACTION you define. The following chart explains:

<CFFILE ACTION="*One of the following attributes*" ....>

TABLE 4-1 <CFFILE> Actions

Action	Attributes
Append	Output
	File
	Mode
	AddNewFile
	Attributes
Copy	Source
	Destination
	Attributes
Delete	File
Move	Source
	Destination
	Attributes
Read	File
	Variable

TABLE 4–1 <CFFILE> Actions *(continued)*

Action	Attributes
ReadBinary	File
	Variable
Rename	Source
	Destination
	Attributes
Upload	Accept
	Destination
	FileField
	NameConflict
	Mode
	Attributes
Write	Output
	File
	Mode
	AddNewFile
	Attributes

For the project we will be working with later in this chapter we are going to work with the ACTION="Upload" attribute.

TABLE 4–2 <CFFILE> Attributes

Attribute	Description
ACTION	Append, Copy, Delete, Move, Read, ReadBinary, ReName, Upload, Write
FILEFIELD	Defines the name of the form field that is passing the file name to <CFFILE>
DESTINATION	Defines the path the file is being uploaded to. In Windows use the backslash (\ ) to separate the directories (C:\inetpub\wwwroot\); in UNIX use the forward slash (/) for directory separators.
NAMECONFLICT	Attribute used to determine what to do if a file conflicts with another file. Error is the default. *Error*—Does not process and ColdFusion will return an error. *Skip*—Does not save the file or pass an error. *Overwrite*—If a file exists with the same name as the uploaded file it is overwritten. *MakeUnique*—If a file exists with the same name as the file being uploaded, ColdFusion will generate a unique name.

TABLE 4-2 <CFFILE> Attributes *(continued)*

Attribute	Description
ACCEPT	Defines what MIME types to accept. Multiple entries are accepted separated by a comma.
MODE	Attribute used only on UNIX machines when ACTION="Create" to set the directory permissions. *MODE="644"*. Not used with Windows.
ATTRIBUTES	ReadOnly, Temporary, Archive, Hidden, System, Normal Defines the type of attributes to set on the file itself.

Now let's take a look at setting up a form to upload your images to the Shelley Biotechnologies **Products** directory in your database.

Script 4-5
cfFile.cfm

```
<!DOCTYPE HTML PUBLIC "-//W3C//DTD HTML 4.0 Transitional//EN">
<HTML>
<HEAD>
   <TITLE>CFFILE</TITLE>
</HEAD>
<BODY>

<H3>CFFILE Upload Screen</H3>
```
1.  ```
    <FORM ACTION="uploadImageComplete.cfm" METHOD="post"
    ENCTYPE="multipart/form-data">
    Name of file:<BR>
    ```
2.  ```
    <INPUT TYPE="file" SIZE="20" NAME="myFile">
    <BR>
    <INPUT TYPE="submit" VALUE="UPLOAD">
    </FORM>

    </BODY>
    </HTML>
    ```

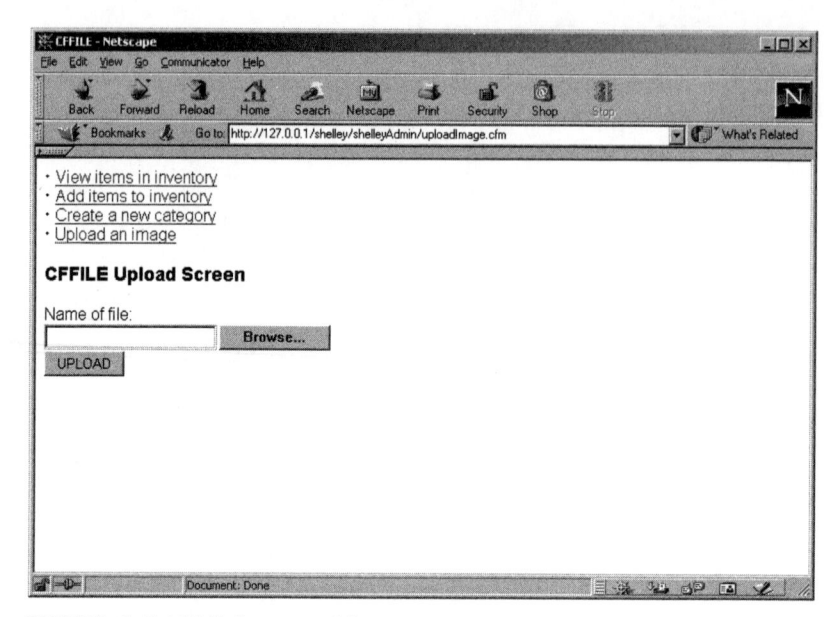

FIGURE 4–5 HTML form used for <CFFILE>.

HOW THIS WORKS

1. Set up the FORM with the METHOD and ACTION. A new attribute is used here called ENCTYPE which defines the encryption type used to upload the file in.
2. Define the name of the field for which your file will be referenced by.

Script 4-6
uploadImage.cfm

```
<!DOCTYPE HTML PUBLIC "-//W3C//DTD HTML 4.0 Transitional//EN">
<HTML>
<HEAD>
   <TITLE>CFFILE - Successful</TITLE>
</HEAD>
<BODY>
```
1. `<CFFILE`
2. `ACTION="Upload"`
3. `FILEFIELD="myFile"`
4. `DESTINATION="C:\Inetpub\wwwroot\shelley\images\products\">`
5. `File was successfully uploaded`
   `</BODY>`
   `</HTML>`

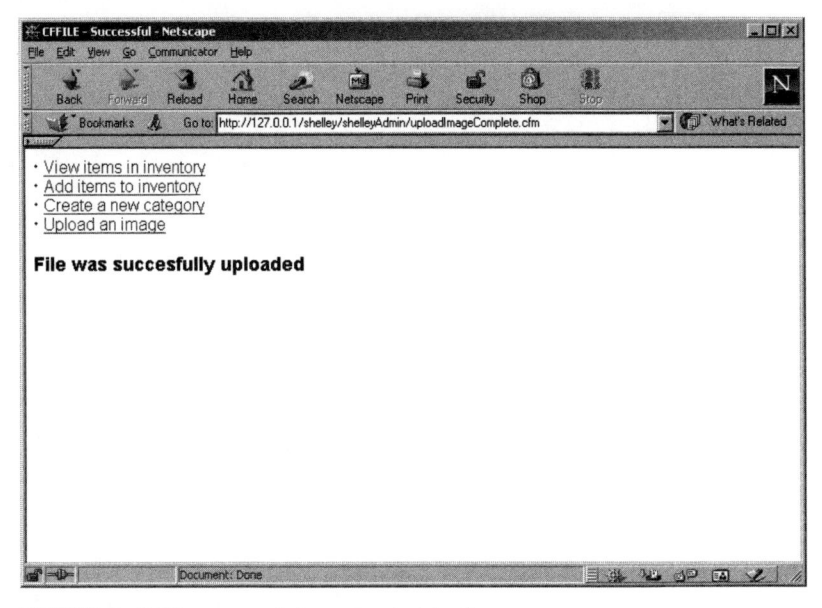

FIGURE 4–6 File successfully uploaded to the server.

HOW THIS WORKS

1. Sets up the `<CFFILE>` tag
2. Defines the ACTION as `'Upload'`
3. Uses the field name that was passed from the FORM from *upLoadImage.cfm*
4. Defines the location the file is to be saved to
5. Displays a message confirming the file was transferred properly. If the file does not upload properly you will never get to this point.

Now you can use this example to upload your images to the Shelley Biotechnologies directory.

<CFDIRECTORY>

`<CFDIRECTORY>` must also be turned on in ColdFusion administrator under the **Basic Settings** screen. If you are using an ISP this might be turned off due to security reasons.

```
<CFDIRECTORY
    ACTION="type"                              Optional
    DIRECTORY="name of directory"              Required
    NAME="name of query"                       Required
    FILTER="filter name"                       Optional
    MODE="permission - UNIX only"              Optional
    SORT="sort type"                           Optional
    NEWDIRECTORY="name of new directory">      Required
                                               (if action="create")
```

TABLE 4-3 <CFDIRECTORY> Attributes

Attribute	Description
ACTION	List (default), Create, Delete, Rename Attribute that uses LIST by default. These are used to decide what type of action to use on the directory.
DIRECTORY	Defines the name of the directory you will be working with. If you are creating a directory this will be the parent directory you will be creating the new directory within.
NAME	REQUIRED if ACTION="List" to specify the output query. Not used for any other ACTION.
FILTER	OPTIONAL if ACTION="List". Used to filter specific types of files to list. FILTER="*.jpg" will return only files with .jpg extensions. Only one filter can be used at a time.
MODE	Attribute used only on UNIX machines when ACTION="Create" to set the directory permissions. MODE="644". Not used with Windows.
SORT	OPTIONAL if ACTION="List". Defines the way you want the directory listed. SORT="dirName" Sort by directory name SORT="dateLastModified" Sort by date SORT="size" Sort by file size You can also use ASC or DESC to sort by ascending or descending order. ASC is used by default. SORT="dirName DESC"
NEWDIRECTORY	REQUIRED if ACTION="Create" to define what the new directory will be called. Ignored for all other types of ACTION.

Script 4-7
cfDirectory.cfm

```
<!DOCTYPE HTML PUBLIC "-//W3C//DTD HTML 4.0 Transitional//EN">
<HTML>
<HEAD>
    <TITLE>CFDIRECTORY</TITLE>
</HEAD>
<BODY>
```

1. `<CFDIRECTORY`
2. `    ACTION="LIST"`
3. `    DIRECTORY="C:\Inetpub\wwwroot\shelley\images\products"`
4. `    NAME="shelleyImages"`
5. `    FILTER="*.jpg"`
6. `    SORT="name ASC">`

```
<TABLE CELLPADDING="0" CELLSPACING="2" BORDER="0">
<TR>
    <TD VALIGN="top" WIDTH="200"><B>FILE NAME</B></TD>
    <TD VALIGN="top" WIDTH="200"><B>FILE SIZE</B></TD>
</TR>
```
7. `<CFOUTPUT QUERY="shelleyImages">`
   `<TR>`
8. `<TD VALIGN="top">#shelleyImages.name#</TD>`
9. `<TD VALIGN="top">#shelleyImages.size#</TD>`

```
</TR>
</CFOUTPUT>
</TABLE>

</BODY>
</HTML>
```

HOW THIS WORKS:

1. Starts the `<CFDIRECTORY>` tag
2. Sets the `ACTION` to "`List`". `List` is selected by default.
3. Defines the path to the directory you will be working with.
4. Gives the `CFDIRECTORY` a name. This is basically the `QUERY` name you will be referring back to in your `<CFOUTPUT>`.
5. Since we're only concerned with seeing the JPEG images in this directory we set the filter to **`FILTER="*.jpg"`**.
6. Sets the `SORT` order to sort by *name* in ascending order.
7. Now you're ready to output the `CFDIRECTORY` information you have captured. Set up the `CFOUTPUT` using the `name` you set in the `CFDIRECTORY` as the query for the `CFOUTPUT`.

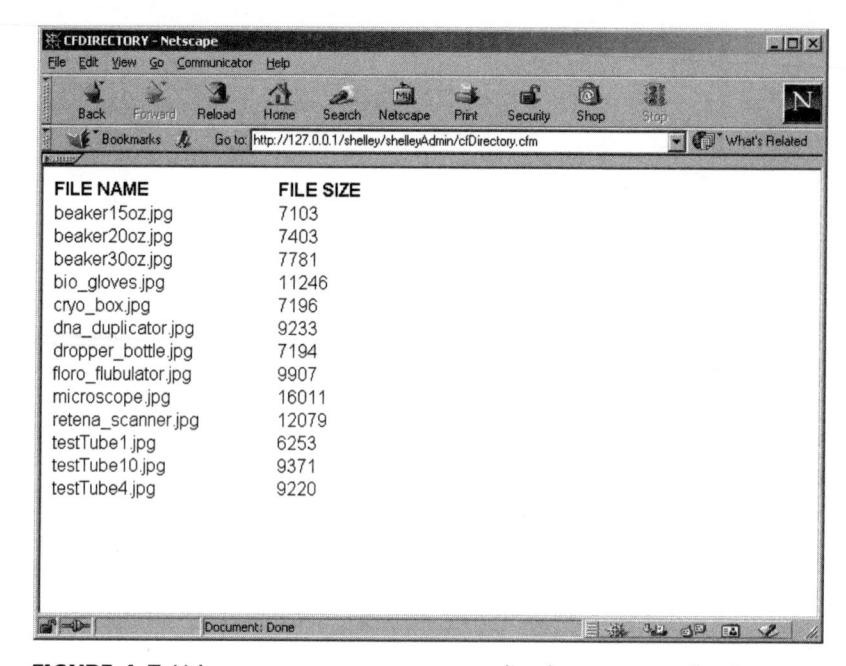

FILE NAME	FILE SIZE
beaker15oz.jpg	7103
beaker20oz.jpg	7403
beaker30oz.jpg	7781
bio_gloves.jpg	11246
cryo_box.jpg	7196
dna_duplicator.jpg	9233
dropper_bottle.jpg	7194
floro_flubulator.jpg	9907
microscope.jpg	16011
retena_scanner.jpg	12079
testTube1.jpg	6253
testTube10.jpg	9371
testTube4.jpg	9220

FIGURE 4-7 Using `<CFDIRECTORY>` you can list the contents of a directory.

8-9. Now you are ready to output the contents of the */shelley/images/products/* directory.

◆ Project III: Adding Records to Your Database

Now that you understand how to pull your records out of the database, read your files with `<CFDIRECTORY>`, and manipulate the data, as well as use `<CFFILE>` to upload your image files, you're ready to start adding all of those items your boss has been asking you to do. If you're worried that some of the prices or descriptions of the current items need to be changed, fear not. In the next section we will look at updating those records. First we need to take a look at adding the records, as we will be using the same template to edit them. So we don't need to do things twice.

Script 4-8
itemManager.cfm

1. ```
   <CFQUERY NAME="listCategories" DATASOURCE="shelleyCatalog"
   DBTYPE="ODBC">
   SELECT   *
   FROM     Category
   </CFQUERY>

   <!DOCTYPE HTML PUBLIC "-//W3C//DTD HTML 4.0 Transitional//EN">
   <HTML>
   <HEAD>
       <TITLE>Shelley Biotech - Administration Screen</TITLE>
   </HEAD>
   <BODY>
   <CFINCLUDE TEMPLATE="_navBar.cfm">
   <H3>Item manager:</H3>

   <CFOUTPUT>
   <FORM ACTION="itemManagerProcess.cfm" METHOD="post">
   ```
2. ```
   <INPUT TYPE="hidden" NAME="method" VALUE="#method#">

   <TABLE BORDER="0" CELLPADDING="2" CELLSPACING="0">
   <TR>
       <TD><B>Name: </B></TD>
       <TD><INPUT TYPE="text" NAME="name" SIZE="20"></TD>
   </TR>
   <TR>
       <TD><B>Price: </B></TD>
       <TD><INPUT TYPE="text" NAME="price" SIZE="20"></TD>
   </TR>
   <TR>
       <TD><B>Weight: </B></TD>
       <TD><INPUT TYPE="text" NAME="weight" SIZE="20"></TD>
   </TR>
   </CFOUTPUT>
   <TR>
   <TD><B>Category: </B></TD>
   <TD>
   ```
3. `    <SELECT NAME="category">`
   ```
   <OPTION VALUE=""></OPTION>
   ```
4. `    <CFOUTPUT QUERY="listCategories">`
5. `    <OPTION VALUE="#listCategories.categoryID#">`
6. `    #listCategories.categoryName#</OPTION>`
7. `    </CFOUTPUT>`
8. ```
       </SELECT>
       </TD>
   </TR>
   <TR>
   ```
   ```

```
        <TD><B>Image: </B></TD>
        <TD>
9.          <CFDIRECTORY
        DIRECTORY="C:\Inetpub\wwwroot\shelley\images\products"
        NAME="shelleyImages" FILTER="*.jpg" SORT="name ASC">
10.         <SELECT NAME="image">
11.         <OPTION VALUE="" SELECTED></OPTION>
12.         <CFOUTPUT QUERY="shelleyImages">
13.         <OPTION VALUE="#shelleyImages.name#">#shelleyImages.name#</
        OPTION>
14.         </CFOUTPUT>
15.         </SELECT>
        </TD>
    </TR>
    <CFOUTPUT>
    <TR>
        <TD VALIGN="top"><B>Description: </B></TD>
        <TD><TEXTAREA NAME="description" WRAP="virtual" COLS="30"
    ROWS="5"></TEXTAREA></TD>
    </TR>
    <TR>
        <TD> </TD>
16.     <TD><INPUT TYPE="submit" VALUE="#method#"></TD>
    </TR>
    </TABLE>
    </FORM>
    </CFOUTPUT>
    </BODY>
    </HTML>
```

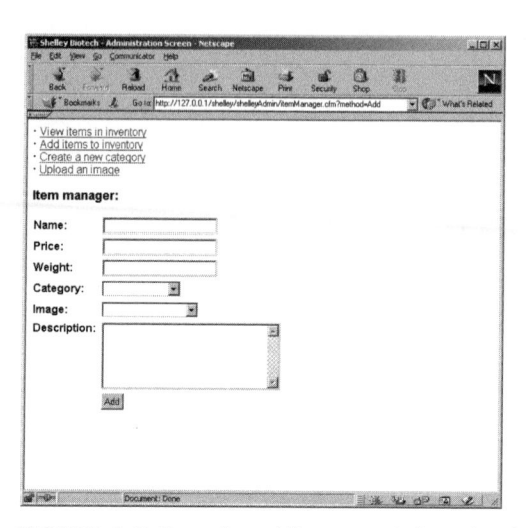

FIGURE 4-8 Form for adding records into the database.

Project III: Adding Records to Your Database   85

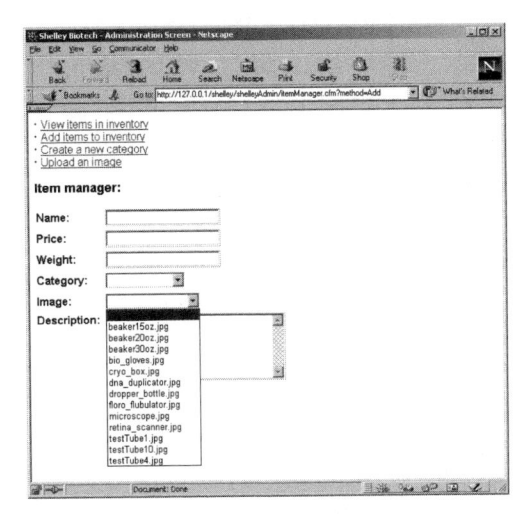

FIGURE 4-9 The image drop-down box is dynamically populated with JPEG files that exist in the specified directory.

HOW THIS WORKS

1. Sets up a query called `listCategories` that pulls the names of the different categories in your **Category** table

2. Sets a hidden field name with the `method` you are passing since you will need this for the next template. You will either have a method of ADD or EDIT depending on what you are doing on this page.

3. Now you are going to be setting up the dynamic SELECT field with the name value of `category`.

4-8. Using the query `listCategories`, you will set the first <OPTION> with the value of `categoryID` in the drop-down form to contain the first record. A new <OPTION> with its associated value is added until all the values have been added into the drop-down menu.

9. The function <CFDIRECTORY> now looks into the directory path `"C:\Inetpub\wwwroot\shelley\images\products"` and filters only files with the extention *.jpg* and sorts them by name in ascending order. The query name for this has been set to `shelleyImages`.

10-15. Using the <OPTION> form field you will loop through as you did with the `listCategories` to list the images that were filtered out with <CFDIRECTORY>.

16. `#method#` holds the value of ADD that was passed and defines the button's VALUE and labels it as such.

♦ Project IV: Editing an Existing Record in Your Database

Looking back at the *viewItems.cfm* template you'll remember we added two links. Now we will take a look at how we are going to edit the listing with the same template as the *itemManager.cfm* only slightly modified. Sure you could create a new template that uses the same layout as *itemManager.cfm* but that's twice the work. And down the road you might want to make some changes to the template or add some new fields for your products and you would have to manage two templates. Why bother when you can do this in one.

```
http://127.0.0.1/shelley/shelleyAdmin/
itemManager.cfm?sku=1&method=Edit
```

In the URL that you are passing to edit an item, you have two variables you are passing: The first is the `sku` variable which is the unique ID of the record followed by the variable `method=Edit`. Using some `<CFIF>` statements to test the conditions you can have ColdFusion pass some code while ignoring others. You can use this in a form field to add a `VALUE` attribute and dynamically fill it with the value of the field in the database that matches the unique `sku` that you passed:

```
<INPUT TYPE="text" NAME="name" SIZE="20"
<CFIF method EQ "Edit">VALUE="#name#"</CFIF>>
```

If you are using the *itemManager.cfm* template but the method you are passing is `Add` then the `<CFIF method EQ "Edit">VALUE="#name#"</CFIF>` statement is ignored and you simply have `<INPUT TYPE="text" NAME="name" SIZE="20">`.

Now we will look at *itemManager.cfm* as we edit the first item: *DNA Duplicator*. The only thing different in this template is the way we are displaying the form fields.

Script 4-9
itemManager.cfm

```
<CFQUERY NAME="listCategories" DATASOURCE="shelleyCatalog"
DBTYPE="ODBC">
SELECT *
FROM    Category
</CFQUERY>

<CFIF URL.method EQ "Edit">
<CFQUERY NAME="editItem" DATASOURCE="shelleyCatalog"
DBTYPE="ODBC">
SELECT *
FROM products, category
WHERE Category.categoryID=Products.category AND sku = sku
</CFQUERY>
</CFIF>

<!DOCTYPE HTML PUBLIC "-//W3C//DTD HTML 4.0 Transitional//EN">
<HTML>
<HEAD>
    <TITLE>Shelley Biotech - Administration Screen</TITLE>
</HEAD>
<BODY>
<CFINCLUDE TEMPLATE="_navBar.cfm">
<H3>Item manager:</H3>

<CFOUTPUT>
```
1. `<CFIF URL.method EQ "add">`
2. `<FORM ACTION="itemManagerProcess.cfm?method=add" METHOD="post">`

3. `<CFELSEIF URL.method EQ "Edit">`
4. `<FORM ACTION="itemManagerProcess.cfm?method=edit&sku=#sku#" METHOD="post">`
5. `<INPUT TYPE="hidden" NAME="sku" VALUE="#sku#">`
6. `</CFIF>`

   `<TABLE BORDER="0" CELLPADDING="2" CELLSPACING="0">`
7. `<CFIF URL.method EQ "Edit">`
8. `<TR>`
9. `   <TD><B>SKU: </B></TD>`
10. `   <TD>#sku#</TD>`
11. `</TR>`
12. `</CFIF>`

    `<TR>`
    `   <TD><B>Name: </B></TD>`
13. `   <TD><INPUT TYPE="text" NAME="name" SIZE="20"`
    `   <CFIF URL.method EQ`
    `   "Edit">VALUE="#editItem.name#"</CFIF>></TD>`

Chapter 4 • Building an Online Catalog

```
        </TR>
        <TR>
            <TD><B>Price: </B></TD>
14.         <TD><INPUT TYPE="text" NAME="price" SIZE="20" <CFIF
    URL.method EQ "Edit">VALUE="#DollarFormat(editItem.price)#"</
    CFIF>></TD>
        </TR>
        <TR>
            <TD><B>Weight: </B></TD>
15.         <TD><INPUT TYPE="text" NAME="weight" SIZE="20" <CFIF
    URL.method EQ "Edit">VALUE="#editItem.weight#"</CFIF>></TD>
        </TR>
    </CFOUTPUT>
        <TR>
            <TD><B>Category: </B></TD>
            <TD><SELECT NAME="category">
16.         <CFIF URL.method EQ "Edit">
            <CFOUTPUT>
            <OPTION VALUE="#editItem.categoryID#">->
            #editItem.categoryName#</OPTION>
            </CFOUTPUT>
            <CFELSE>
            <OPTION VALUE=""></OPTION>
            </CFIF>

            <CFOUTPUT QUERY="listCategories">
            <OPTION VALUE="#listCategories.categoryID#">
            #listCategories.categoryName#</OPTION>
            </CFOUTPUT>
            </SELECT>
            </TD>
        </TR>
        <TR>
            <TD><B>Image: </B></TD>
            <TD>
            <CFDIRECTORY DIRECTORY=
            "C:\Inetpub\wwwroot\shelley\images\products"
            NAME="shelleyImages"
            FILTER="*.jpg" SORT="name ASC">
            <SELECT NAME="image">
            <CFOUTPUT>
17.         <CFIF URL.method EQ "Edit">
            <OPTION VALUE="#editItem.image#" SELECTED>->
            #editItem.image#</OPTION>
            <CFELSE>
            <OPTION VALUE="" SELECTED></OPTION>
            </CFIF>
            </CFOUTPUT>

            <CFOUTPUT QUERY="shelleyImages">
            <OPTION VALUE="#shelleyImages.name#">
```

Project IV: Editing an Existing Record in Your Database

```
            #shelleyImages.name#</OPTION>
         </CFOUTPUT>
         </SELECT>
      </TD>
   </TR>
   <CFOUTPUT>
   <TR>
      <TD VALIGN="top"><B>Description: </B></TD>
      <TD>
18.      <TEXTAREA NAME="description" WRAP="virtual" COLS="30"
         ROWS="5"><CFIF URL.method EQ "Edit">#editItem.description#
         </CFIF></TEXTAREA>
      </TD>
   </TR>
   <TR>
      <TD> </TD>
      <TD><INPUT TYPE="submit" VALUE="#method#"></TD>
   </TR>
   </TABLE>
   </FORM>
   </CFOUTPUT>
   </BODY>
   </HTML>
```

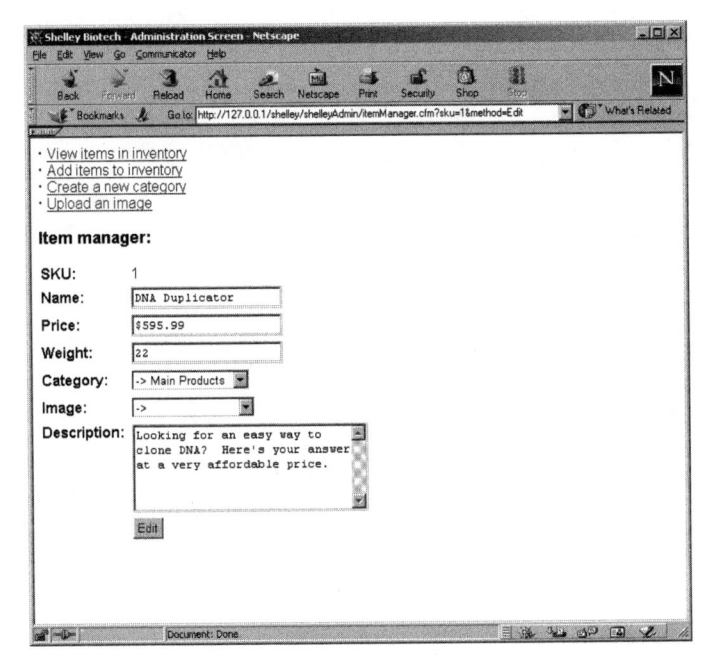

FIGURE 4–10 Testing the condition of URL.method you can use the same form for adding a new record to populate it with an existing record's information.

HOW THIS WORKS

1-2. If the URL.method equals the value ADD, then the following FORM header is passed on line 2.

3-5. If the URL.method equals the value EDIT, then the following FORM header is passed on line 4 with the sku value attached. Also a hidden value for sku is passed to keep track of which item we're working with.

6. Close the CFIF statement.

7-12. Test to see if the URL.method equals the value EDIT. If so, display a table row with the value of the sku number.

13-18. Test to see if the value of URL.method equals EDIT. If so then display the VALUE attribute in the form field and populate it with the fields value pulled from the editItem query.

◆ Project V: Processing the Information

Now that you've built the front end for adding or editing a listing with the *itemManager.cfm* page, you need to go one step further. I know you were hoping that it would just magically end there and somehow things would find their way into the database. Fear not for there is not much more to do here to have your information written to the database. We will be covering three different processes here:

- Adding a record
- Updating a record
- Deleting a record

On *itemManager.cfm* you'll notice that the FORM ACTION called the page *itemManagerProcess.cfm* to send all the fields to. We are now going to work on building this page to process this information to the database.

There are two different ways to insert data into the database. There is the SQL INSERT INTO statement in which you must specify what fields are going where into the table. You can also use <CFINSERT> to do this. Each has its strengths as well as its weaknesses. First we will look at the SQL way:

Adding a Record

SQL INSERT INTO

1. `<CFQUERY DATASOURCE="shelleyCatalog" DBTYPE="ODBC">`
2. `INSERT INTO products(name, price, weight, category, image, description)`
3. `VALUES('#name#', #price#, #weight#, #category#, '#image#', '#description#')`
   `</CFQUERY>`

HOW THIS WORKS

1. Names the data source you will be using.
2. You need to specify the name of the table you will be inserting the fields into. Using the SQL `INSERT INTO` function followed by the name of the table you will specify the fields in that table.
3. Next you give the names of the fields that were passed from *itemManager.cfm* in the same order as you specified with the `INSERT INTO`.

<CFINSERT>

`<CFINSERT>` quite possibly can be one of your best friends! It automates the process of inserting fields from a form collection into a table. This saves you from having to use `<CFQUERY>` to create an insert into `query`. You can choose which form fields to enter into the table or use the standard usage and insert all fields in the table. Note that the names of the form elements must match the field names in your table. The most used attributes for `<CFINSERT>` are as follows:

`<CFINSERT`	
`TABLENAME="table name"`	Required
`DATASOURCE="dataSource name"`	Required
`FORMFIELDS="fields passed"`	Optional
`USERNAME="username"`	Optional
`PASSWORD="password">`	Optional
`DBTYPE="driver type"`	Optional
`DBSERVER="server"`	Optional
`DBNAME="database name"`	Optional
`TABLEOWNER="table owner"`	Optional
`TABLEQUALIFIER="table qualifier"`	Optional
`PROVIDER="COM provider"`	Optional
`PROVIDERDSN="datasource name">`	Optional

TABLE 4-4 <CFINSERT> Attributes

Attribute	Description
TABLENAME	The name of the table you wish to insert into.
DATASOURCE	The name of the data source you are working with.
FORMFIELDS	Specifies the fields you wish to insert into. If omitted ColdFusion will enter a value for all fields in the specified table. `FORMFIELDS="name, email, address"`
USERNAME	Username is required from database systems such as SQL Server that use named security.
PASSWORD	Password to the username you are using to access the database management system.
DBTYPE	Database driver type (DB2, Informix73, ODBC, OLEDB, Oracle73, Oracle80, Sybase11). ODBC is the default.
DBSERVER	Defines the name of the database server. For native database drivers only.
DBNAME	Database name (Sybase11 only).
TABLEOWNER	Defines the table owner if your database calls for it.
TABLEQUALIFIER	Defines the table qualifier if your database calls for it.
PROVIDER	COM provider. Only used with OLE-DB.
PROVIDERDSN	Data source name for COM provider. Only used with OLE-DB.

1. `<CFINSERT DATASOURCE="shelleyCatalog" TABLENAME="products">`

HOW THIS WORKS

1. Names the DATASOURCE you will be using as well as the table you will be doing the insert into.

<CFINSERT> is really that simple and you will probably use it most of the time, although, as we mentioned before, there are some drawbacks. <CFINSERT> will NOT insert values that are not part of the form. By default all form fields passed are inserted with the <CFINSERT> function. You can use the FORMFIELDS attribute to insert specific form fields.

```
<CFINSERT DATASOURCE="shelleyCatalog"
TABLENAME="products"
FORMFIELDS="name, price, weight, category, image, description">
```

Updating a Record

SQL UPDATE

```
1. <CFQUERY DATASOURCE="shelleyCatalog" DBTYPE="ODBC">
2. UPDATE products
3. SET    name='#name#',
4.        price=#price#,
5.        weight=#weight#,
6.        category=#category#,
7.        image='#image#',
8.        description='#description#'
9. WHERE  sku=#URL.sku#
   </CFQUERY>
```

HOW THIS WORKS

1. Names the data source you will be using.
2. Using the SQL function UPDATE, specifies the table you will be using for this operation.
3-8. Using the SQL function SET, specifies the field names in the table to equal the fields being passed from the FORM.
9. Using the SQL function WHERE, you will let the table know which record to update. Notice the #URL.sku# doesn't have single quotes around it. This is because you are passing a numeric character and they aren't needed.

<CFUPDATE>

```
<CFUPDATE
TABLENAME="table name"                          Required
DATASOURCE="dataSource name"                    Required
FORMFIELDS="fields passed"                      Optional
USERNAME="username"                             Optional
PASSWORD="password">                            Optional
DBTYPE="driver type"                            Optional
DBSERVER="server"                               Optional
DBNAME="database name"                          Optional
TABLEOWNER="table owner"                        Optional
TABLEQUALIFIER="table qualifier"                Optional
PROVIDER="COM provider"                         Optional
PROVIDERDSN="datasource name">                  Optional
```

Chapter 4 • Building an Online Catalog

TABLE 4-5 <CFUPDATE> Attributes

Attribute	Description
TABLENAME	The name of the table you wish to update.
DATASOURCE	The name of the data source you are working with.
FORMFIELDS	Used to specify the fields you wish to update. If omitted ColdFusion will enter a value for all fields in the specified table. `FORMFIELDS="name, email, address"`
USERNAME	Username is required from database systems such as SQL Server that use named security.
PASSWORD	Password to the username you are using to access the database management system.
DBTYPE	Database driver type (DB2, Informix73, ODBC, OLEDB, Oracle73, Oracle80, Sybase11). ODBC is the default.
DBSERVER	Defines the name of the database server. For native database drivers only.
DBNAME	Database name (Sybase11 only).
TABLEOWNER	Defines the table owner if your database calls for it.
TABLEQUALIFIER	Defines the table qualifier if your database calls for it.
PROVIDER	COM provider. Only used with OLE-DB.
PROVIDERDSN	Data source name for COM provider. Only used with OLE-DB.

1. `<CFUPDATE DATASOURCE="shelleyCatalog" TABLENAME="products">`

HOW THIS WORKS

1. Names the DATASOURCE you will be using as well as the table you will be updating.

<CFUPDATE> works the same way as <CFINSERT>. There are drawbacks to it as well in that you can only update formfields. By default all fields passed are updated with the <CFUPDATE> function. If you would like to only update specific fields you can specify this with the FORMFIELDS attribute. CFUPDATE will only work on tables with a primary key defined.

```
<CFUPDATE DATASOURCE="shelleyCatalog"
TABLENAME="products"
FORMFIELDS="name, price, weight, category, image, description">
```

Deleting a Record

You're probably thinking there is going to be some ColdFusion tag like `<CFDELETE>` that will work here. Unfortunately there is not and the only way to delete a record is to use SQL. Do not worry as this task is actually quite simple.

1. `<CFQUERY DATASOURCE="shelleyCatalog">`
2. `DELETE FROM products`
3. `WHERE sku=#URL.sku#`
   `</CFQUERY>`

HOW THIS WORKS

1. Names the `DATASOURCE` you will be using.
2. Using the SQL function `DELETE FROM`, specifies the table name.
3. Using the SQL function `WHERE`, you will let the table know which record to actually delete.

That wasn't too hard, was it? Now using a series of `<CFIF>` functions we can put together the *itemManagerProcess.cfm* page to handle each of these depending on the value of the `#method#` variable that is passed.

Script 4-10
itemManagerProcess.cfm

```
<!DOCTYPE HTML PUBLIC "-//W3C//DTD HTML 4.0 Transitional//EN">
<HTML>
<HEAD>
   <TITLE>Shelley Biotech - Administration Screen</TITLE>
</HEAD>
<BODY>
<CFINCLUDE TEMPLATE="_navBar.cfm">
<H3>Item manager: <CFOUTPUT>#method#</CFOUTPUT></H3>

<CFIF method EQ "edit">
<CFUPDATE DATASOURCE="shelleyCatalog" TABLENAME="products"
FORMFIELDS="name, price, weight, category, image, description">
<CFOUTPUT>#name# has been updated in the database</CFOUTPUT>

<CFELSEIF method EQ "delete">
```

```
<CFQUERY DATASOURCE="shelleyCatalog">
DELETE FROM products
WHERE sku=#URL.sku#
</CFQUERY>
<CFOUTPUT>The item has been deleted from the database</CFOUTPUT>

<CFELSEIF method EQ "add">
<CFINSERT DATASOURCE="shelleyCatalog" TABLENAME="products"
FORMFIELDS="name, price, weight, category, image, description">
<CFOUTPUT>#name# has been entered into the database</CFOUTPUT>
</CFIF>

</BODY>
</HTML>
```

◆ Project VI: User Pages

Now that we've set up the administration section to completely manage your site, we need to take a look at setting up the front-end user pages. Go back to your *_header.cfm* file and set up a link for the Products link to point to *products.cfm*:

```
<A HREF="products.cfm">
<IMG SRC="images/shelleyProducts.gif" ALT="Products" BORDER="0"></A>
```

Script 4-11
products.cfm

```
         <CFQUERY NAME="listCategory" DATASOURCE="shelleyCatalog"
         DBTYPE="ODBC">
1.       SELECT    categoryID,
                   categoryName
2.       FROM      Category
3.       ORDER BY categoryName ASC
         </CFQUERY>

         <!DOCTYPE HTML PUBLIC "-//W3C//DTD HTML 4.0 Transitional//EN">
         <HTML>
         <HEAD>
            <TITLE>Products</TITLE>
         </HEAD>
         <BODY>

         <CFINCLUDE TEMPLATE="_header.cfm">
         <BR>

4.       <CFIF IsDefined("URL.category")>
```

```
 5.   <CFQUERY NAME="listItems" DATASOURCE="shelleyCatalog"
      DBTYPE="ODBC">
 6.   SELECT    name,
               price,
               description
 7.   FROM Products
 8.   WHERE category=#URL.category#
 9.   ORDER BY name ASC
10.   </CFQUERY>

11.   <TABLE BORDER="0" CELLPADDING="0" CELLSPACING="0" WIDTH="600">
12.   <CFOUTPUT QUERY="listItems">
13.   <TR>
14.      <TD VALIGN="top" WIDTH="80%"><A HREF=
         "productDescription.cfm?category=#category#&name=
         #URLEncodedFormat(listItems.name)#">#name#</A></TD>
15.      <TD VALIGN="top" WIDTH="20%">#DollarFormat(listItems.price)
         #</TD>
16.   </TR>
17.   <TR>
18.      <TD VALIGN="top" COLSPAN="2">#listItems.description#</TD>
19.   </TR>
20.   <TR>
21.      <TD VALIGN="top" COLSPAN="2"> </TD>
22.   </TR>
23.   </CFOUTPUT>
24.   </TABLE>
25.   <CFINCLUDE TEMPLATE="_footer.cfm">
26.   </BODY>
27.   </HTML>
28.   <CFABORT>
29.   </CFIF>

30.   <TABLE BORDER="0" CELLPADDING="0" CELLSPACING="0" WIDTH="600">
31.   <TR>
32.      <TD VALIGN="top">
33.      <CFOUTPUT QUERY="listCategory">
34.      <A HREF="products.cfm?category=
         #listCategory.categoryID#">#listCategory.categoryName#
         </A><BR>
35.      </CFOUTPUT>
36.      </TD>
37.   </TR>
38.   </TABLE>
39.   <BR>
40.   <BR>
41.   <BR>
42.   <CFINCLUDE TEMPLATE="_footer.cfm">
43.   </BODY>
44.   </HTML>
```

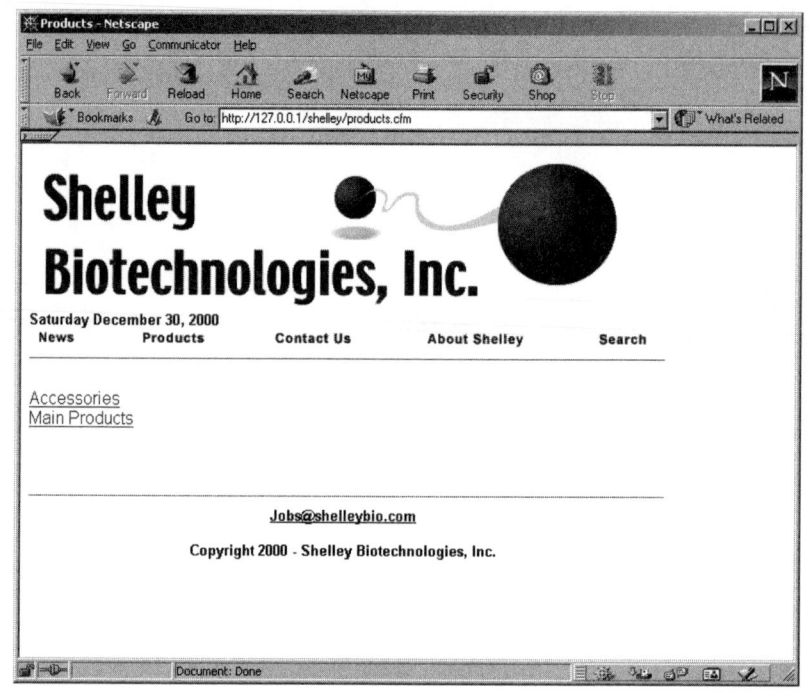

FIGURE 4-11 View the list of category names.

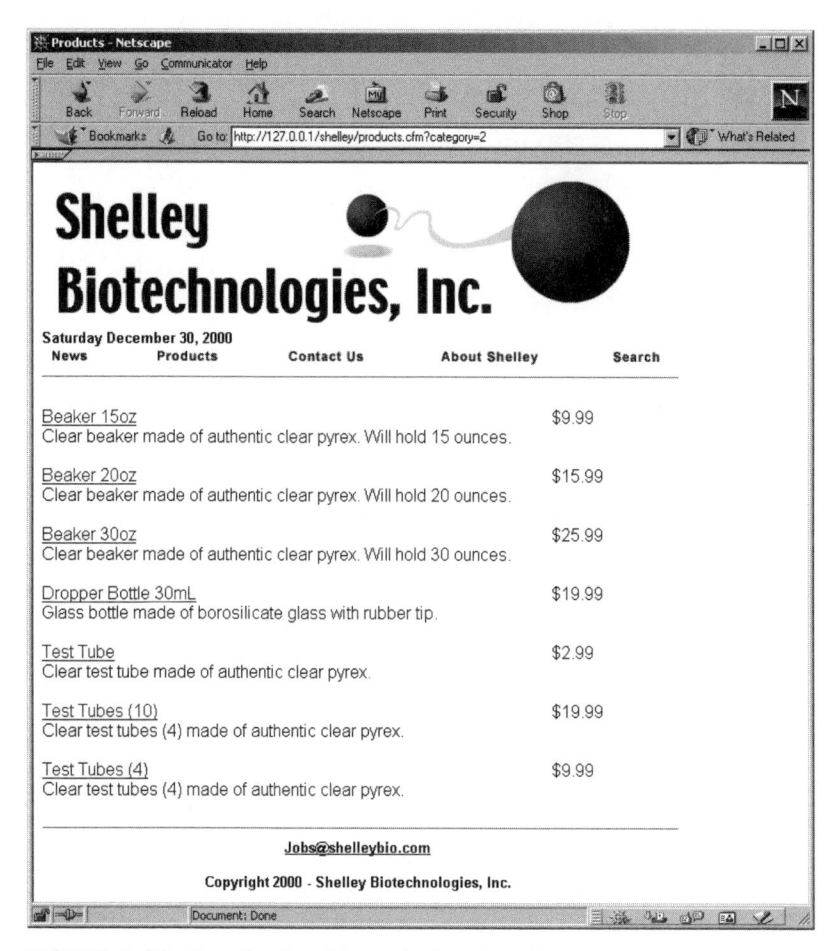

FIGURE 4-12 View the list of items in Category 2.

This page builds two types of lists depending on what is being passed in the URL. If you are first coming to this page and no variables are being passed in the URL then one part of the form is passed (lines 30–44) and lists the category names. Once you select one of those category names, the parameter `category` is passed to the URL with the value of that category and the page is loaded again. The function `IsDefined()` is used to see if the category variable exists. This time since it is, a new piece of code is executed (lines 5–28) to list all the products in that category.

HOW THIS WORKS

- **1-2.** Selects the fields `categoryID` and `categoryName` from the **Category** table.
- **3.** `ORDER` the listings by the `categoryName` in ascending (ASC) order.
- **3-9.** Using the `IsDefined` function we test to see if the variable `URL.category` was passed. If this variable exists, the code in lines 4 through 29 will execute. If the variable `URL.category` is not being passed, as is the case when you first load *products.cfm* (Figure 4-11), this piece of code is ignored and lines 30 through 44 are executed.

If `URL.category` **is passed:**

- **6-7.** Selects the fields *name, price, description* from the **Products** table
- **8.** Pulls only the information where the *category* field has the value of `#category#` which was passed in the URL.
- **14.** Links to the URL *productDescription.cfm* where a more detailed description awaits. You will be passing the same `#category#` variable as well as the `#name#` variable in `URLEncodedFormat()` in case the products has multiple words or special characters.
- **28.** Finally, if you are in this part of the code then you will not want the rest of the code to execute so you will use the `<CFABORT>` function to hop out of the code.
- **29.** Ends the `<CFIF>` function you started on line 4.
- **30-44.** If the `category` parameter was never passed to the URL then lines 30-44 would execute.

Script 4-12
productDescription.cfm

```
    <CFQUERY NAME="describeItem" DATASOURCE="shelleyCatalog"
    DBTYPE="ODBC">
1.  SELECT *
2.  FROM    Products
3.  WHERE category=#URL.category# AND name='#URL.name#'
    </CFQUERY>

    <!DOCTYPE HTML PUBLIC "-//W3C//DTD HTML 4.0 Transitional//EN">
    <HTML>
    <HEAD>
        <TITLE>Products</TITLE>
    </HEAD>
```

```
<BODY>

<CFINCLUDE TEMPLATE="_header.cfm">
<BR>

<TABLE BORDER="0" CELLPADDING="0" CELLSPACING="0" WIDTH="600">

<CFOUTPUT QUERY="describeItem">
<TR>
   <TD VALIGN="top" WIDTH="80<B>#describeItem.name#</B></A></TD>
   <TD VALIGN="top" WIDTH="20%" ROWSPAN="4"><IMG SRC="images/products/#describeItem.image#"></TD>
</TR>
<TR>
   <TD VALIGN="top">Price: #DollarFormat(describeItem.price)#</TD>
</TR>
<TR>
   <TD VALIGN="top">Weight: #describeItem.weight#</TD>
</TR>
<TR>
   <TD VALIGN="top">#describeItem.description#</TD>
</TR>
</CFOUTPUT>
</TABLE>
<BR>
<BR>
<BR>
<A HREF="JavaScript:(history.back())">&lt;&lt;Back</A>
<CFINCLUDE TEMPLATE="_footer.cfm">
</BODY>
</HTML>
```

NOTE

Make sure you have gone through an added the image names to your database table or the images will not appear.

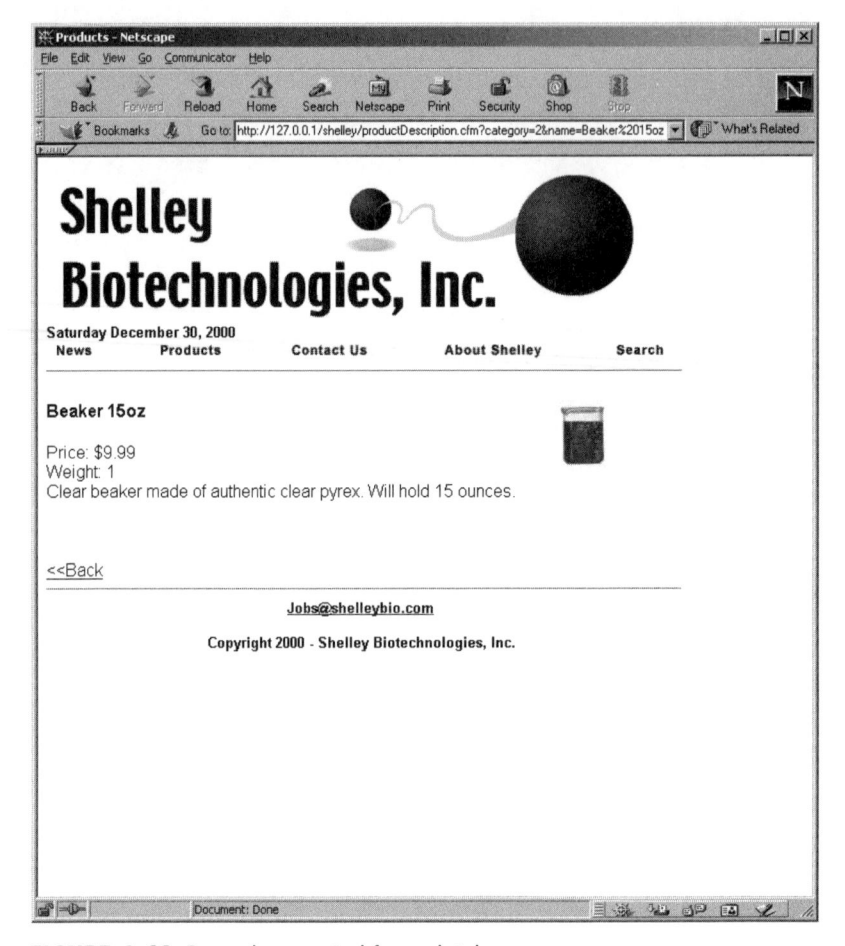

FIGURE 4-13 Record requested from database.

HOW THIS WORKS

1-2. SELECT everything (*) from the *Products* field.
3. Now we will be using the two parameters (URL.category and URL.name) passed in the URL to select the exact record we requested from the database.

◆ Recap

Using the techniques we covered in this chapter and with some minor modifications you can easily build a nice database-driven catalog for your website where you can add or modify content and products on the fly. With the use of functions such as `IsDefined`, `<CFINCLUDE>` and `IF` loops, your code can determine which parts of code to use to build the pages.

◆ Advanced Project

To make your life a little easier in the long term and while programming, go back and create an *application.cfm* file and set up values for the following items:

- Data source name
- Colors for the table rows
- Common fonts
- An error page

Go back to the Administration portion of the Shelley Technologies site and create a template for the `'Create a New Category'` listing in your top menu.

5 Sending Email

IN THIS CHAPTER

- <CFMAIL>
- <CFFORM>
- <CFINPUT>
  - <CFSWITCH> <CFCASE> and <CFDEFAULTCASE> tags
- Project I: Sign Up!
- <CFPOP>
- Project II: Retrieving Your Email from a POP Server
- New Functions
  - <CFMAIL>
  - <CFFORM>
  - <CFINPUT>
  - <CFSWITCH>
  - <CFCASE>
  - <CFDEFAULTCASE>
  - <CFPOP>
- Recap
- Advanced Project

Email is the standard for Internet communication these days. Fortunately for a ColdFusion developer it's very easy to harness the power of email on your website. The most common thing a person can do with email on the website is receive comments from users about the site. The projects in this chapter will deal with using the <CFMAIL> and <CFPOP> tags within the ColdFusion language. Each of these tags makes it a snap for interacting with email and your clients.

◆ <CFMAIL>

```
<CFMAIL
    TO="email address"                          Required
    FROM="email address"                        Required
    CC="email address"                          Optional
    BCC="email address"                         Optional
    SUBJECT="email subject"                     Required
    TYPE="html"                                 Optional
    MAXROWS="number"                            Optional
    MIMEATTACH="path to file"                   Optional
    QUERY="query name"                          Optional
    GROUP="query column"                        Optional
    GROUPCASESENSITIVE="yes or no"              Optional
    STARTROW="row number"                       Optional
    SERVER="server address"                     Required
    PORT="port number"                          Optional
    MAILERID="mailer ID"                        Optional
    TIMEOUT="timeout seconds">                  Optional
```

TABLE 5–1 <CFMAIL> Attributes

Attribute	Description
TO	Defines the email address of the person you want to mail. Can be a comma-separated list for multiple recipients. Can also be a ColdFusion variable with the recipient's email address.
FROM	Defines the email address or identity of the person sending the email.
CC	A carbon copy of the email will be sent to the people in this list.

TABLE 5-1 <CFMAIL> Attributes *(continued)*

Attribute	Description
BCC	Blind Carbon Copy emails will be sent to the addresses specified here.
SUBJECT	Defines the subject of the email.
TYPE	Only HTML can be used in this attribute. This tells the recipient's client that HTML tags need to be processed when reading this message.
MAXROWS	Specifies the total number of emails you want to send with this request.
MIMEATTACH	Specifies the path of a file to be attached. The file will be encoded in MIME format.
QUERY	Defines a query to be used to "loop" through and send multiple email messages. Specifies the query's name you wish to use and any fields selected in the query can be used in the body of the message.
GROUP	This allows you to group the results of the Query tag. This will let you group all common records to be mailed on one email. A common scenario would include grouping transactions together for one common field, such as CustomerID.
GROUPCASESENSITIVE	This will group with regard to case sensitivity. Setting this to NO will create grouping regardless of case. Default is set to YES.
STARTROW	Specifies the row to start processing on when using a query.
SERVER	Defines the SMTP server you want to use when sending email. If no value is given, the default value set in the ColdFusion Administrator is used.
PORT	Defines the port on which the SMTP server resides. Commonly set to port 25.
MAILERID	Specifies the MailerID that is passed to the SMTP server header. Default is ColdFusion Application Server.
TIMEOUT	Determines the number of seconds to wait while trying to connect to your SMTP server.

`<CFMAIL>` is pretty self-explanatory in the name itself! It harnesses the power of dealing with email through one tidy little tag. Some of the things you can do with `<CFMAIL>` are:

- Send your users email updates when your website has been changed or has new products or services to offer.
- Allow your users to send you email with suggestions or comments about your website.
- Confirm purchases of items purchased on your e-commerce website.

That list of attributes may look intimidating, but you don't have to use all of them to make it work for your purposes! You only need a few simple lines of code to create email messages. Let's say you had the following code on a page and executed it.

```
<CFMAIL TO="mike@polarisman.com"
FROM="webmaster@shelleybiotechnologies.com"
SUBJECT="Thanks for stopping by">
Greetings Mike!

Thanks for stopping by our website. Hope you found everything you
need! Come back often to check out our special pricing on all your
bio-tech needs!

Shelley Biotechnologies Webmaster
</CFMAIL>
```

```
From:    webmaster@shelleybiotechnologies.com
To:      mike@polarisman.com
CC:
Subject: Thanks for stopping by


Greetings Mike!

Thanks for stopping by our website. Hope you found everything
you need! Come back often to check out our special pricing on
all your bio-tech needs!

Shelley Biotechnologies Webmaster
```

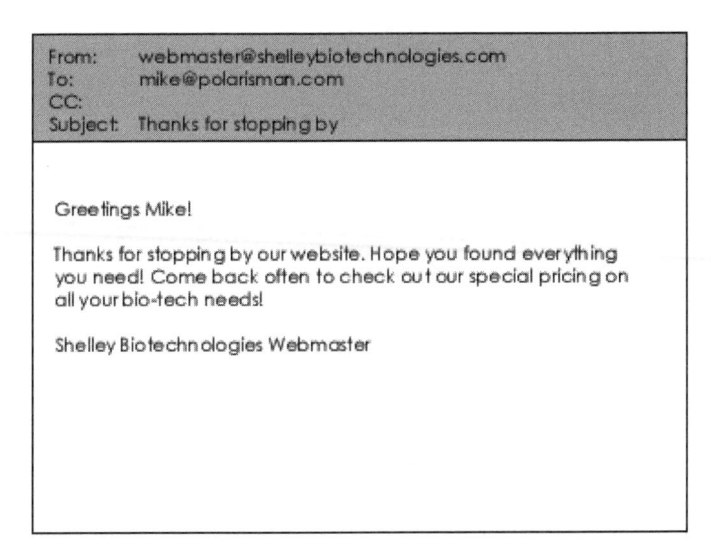

FIGURE 5-1 Results of email message.

While this is a good example of how to use <CFMAIL>, it's not very practical. In most cases, you'll be using dynamic content from your website to send email to your clients. Project I will use a form on your website to allow a user to sign up for an optional email list. But before we jump into that, we're going to explain some of the new tags that are used in this project.

◆ <CFFORM>

```
<CFFORM
NAME="form name"                    Required
ACTION="filename"                   Required
METHOD="get or post"                Required
PASSTHROUGH="elements"              Optional
ENCTYPE="mime type"                 Optional
ENABLECAB="yes or no"               Optional
TARGET="window"                     Optional
ONSUBMIT="JavaScript">              Optional
```

TABLE 5-2 <CFFORM> Attributes

Attribute	Description
NAME	Defines the name of the form you wish to create.
ACTION	Defines the template you wish to pass the form to for processing.
METHOD	Defines the method of the form. Either GET or POST.
PASSTHROUGH	Used to pass form elements that are not supported by <CFFORM> to the browser.
ENCTYPE	Defines the MIME type that is used to encode data.
ENABLECAB	This option allows users to download JAVA-based CAB files to their machines for use with <CFFORM> controls.
TARGET	Specifies which window frame you wish to get or post to.
ONSUBMIT	JavaScript routine you wish to execute when the form is submitted.

<CFFORM> functionally does the same thing as an HTML form. It will post the results to the page of your choice. Using <CFFORM> will also make validating your form elements much easier. Tradi-

tionally the developer had to create the client side validation such as JavaScript or VBScript. <CFFORM> will create the client side code on the fly, allowing you to spend more time using ColdFusion and less on JavaScript.

◆ <CFINPUT>

```
<CFINPUT
   TYPE="form type"                        Optional
   NAME="form element name"                Required
   REQUIRED="yes or no"                    Optional
   RANGE="min, max"                        Optional
   VALUE="preset value"                    Optional
   MAXLENGTH="numeric"                     Optional
   MESSAGE="message"                       Optional
   ONERROR="JavaScript function"           Optional
   SIZE="numeric"                          Optional
   ONVALIDATE="JavaScript function"        Optional
   VALIDATE="validation type"              Optional
   CHECKED="yes or no"                     Optional
   PASSTHROUGH="elements">                 Optional
```

TABLE 5-3 <CFINPUT> Attributes

Attribute	Description
TYPE	Specifies which type of form type to use. Valid entries are text, checkbox, radio, and password. Default value is text.
NAME	Defines the name of the form element.
REQUIRED	Yes or no value is valid. Default set to no.
RANGE	Valid for numeric data only. Specifies the minimum value and maximum value separated by a comma.
VALUE	Sets the initial value of the element.
MAXLENGTH	When type is text, specifies how many characters can be inputted.
MESSAGE	Defines the message to display if the validation fails.
ONERROR	Allows the use of a JavaScript function in the event that validation fails.
SIZE	Defines the size of the form element.
ONVALIDATE	Allows the use of a JavaScript function to validate the form input.

TABLE 5-3 <CFINPUT> Attributes *(continued)*

Attribute	Description
VALIDATE	Used to specify what type of validation ColdFusion should use on the field. Valid entries are date, eurodate, time, float, integer, telephone, zipcode, creditcard, and social_security_number.
CHECKED	Used with the checkbox control; yes or no are valid entries.
PASSTHROUGH	Used to pass form elements that are not supported by <CFFORM> to the browser.

ColdFusion also gives you the functionality to use the <CFINPUT> tag. It acts similarly to the HTML tag <INPUT> but allows for more interaction and validation. <CFINPUT> can take the validation routines explained in the <CFFORM> section and put them into action with the following attributes:

Example Usage of <CFFORM> **and** <CFINPUT>:

```
<CFFORM ACTION="myForm.cfm" METHOD="post" NAME="myForm">
   <CFINPUT TYPE="text" NAME="Country">
</CFFORM>
```

<CFSWITCH> <CFCASE> and <CFDEFAULTCASE> Tags

These three tags are used in conjunction with evaluating an expression. This works the same as the switch statement of C++ or select case statement of Visual Basic/ASP development. The <CFSWITCH> tag has one attribute called expression. You would supply the expression you want to evaluate in this attribute. The <CFCASE> tag outlines the possible values of your expression. You can have multiple responses within a case entry. Simply delimit the possible answers with a character of your choice and specify that character in the delimiter attribute of the tag. If none of the expected values are found, anything between the <CFDEFAULTCASE> tag is executed.

```
<CFSET authors="Micah">
<CFSWITCH EXPRESSION="#authors#">
   <CFCASE VALUE="Mike,Micah" DELIMITERS=",">
       Correct Answer!
   </CFCASE>
   <CFDEFAULTCASE>
       Wrong Answer!
   </CFDEFAULTCASE>
</CFSWITCH>
```

The expression (or variable in this case) called authors is the one to be evaluated. This logic is considered very similar to a series of `<CFIF><CFELSEIF><CFELSE>` statements. The benefit `<CFSWITCH>` has in processing time is considerably less since when the value is found, the code is executed and processing is passed to the next line. If you use the `<CFIF>` method, every statement must be checked before moving on. Generally performance will be better with the `<CFSWITCH>` statement, so use it when you can!

◆ Project I: Sign Up!

Let's start out by adding a link to the email list page. Go back to your *_header.cfm* file and set up a link for the **Contact Us** link to point to *emailList.cfm*, which we will create next:

```
<A HREF="emailList.cfm">
<IMG SRC="images/shelleyContactUs.gif" ALT="Contact Us" BORDER="0">
</A>
```

You've seen them all over the Internet by now. Sometimes email can be annoying, especially if you don't ask for it. In this case, the boss wants to have a way she can reach a new customer base from the Internet. Email is the perfect solution for this common marketing technique. This project will allow users to enter all their information and sign up for an email list if they wish. It also makes use of the **Products** table in the *shelleyCatalog* data source.

Script 5-1
emailList.cfm

```
<!DOCTYPE HTML PUBLIC "-//W3C//DTD HTML 4.0 Transitional//EN">
<HTML>
<HEAD>
    <TITLE>Shelley Biotechnologies E-Mail List</TITLE>
</HEAD>
<BODY>
<CFINCLUDE TEMPLATE="_header.cfm">
<BR>
<H3>Shelley Biotechnologies E-mail List</H3>
```
1. `<CFIF IsDefined("URL.addMe")>`
2. `<CFINSERT DATASOURCE="shelleyCatalog" TABLENAME="Customer">`

3. `<BR>Thanks! <CFIF FORM.mailingList EQ 'Yes'>You have been added to the mailing list. </CFIF> <BR> Watch your email for your free gift!`
4. `<CFINCLUDE TEMPLATE="freeGift.cfm">`
5. `<CFELSE>`
    `<BR>Please sign-up for your free gift from Shelley!<BR>`
6. `<CFFORM ACTION="emailList.cfm?addMe=yes" NAME="mailForm" METHOD="post">`
    `<TABLE BORDER="0" CELLPADDING="0" CELLSPACING="2">`
    `<TR>`
    `    <TD>First Name</TD>`
7. `    <TD><CFINPUT TYPE="text" NAME="firstName" REQUIRED="yes" MESSAGE="You must provide a first name."></TD>`
    `</TR>`
    `<TR>`
    `    <TD>Last Name</TD>`
8. `    <TD><CFINPUT TYPE="text" NAME="lastName" REQUIRED="yes" MESSAGE="You must provide a last name."></TD>`
    `</TR>`
    `<TR>`
    `    <TD>Address</TD>`
9. `    <TD><CFINPUT TYPE="text" NAME="address" REQUIRED="yes" MESSAGE="You must provide an address."></TD>`
    `</TR>`
    `<TR>`
    `    <TD>City</TD>`
10. `    <TD><CFINPUT TYPE="text" NAME="city" REQUIRED="yes" MESSAGE="You must provide a city."></TD>`
    `</TR>`
    `<TR>`
    `    <TD>State/Province</TD>`
11. `    <TD><CFINPUT TYPE="text" NAME="state" REQUIRED="yes" MESSAGE="You must provide a state/province."></TD>`
    `</TR>`
    `<TR>`
    `    <TD>Zip/PC</TD>`
12. `    <TD><CFINPUT TYPE="text" NAME="zip" REQUIRED="yes" VALIDATE="zipcode" MESSAGE="Please provide a 5 or 9 digit zipcode"></TD>`
    `</TR>`
    `<TR>`
    `    <TD>Country</TD>`
13. `    <TD><CFINPUT TYPE="text" NAME="country"></TD>`
    `</TR>`
    `<TR>`
    `    <TD>Phone</TD>`
14. `    <TD><CFINPUT TYPE="text" NAME="phone"></TD>`
    `</TR>`
    `<TR>`

```
          <TD>Email</TD>
15.       <TD><CFINPUT TYPE="text" NAME="email"></TD>
     </TR>
     </TABLE>
     Include you on the mailing list?<BR>
16.  Yes <CFINPUT TYPE="radio" NAME="mailingList" VALUE="yes"
     CHECKED="yes">
17.  No <CFINPUT TYPE="radio" NAME="mailingList" VALUE="no"><BR>
18.  <INPUT TYPE="submit" VALUE=" Submit Form ">
19.  <INPUT TYPE="reset" VALUE=" Reset Form ">
     </CFFORM>
     </CFIF>
     </BODY>
     </HTML>
```

HOW THIS WORKS

1. The `<CFIF>` statement is evaluating the URL parameter called `addMe`. If this is not found, processing skips to the `<CFELSE>` block. Upon entry to the page processing should start there.
2. `<CFINSERT>` adds the information from the form into the **Customers** table.
3. This `<CFIF>` tag evaluates the value of the form variable called `mailingList`. If the user requests to be added to the mailing list, the appropriate message is displayed.
4. `<CFINCLUDE>` will include the *freeGift.cfm* file. This file will send an email confirmation to the user. This file will be outlined below.
5. This `<CFELSE>` matches with the `<CFIF>` statement found in line 1. This marks the code to be executed when a user first requests this page.
6. `<CFFORM>` is used to mark the start of an HTML form. Notice the action of the form adds a URL parameter called `addMe`. This was referenced in line 1 to tell ColdFusion to execute the lines of code to add the user to the database.
7-19. These lines use the `<CFINPUT>` tag to capture the data from the user. `<CFINPUT>` makes use of many parameters including the `required` parameter. If a value is left blank for the last name a JavaScript routine will execute and let the user know they need to correct the information. The message you wish to display is stored in the `message` attribute.
12. `<CFINPUT>` has some built-in validations that are very useful. In this example we are using the `Validate` attribute.

Since we are requiring a ZIP code, supply `zipcode` as the validation parameter. This will hold the text box to be a numeric value of either 5 or 9 characters.

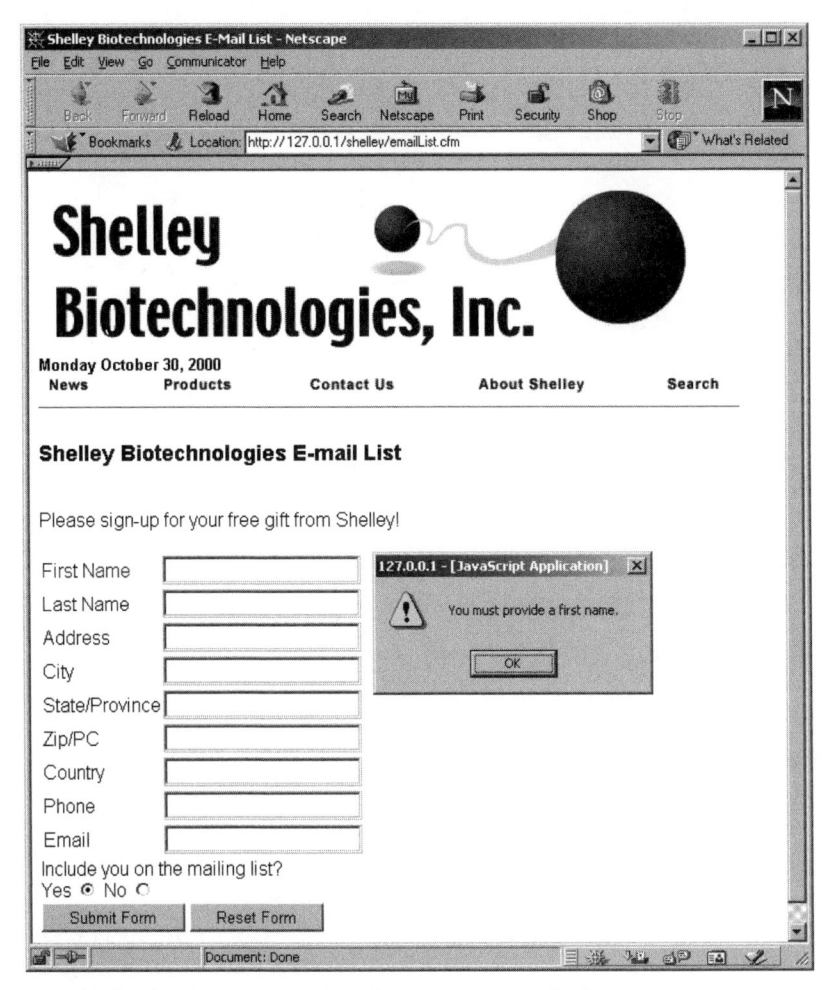

FIGURE 5-2 Error message if no first name is supplied.

Once the main file is complete we can examine the logic behind the email your users will get. Below is the code that will allow us to send our users a free gift. If the users sign up for the email list, they are entitled to two free gifts!

Script 5-2
freegift.cfm

1. `<CFSWITCH EXPRESSION="#FORM.mailingList#">`
2. `<CFCASE VALUE="Yes">`
3. `<CFSET emailBody="Thanks for signing up for our mailing list! Since you signed up, you will receive 2 free gifts!">`
4. `</CFCASE>`
5. `<CFCASE VALUE="No">`
6. `<CFSET emailBody="Thanks for visiting our website, a free gift will be on the way via email shortly!">`
7. `</CFCASE>`
8. `<CFDEFAULTCASE>`
9. `<CFSET emailBody="Sorry, an error has occurred, please contact us">`
10. `</CFDEFAULTCASE>`
11. `</CFSWITCH>`
12. `<CFMAIL TO="#FORM.email#"`
13. `FROM="webmaster@shelleybiotechnologies.com"`
14. `SUBJECT="Greetings from Shelley Biotechnologies!">`
15. `Greetings #FORM.FirstName#!`
16. `#emailBody#`
17. `Thanks!`
18. `Shelley Biotechnologies Webmaster`
19. `</CFMAIL>`

HOW THIS WORKS

1. The `<CFSWITCH>` statement is set to evaluate the form element called `mailingList`.
2-4. `<CFCASE>` outlines one of the possible responses. If the variable is evaluated to "Yes" then the body of the email is set with the `emailBody` variable.
5-7. This `<CFCASE>` also evaluated the value of `mailingList`. This time if it evaluates to "No" a different message for the email is assigned to the variable `emailBody`.
8-10. If none of the specified values within the `<CFCASE>` statements are equal to the expression then the code between the `<CFDEFAULTCASE>` tags is executed. In this case, since we know there are only two possibilities, the default value should never occur.
11-19. Once we have the variables set up for our mail message we can send it to the user with `<CFMAIL>`. We supply the user's email address in the `TO` attribute and the body of the email is set between the `<CFMAIL>` and `</CFMAIL>` tags. We can now dynamically place the variable for the email body into this message.

◆ <CFPOP>

```
<CFPOP
    SERVER="server address"                    Required
    PORT="port number"                         Optional
    USERNAME="username"                        Optional
    PASSWORD="password"                        Optional
    ACTION="action name"                       Optional
    NAME="name"                                Optional
    MESSAGENUMBER="number"                     Optional
    ATTACHMENTPATH="path"                      Optional
    TIMEOUT="timeout seconds"                  Optional
    MAXROWS="number"                           Optional
    STARTROW="row number"                      Optional
    GENERATEUNIQUEFILENAMES="yes or no">       Optional
```

TABLE 5-4 <CFPOP> Attributes

Attribute	Description
SERVER	Name or IP address of the mail server you wish to use.
PORT	Optional: Defaults to the standard 110 port for mail servers.
USERNAME	Defines the username of the account you wish to log in to.
PASSWORD	Defines the password of the username account.
ACTION	There are three methods of action allowed: GetAll retrieves all information. GetHeaderOnly retrieves only header information of the messages. Delete deletes the messages from the server.
NAME	Used to name the collection of messages for use with a <CFOUTPUT> statement.
MESSAGENUMBER	Used to retrieve a specific message number in the mailbox.
ATTACHMENTPATH	This option allows attachments to be written to a specific directory on the server.
TIMEOUT	Defines the maximum number of seconds for a request to be completed.
MAXROWS	Defines how many messages to retrieve from the mail server.

TABLE 5-4 <CFPOP> Attributes *(continued)*

Attribute	Description
STARTROW	Starts retrieving messages from this position.
GENERATEUNIQUE-FILENAMES	Default is no; will generate unique file names when downloading attachments from an email message.

The <CFPOP> tag is used to interact with email servers. It can retrieve email from the specified server and display the contents to a web browser. This is a good alternative to use if you are traveling and need to check your mail often.

◆ Project II: Retrieving Your Email from a POP Server

There are many web-based clients out on the Internet today. These would include applications like Hotmail or Yahoo Mail to name a couple. You can also offer your users their own personalized web-based mail control panel. This would be a great way to drive traffic to your site and keep them coming back. Using <CFPOP> can make this dream of more hits a reality.

Script 5-3
getMail.cfm

```
1.  <CFPARAM NAME="userName" DEFAULT="">
2.  <CFPARAM NAME="password" DEFAULT="">
3.  <CFPARAM NAME="mailServer" DEFAULT="">

4.  <CFOUTPUT>
5.  <FORM ACTION="getMail.cfm?getMessages=yes" METHOD="post">
6.  Email Server
7.  <INPUT TYPE="text" NAME="mailServer" VALUE="#mailServer#"><BR>
8.  UserName
9.  <INPUT TYPE="text" NAME="userName" VALUE="#userName#" SIZE="25"><BR>
10. Password <INPUT TYPE="password" NAME="password" VALUE="#password#"><BR><BR>
11. <INPUT TYPE="submit" VALUE="get Messages ">
12. </FORM>
13. </CFOUTPUT>
```

Project II: Retrieving Your Email from a POP Server

```
14.     <CFIF IsDefined("URL.getMessages")>
15.        <CFPOP SERVER="#mailServer#" USERNAME="#userName#"
        PASSWORD="#password#" ACTION="getHeaderOnly"
        NAME="getMessages">
16.        <FORM ACTION="getMail.cfm?getMessages=yes&getDetail=yes"
        METHOD="post">
           <CFOUTPUT>
17.        <INPUT TYPE="hidden" NAME="mailServer"
        VALUE="#mailServer#">
18.        <INPUT TYPE="hidden" NAME="userName" VALUE="#userName#">
19.        <INPUT TYPE="hidden" NAME="password" VALUE="#password#">
20.        </CFOUTPUT>
21.        <H3><CFOUTPUT>#getMessages.RecordCount#</CFOUTPUT>Messages
        in your Inbox</H3>
22.        <CFOUTPUT QUERY="getMessages">
23.        View Message <INPUT TYPE="submit" NAME="gessageNumber"
        VALUE="#CurrentRow#"> :</B> From: #from# -- Subject:
        #subject#
           </CFOUTPUT>
           </FORM>
           <BR><BR><BR>
           <HR>
24.        <CFIF IsDefined("URL.getDetail")>
25.           <CFPOP SERVER="#mailServer#" USERNAME="#userName#"
        PASSWORD="#password#" ACTION="getAll" NAME="getDetail"
        MESSAGENUMBER="#messageNumber#">
26.           <CFOUTPUT QUERY="getDetail">
27.           #body#
28.           </CFOUTPUT>
           </CFIF>
        </CFIF>
```

HOW THIS WORKS

1-3. The `<CFPARAM>` tags set the required variables to blanks if the variables are not present. The first load of this page will result in no values for these variables. When the form is submitted, the values will be replaced by the values the user has entered.

4-13. This piece of code sets up the form used to get the mail server information. Provides a `userName`, `password`, and `hostname` to the mail server and you are set to get your mail.

14. The `<CFIF>` statement tests for the existence of the `getMessages` parameter that is supplied on the query string in the `<FORM>` tag. If this variable is present, then we know to get the mail headers.

15. **The** `<CFPOP>` tag that will go to the specified mail server with the `userName` and `password` that was provided in the form. The `ACTION` in this case is `getHeaderOnly`. This will only retrieve the header information of the email messages.

16-19. The `<FORM>` element is set up with the three mail server variables as hidden fields. This allows us to keep the current values of these variables so we can log in again to retrieve the message details.

21. This line uses the `RecordCount` property of `<CFPOP>`. It's used in conjunction with the name of the `<CFPOP>` request, in this case it's `getMessages`. This will return how many email messages you have in your inbox.

22-23. Through the use of the `<CFOUTPUT>` tag, you can loop through the mail collection just as you would a query collection from a database. Using the `from`, `subject`, and `CurrentRow` parameters we are able to retrieve the information about each mail message and create a submit button with each.

24. This `<CFIF>` statement works the same way as the one in line 17. If the requested parameter (`getDetail`) is supplied it tells us we have to retrieve that email message.

25. This `<CFPOP>` statement uses the hidden variables set in line 21 to log in to the mail server and get a specific message. `ACTION` is set to `getAll` so all information about a message is retrieved. The `messageNumber` parameter is also set to the value supplied in the form element. This tells ColdFusion to select only this message number.

26-28. Once we have executed the `<CFPOP>` statement we can now loop through the collection with `<CFOUTPUT>`. In this case, we have only one record to display. The `body` variable is available to display the body of the email to the browser.

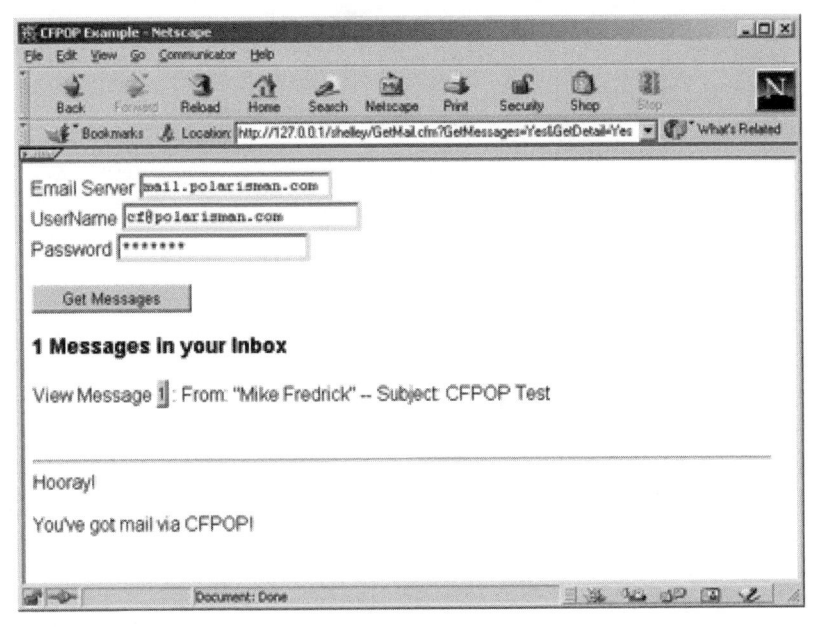

FIGURE 5-3 Results of <CFPOP> query.

◆ Recap

This chapter gave you a basic understanding of some of the email operations you can use with ColdFusion. <CFMAIL> is a powerful tool you can use to send your users important information about your website. <CFPOP> can also add dynamic content to your website. Either tool will help every webmaster achieve their goal of increasing their site's popularity.

◆ Advanced Project

A lot of times you'll have the need to send emails to all of your registered users letting them know of upcoming deals, or major site revisions. Instead of sending out a generic message to all of them, why not personalize it?

Using the **Customer** table, send each of your customers an email using the `email`, `firstName`, and `lastName` fields with <CFMAIL>.

6 Searching the Site

In This Chapter

- PreserveSingleQuotes
- <CFTABLE> and <CFCOL>
- Project I: Search Engines 'R' Us
- Using Verity with ColdFusion
- Project II: Collection Management
- Project III: Searching with Verity
- New Functions
  - PreserveSingleQuotes
  - <CFTABLE>
  - <CFCOL>
  - <CFSELECT>
  - <CFCOLLECTION>
  - <CFINDEX>
  - <CFSEARCH>
- Recap
- Advanced Project

Chapter 6 • Searching the Site

One of the most common things found on a website is its searching capability. This allows the users to find what they want on a website without navigating the whole site to find it. There are some easy techniques that can be used to create a search interface for your website. First we'll look into searching the products database using SQL. This is a simple solution you can get up and running very quickly to display information to your users. Then we'll take a look at using the Verity full-text search engine service and the tags ColdFusion provides to interface it.

◆ PreserveSingleQuotes

This function allows you to evaluate a character string that has single quotes (') in it. When evaluating strings, ColdFusion will try to escape (or double if you like to think of it that way) any single quotes it encounters. This is most commonly used when evaluating a string to be used in an SQL statement. If this is not done the SQL statement will not execute properly.

```
<CFSET authors = "'Micah','Mike'">

<CFQUERY...>
   SELECT *
   FROM Authors
   WHERE firstName IN (#PreserveSingleQuotes(authors)#)
</CFQUERY>
```

This example will take the `authors` variable and search for any of the values in the **Authors** table that has a `firstName` of Mike or Micah.

◆ <CFTABLE> and <CFCOL>

`<CFTABLE>` allows you to format query results with ease. Used in conjunction with the `<CFCOL>` tag, you can have a preformatted text (`<PRE>`) or a standard HTML table. Below are the attributes for `<CFTABLE>` and `<CFCOL>`.

<CFTABLE>

```
<CFTABLE
    QUERY="name of query"                Required
    MAXROWS="number"                     Optional
    STARTROW="number"                    Optional
    COLSPACING="number"                  Optional
    HEADERLINES="number"                 Optional
    HTMLTABLE                            Optional
    BORDER="number"                      Optional
    COLHEADERS="yes or no">              Optional
```

TABLE 6-1 <CFTABLE> Attributes

Attribute	Description
QUERY	Defines the name of the query you wish to pull the data from.
MAXROWS	Defines the maximum number of rows you wish to display.
STARTROW	Defines the row you wish to start on with your query.
COLSPACING	Defines how many spaces you wish to place between columns. Default is 2.
HEADERLINES	Indicates how many lines you wish to use in the header of the table. Default is 2.
HTMLTABLE	Using this option will render a HTML 3.0 table versus preformatted text. No attribute is given.
BORDER	Defines the border size of the table.
COLHEADERS	Yes/No option. Allows you to use the HEADER option of <CFCOL> to place headers with the data.

<CFCOL>

```
<CFCOL
    HEADER="header text"                 Optional
    WIDTH="number"                       Optional
    ALIGN="alignment position"           Optional
    TEXT="text">                         Optional
```

TABLE 6-2 <CFCOL> Attributes

Attribute	Description
HEADER	Defines the text to use in the column's header.
WIDTH	Defines the width of the column in characters. Default is 20 and any data that is more than 20 will be truncated if not otherwise set.
ALIGN	Defines the alignment in the table: center, left, or right.
TEXT	Defines the text you wish to display in this column. Usually a variable from the QUERY you are using in <CFTABLE>. Can be formatted with bold or any other formatting tags.

<CFTABLE> and <CFCOL> are exclusive tags to one another. <CFCOL> can only be used inside <CFTABLE></CFTABLE> tags. The following project will take advantage of these two tags, which will make displaying the data much easier.

Since we have gotten that out of the way we can jump into Project I. This project will search the *shelleyCatalog* **Products** table. We are going to give the user the option to use an explicit or wildcard search. An explicit search is one that returns an exact match of the search criteria. A wildcard search is more commonly used to return results that are like the user input.

◆ Project I: Search Engines 'R' Us

Go back to your *_header.cfm* file and set up a link for the Search link to point to *search.cfm*:

```
<A HREF="search.cfm">
<IMG SRC="images/shelleySearch.gif" ALT="Search" BORDER="0"></A>
```

Script 6-1
search.cfm

```
<!DOCTYPE HTML PUBLIC "-//W3C//DTD HTML 4.0 Transitional//EN">
<HTML>
<HEAD>
    <TITLE>Search</TITLE>
</HEAD>
<BODY>
```

```
    <CFINCLUDE TEMPLATE="_header.cfm">

1.  <CFPARAM NAME="searchPhrase" DEFAULT="">
2.  <FORM ACTION="search.cfm?search=Yes" METHOD="post"
3.  NAME="searchForm">
4.  Search Phrase <INPUT TYPE="Text" NAME="searchPhrase"
5.  VALUE="<CFOUTPUT>#searchPhrase#</CFOUTPUT>"><BR><BR>
6.  Explicit Search <INPUT TYPE="Radio" NAME="searchType"
7.  VALUE="Explicit" CHECKED>
8.  Wildcard Search <INPUT TYPE="Radio" NAME="searchType"
9.  VALUE="WildCard"><BR><BR>
10. <INPUT TYPE="Submit" VALUE=" Search Shelley Products ">
11. </FORM>
12. <CFIF IsDefined("URL.search")>
13.    <CFSWITCH EXPRESSION="#Form.searchType#">
14.        <CFCASE VALUE="Explicit">
15.        <CFSET SQL="WHERE description = '" &
    #Form.searchPhrase#
16.        & "' OR name='" & #Form.searchPhrase# & "'">
17.        </CFCASE>
18.        <CFCASE VALUE="wildCard">
19.        <CFSET Sql="WHERE description LIKE '%" &
20.        #Form.searchPhrase# & "%' OR name LIKE '%" &
21.        #Form.searchPhrase# & "%'">
22.        </CFCASE>
23.    </CFSWITCH>
24.    <CFQUERY DATASOURCE="shelleyCatalog" NAME="searchProducts">
25.        SELECT * FROM Products
26.        #PreserveSingleQuotes(Sql)#
27.        ORDER BY Sku
28.    </CFQUERY>
29.    <CFIF searchProducts.RecordCount GT 0>
30.    <CFOUTPUT>
31.        <B>#searchProducts.RecordCount#</B> product(s)
    matched your
32.        query. <BR><BR>
33.        <CFTABLE QUERY="searchProducts" COLHEADERS="Yes"
34.        HTMLTABLE="Yes">
35.            <CFCOL WIDTH="5" HEADER="<B>SKU</B>"
36.            ALIGN="Center" TEXT="#sku#">
37.            <CFCOL WIDTH="10" HEADER="<B>Name</B>"
38.            ALIGN="Center" TEXT="#name#">
39.            <CFCOL WIDTH="10" HEADER="<B>Price</B>"
40.            ALIGN="Center" TEXT="#DollarFormat(price)#">
41.            <CFCOL WIDTH="25" HEADER="<B>Description</B>"
42.            ALIGN="Center" TEXT="#description#">
43.            <CFCOL WIDTH="5" HEADER="<B>Weight</B>"
44.            ALIGN="Center" TEXT="#weight#">
```

128 Chapter 6 • Searching the Site

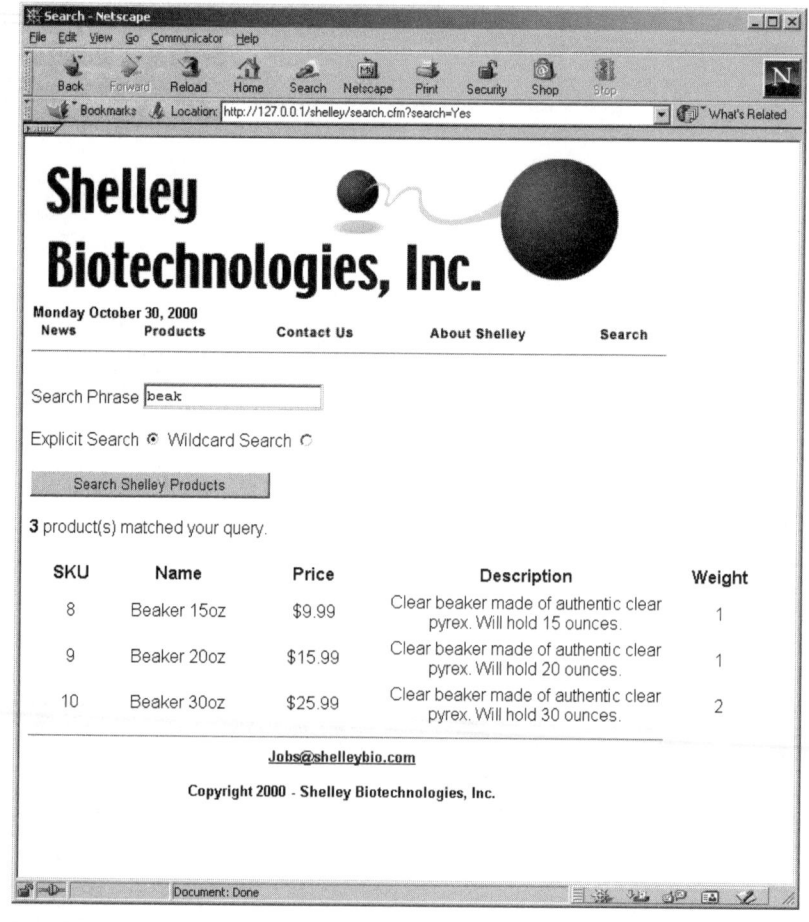

```
45.           </CFTABLE>
46.        </CFOUTPUT>
47.     <CFELSE>
48.        Sorry, No records were returned from your request.
49.     </CFIF>
50.  </CFIF>
     <CFINCLUDE TEMPLATE="_footer.cfm">
</BODY>
</HTML>
```

FIGURE 6-1 Results from searching the *shelleyCatalog* **Products** table.

HOW THIS WORKS

1. `<CFPARAM>` defines a default variable `searchPhrase`. When the page is loaded, the `searchPhrase` variable is not defined when we try to display it in the value of the `searchPhrase` textbox. By setting the value to blanks, we avoid this error.

2-11. This form sets the stage for input to get the user's request. It has an action of `search.cfm?Search=Yes`. Like chapters past, this will tell ColdFusion to process the form input later in the code. We also place the value of the `searchPhrase` variable. This form also has a radio button control on it. It allows you to select an explicit search or a wildcard search.

12. This `<CFIF>` statement triggers the search of the requested products. When the search URL parameter is detected from the form input, this section of code will be executed to find any matches.

13-23. The first thing we have to do is create the SQL statement used to search the **Products** table. Depending on which type of search we want to do, we'll create a different SQL statement. You have two options, either an explicit or a wildcard search. An explicit search will look for an exact match in the description and name fields. Using a wildcard search you can "guess" at the product and possibly come up with results. For example, if you use "Beak" as the search expression then you will come up with all the beaker products. We take advantage of the `<CFSWITCH>` statement to evaluate the radio button input and build the correct statement.

24-28. Now that we have a SQL statement we can execute it with `<CFQUERY>`. The first part of the query selects all the records in the **Products** table. Now we use the `PreserveSingleQuotes` function along with the SQL variable to execute the specific search. The `PreserveSingleQuotes` function will tell ColdFusion NOT to escape single quotes found in the variable. If they were escaped, the SQL statement would be invalid and cause an error.

29. We can now evaluate the `RecordCount` of the query we just executed. If any records are returned we want to display them. If no records are returned, then we will display a message.

33-45. Once we have records to display we'll take advantage of the `<CFTABLE>` tag. This tag is very useful to place query results in a table. First you start with the `<CFTABLE>` tag and attach some attributes. HTMLTABLE is set to yes to display an HTML table on the page. COLHEADERS allow the user to place headers on each column in conjunction with the `<CFCOL>` tag. Place one `<CFCOL>` for each column you wish to display. From this point, place the text you wish to display within the TEXT attribute.

There you have it, a simple, effective searching tool for your website. If you have the need to do some heavy duty searching, then the next section about Verity is right up your alley.

◆ Using Verity with ColdFusion

Now that we have done some basic database searching we can talk about how ColdFusion integrates with Verity full-text searching. Verity, a product that comes with ColdFusion, allows you to easily create a collection of data for users to search. With a new technology comes a few new tags. We'll give you the heads-up on what they do and then jump into the project.

<CFCOLLECTION>

The `<CFCOLLECTION>` tag is used to create and maintain collections of data. This data can be from a database or it can be files such as HTML documents or even Microsoft Office documents. `<CFCOLLECTION>` allows you to create new collections or map to existing Verity collections by giving them an alias. It also supports the use of multiple languages when the International Search Pack is installed.

```
<CFCOLLECTION
ACTION="type"                              Required
COLLECTION="collection name"               Required
PATH="path"                                Required
LANGUAGE="language type">                  Optional
```

TABLE 6-3 <CFCOLLECTION> Attributes

Attribute	Description
ACTION	Action to perform, five are valid: "Create" a new collection, "Repair" a corrupt collection, "Delete" a collection, "Optimize" to reorganize the collection, "Map" to assign an alias to an existing Verity collection.
COLLECTION	Defines the name of the collection or alias you wish to use.
PATH	Required for "Create" and "Map". Specifies the path of the collection or alias you wish to access. This can be anywhere, but is typically in the <install drive>/CFUSION/Collections folder.
LANGUAGE	Defines the language to create the collection in; default is English. Installs the ColdFusion International Search Pack to use different international languages.

<CFINDEX>

The <CFINDEX> tag is used to populate collections created with the <CFCOLLECTION> tag or via the ColdFusion administrator. There are many attributes that allow the administrator to manipulate collections. In most cases this indexing can be done when users enter new data into a database. This cuts down on data maintenance as well as keeping your collections up to date.

```
<CFINDEX
ACTION="type"                              Optional
COLLECTION="collection name"               Required
TYPE="type"                                Optional
TITLE="language type"                      Required
                                           If using custom
KEY="unique identifier"                    Optional
BODY="column name(s)"                      Optional
CUSTOM1="custom"                           Optional
CUSTOM2="custom"                           Optional
URLPATH="URL path"                         Optional
EXTENSIONS="list of extensions"            Optional
QUERY="query name"                         Optional
RECURSE="yes or no"                        Optional
EXTERNAL="yes or no"                       Optional
LANGUAGE="language type">                  Optional
```

TABLE 6-4 <CFINDEX> Attributes

Attribute	Description
ACTION	Specifies the action to take against the specified collection. "Update" updates the index along with any associated keys. "Delete" deletes a key specified in the "Key" attribute. "Purge" clears the index. "Refresh" clears the current collection before it repopulates it with new data. "Optimize" optimizes the collection.
COLLECTION	Defines the name of the collection or alias you wish to use.
TYPE	Specifies what type of data is being indexed. "File" indexes files. "Path" indexes all files that are allowed by the EXTENSIONS attribute. "Custom" indexes custom results from a ColdFusion query.
TITLE	Required for type "custom". This specifies either a valid collection name or a query column name.
KEY	Defines a unique identifier for a record in the index. Documents file name when type is "file". A fully qualified path when type is "path". A unique identifier when type is "custom" such as a primary key in a table. A query column name for any other type.
BODY	Defines either text to index or a column name to index. Columns can be comma separated.
CUSTOM1	Places any data that you wish to pass into the collection to be associated with the records. For instance, you might want to place the price of an item in the collection along with the description.
CUSTOM2	Used the same way as Custom1.
URLPATH	Defines the URL path for files.
EXTENSIONS	Defines a comma-separated list of extensions ColdFusion will use to index files.
QUERY	Specifies the query to use when populating a collection.
RECURSE	Yes/No tells ColdFusion to process directories below the specified directory.
EXTERNAL	States that native Verity tools are being used with this indexing operation.
LANGUAGE	Defines the language to create the collection in. Default is English. Installs the ColdFusion International Search Pack to use different international languages.

<CFSELECT>

<CFSELECT> is used with the <CFFORM> tags. It gives developers an easy way to populate a list box control. It will take data from a ColdFusion query and create the list box dynamically in one statement.

```
<CFSELECT
    NAME="name"                              Required
    REQUIRED="yes or no"                     Optional
    MESSAGE="message"                        Optional
    ONERROR="JavaScript function"            Optional
    MULTIPLE="yes or no"                     Optional
    QUERY="query name"                       Optional
    SELECTED="value"                         Optional
    VALUE="text"                             Optional
    DISPLAY="text"                           Optional
    PASSTHROUGH="HTML attributes">           Optional
```

TABLE 6-5 <CFSELECT> Attributes

Attribute	Description
NAME	Defines the name of the list box control.
REQUIRED	Default is no. If this field is a required element of the form then set the value to yes.
MESSAGE	Defines the message to display if the field is required and no selection was made.
ONERROR	Defines the custom JavaScript function to execute if validation fails.
MULTIPLE	Default is no. Allows multiple selections when set to yes.
QUERY	Defines the name of the query to be used in the drop-down box.
SELECTED	Enter a value that will match one result from the query to pre-select this option.
VALUE	Defines the value that you wish to be passed when the form is submitted.
DISPLAY	Defaults to the "value" parameter if not specified. Value is displayed in the drop-down box.
PASSTHROUGH	If you wish to use attributes that are not supported by <CFSELECT> then you can use PASSTHROUGH to send them to the form.

◆ Project II: Collection Management

This project will allow us to put the collection management tags into action. This template will give us the ability to use <CFCOLLECTION> to create, repair, delete, and optimize collections. Once a collection is created, we will need to fill it with some data. We can use the <CFINDEX> tag to index the data in the **Products** table. This will let us search the collection in Project III later in the chapter.

Script 6-2
verityControlPanel.cfm

```
1.  <CFPARAM NAME="collectionPath"
2.  DEFAULT="D:\CFUSION\Verity\Collections\">
3.  <CFIF IsDefined("URL.Go")>
4.    <CFOUTPUT>
5.    <CFSWITCH EXPRESSION=#FORM.action#>
6.     <CFCASE VALUE="Create">
7.      <CFCOLLECTION ACTION="CREATE"
8.       COLLECTION="#FORM.collectionName#"
   PATH="#collectionPath#">
9.       Collection <B>#FORM.collectionName#</B> created.
10.    </CFCASE>
11.    <CFCASE VALUE="Repair">
12.     <CFCOLLECTION ACTION="Repair"
        COLLECTION="#FORM.name#">
13.     Collection <B>#FORM.name#</B> repaired.
14.    </CFCASE>
15.    <CFCASE VALUE="Optimize">
16.     <CFCOLLECTION ACTION="OPTIMIZE"
17.      COLLECTION="#FORM.name#">
18.     Collection <B>#FORM.name#</B> optimized.
19.    </CFCASE>
20.    <CFCASE VALUE="Delete">
21.     <CFCOLLECTION ACTION="DELETE"
22.      COLLECTION="#FORM.name#">
23.     Collection <B>#FORM.name#</B> deleted.
24.    </CFCASE>
25.    <CFCASE VALUE="Index">
26.     <CFQUERY NAME="Products" DATASOURCE="shelleyCatalog">
27.      SELECT * FROM Products
28.     </CFQUERY>
29.     <CFINDEX COLLECTION="#FORM.name#" ACTION="UPDATE"
30.      TYPE="CUSTOM" TITLE="name" KEY="sku"
31.      BODY="description" QUERY="Products">
32.     Collection <B>#FORM.name#</B> indexed.
33.    </CFCASE>
```

```
34.    </CFSWITCH>
35.    </CFOUTPUT>
36.    </CFIF>

37.    <CFDIRECTORY ACTION="LIST" DIRECTORY="#collectionPath#"
38.    NAME="myCollections" SORT="name DESC">
39.    <CFFORM ACTION="verityControlPanel.cfm?Go=Yes" METHOD="POST"
40.    NAME="MyForm">
41.    <SELECT NAME="action">
42.       <OPTION VALUE="Create">Create Collection</OPTION>
43.       <OPTION VALUE="Optimize">Optimize Collection</OPTION>
44.       <OPTION VALUE="Repair">Repair Collection</OPTION>
45.       <OPTION VALUE="Delete">Delete Collection</OPTION>
46.       <OPTION VALUE="Index">Index Collection</OPTION>
47.    </SELECT>
48.    <CFSELECT NAME="Name" QUERY="myCollections" DISPLAY="name"
49.    VALUE="name"></CFSELECT>
50.    <BR>Add a new collection:
51.    <CFINPUT TYPE="Text" NAME="collectionName">
52.    <INPUT TYPE="Submit" VALUE=" Go! ">
53.    </CFFORM>
```

HOW THIS WORKS

1-2. `<CFPARAM>` sets the initial value for the `collectionPath` variable. This variable holds the path where the collections are to be accessed. This makes it easier to refer to this variable for that information throughout the code.

3. Once the user selects the option to execute, this `<CFIF>` statement will execute. Like many of the other examples, this keys off a URL parameter "go" passed from the submittal of the form.

5. This `<CFSWITCH>` statement evaluates the action from the form variable `action`. When one of the values is found, the appropriate `<CFCASE>` statement is executed.

6-24. This set of code will evaluate the action variable and execute the proper code based on the value of action. In these four cases we are using the `<CFCOLLECTION>` tag to either create, repair, delete, or optimize a collection. If you are choosing to create a collection, you must fill a name in the `collectionName` input box. The remaining three actions use two parameters: `COLLECTION`, which refers to the name of the collection to manipulate, and `ACTION`, which tells ColdFusion what to do with it.

25-33. If the user is choosing to index the collection, we use the `<CFINDEX>` tag to accomplish it. The first thing we have to do is to create a query to index. Lines 26-28 simply select all products in the **Products** table. Once we have some data to populate we can input this into the `<CFINDEX>` tag. Action is specified as `"Update"` to update the collection. The type is set to `custom` to tell ColdFusion to expect data from a query. Setting the title to `"name"` will store the name of the product for display when searched. This is also true for the key and the body tags. Finally, the query attribute is set to the name of the query we created above.

37-38. Instead of requiring us to remember the names of the collections we can use the `<CFDIRECTORY>` tag to retrieve all the collections in the `<collectionPath>` directory. This makes it easy for us to select the one we want to work with. All collections are created with the name you specify as the root directory. So we can simply get a directory listing and go from there.
Note that there will be the "." and ".." directories in this listing which can be ignored as they aren't valid collections.

39-53. This is the form that captures the input from the user. It's a standard `<CFFORM>` with the addition of the `<CFSELECT>` tag. `<CFSELECT>` gives us an easy way to create a select box control from a query. Place the name of the query in the `QUERY` attribute. The `DISPLAY` attribute is what is displayed to the user, while the `VALUE` attribute is what will be passed when the form is submitted.

NOTE
Before you continue on with this chapter you will need to select: `Create Collection` and name it `shelleyProducts`. Then you will need to run `Index Collection` on `shelleyProducts`. This is the collection we will be using later to search for products from the *shelleyCatalog* database.

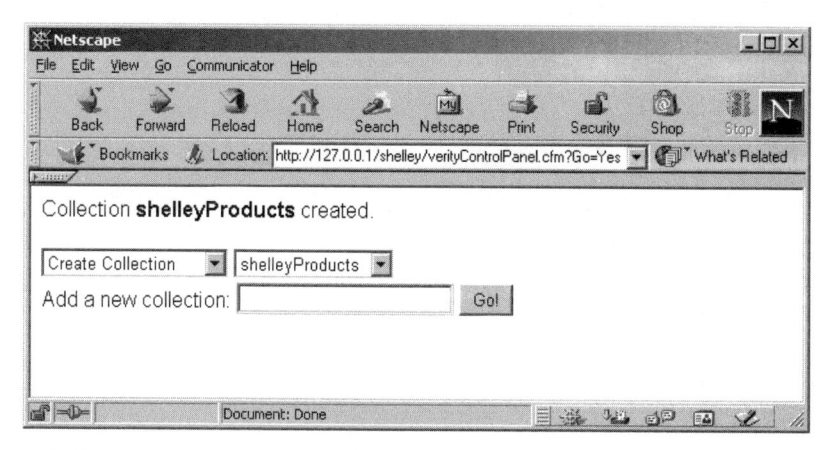

FIGURE 6-2 Create the collection.

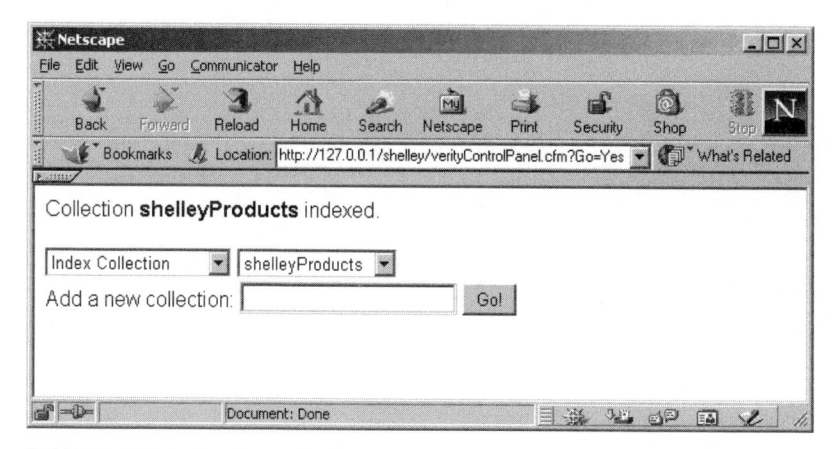

FIGURE 6-3 Index the collection.

◆ Project III: Searching with Verity

Since we have created a collection and it is full of data we can now start to use it! We can take the existing *search.cfm* file and make some small modifications to make it work with Verity. We will use the `<CFSEARCH>` tag to search the collection for the desired products. Let's introduce that tag and move into the project.

<CFSEARCH>

```
<CFSELECT
    NAME="query name"                      Required
    COLLECTION="name of collection"        Required
    TYPE="simple or explicit"              Optional
    CRITERIA="criteria to search"          Optional
    MAXROWS="number"                       Optional
    STARTROW="number"                      Optional
    EXTERNAL="yes or no"                   Optional
    LANGUAGE="language type"               Optional
```

TABLE 6-6 <CFSEARCH) Attributes

Attribute	Description
NAME	The name of the query.
COLLECTION	The collection you wish to search against. You may search multiple collections by separating them by a comma. You may also use external (created with Verity native tools) collections, however you must supply an absolute path to those files.
TYPE	SIMPLE and EXPLICIT are valid entries. Simple mode includes some operators within your search, while Explicit requires the user to supply those operators.
CRITERIA	The criteria that you want to search on.
MAXROWS	Specifies how many rows to return from the query.
STARTROW	Allows you to pick on which row to start displaying results.
EXTERNAL	Allows you to specify a native Verity collection to be used in the search. Must fully qualify the path in the COLLECTION attribute.
LANGUAGE	With the International Search Pack installed you can choose from other languages to search on.

Script 6-3
cfsearch.cfm

```
    <!DOCTYPE HTML PUBLIC "-//W3C//DTD HTML 4.0 Transitional//EN">
    <HTML>
    <HEAD>
        <TITLE>Search</TITLE>
    </HEAD>
    <BODY>
    <CFINCLUDE TEMPLATE="_header.cfm">
1.  <CFPARAM NAME="searchPhrase" DEFAULT="">
2.  <FORM ACTION="cfsearch.cfm?Search=Yes" METHOD="post"
3.  NAME="searchForm">
4.  Search Phrase <INPUT TYPE="Text" NAME="searchPhrase"
5.  VALUE="<CFOUTPUT>#searchPhrase#</CFOUTPUT>"><BR><BR>
6.   <INPUT TYPE="Submit" VALUE=" Search Shelley Products ">
7.  </FORM>
8.  <CFIF IsDefined("URL.Search")>
9.      <CFSEARCH NAME="searchProducts"
    COLLECTION="shelleyProducts"
10.     CRITERIA="#FORM.searchPhrase#">
11.     <CFIF searchProducts.RecordCount GT 0>
12.     <CFOUTPUT>
13.     <B>#searchProducts.RecordCount#</B> product(s) matched your
    query.
14.     <CFTABLE QUERY="searchProducts" COLHEADERS="Yes"
15.     HTMLTABLE="Yes">
16.     <CFCOL WIDTH="10" ALIGN="LEFT" HEADER="Score"
17.     TEXT="#Round(score * 100)#">
18.     <CFCOL WIDTH="25" ALIGN="LEFT" HEADER="URL" TEXT="<a
19.     href='viewProduct.cfm?Key=#key#'>#title#</a>">
20.     <CFCOL WIDTH="65" ALIGN="LEFT" HEADER="Summary"
21.     TEXT="#summary#">
22.     </CFTABLE>
23.     </CFOUTPUT>
24.     <CFELSE>
25.     Sorry, No records were returned from your request.
26.     </CFIF>
27. </CFIF>
    <CFINCLUDE TEMPLATE="_footer.cfm">
    </BODY>
    </HTML>
```

140 Chapter 6 • Searching the Site

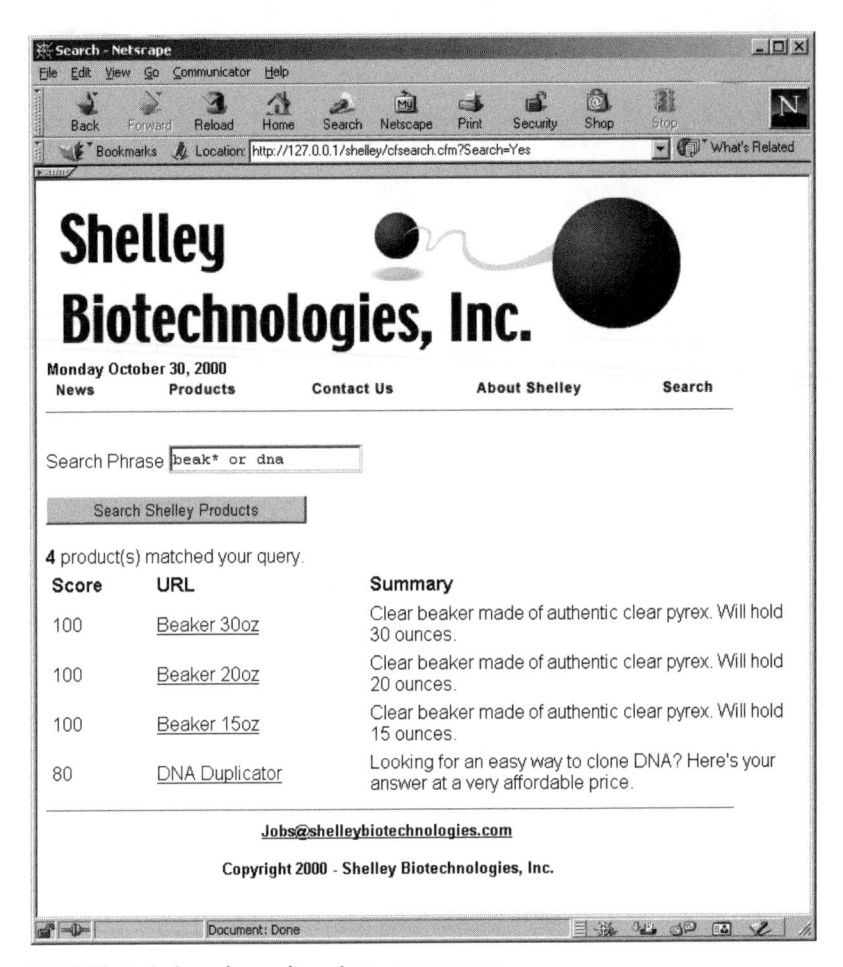

FIGURE 6-4 Search results using `<CFSEARCH>`.

HOW THIS WORKS

1. `<CFPARAM>` defines a default variable `searchPhrase`. When the page is loaded, the `searchPhrase` variable is not defined when we try to display it in the value of the `searchPhrase` textbox. By setting the value to blanks, we avoid this error.

2-7. This form sets up the stage for input to get the user's request. It has an action of `search.cfm?Search=Yes`. Like chapters past, this will tell ColdFusion to process the form input later in the code. We also place the value of the `searchPhrase` variable.

8. This `<CFIF>` statement triggers the search of the requested products. When the "`search`" URL parameter is detected from the form input, this section of code will be executed to find any matches.
9-10. `<CFSEARCH>` is now invoked to search the *shelleyProducts* collection we created in Project II. The last piece of information we supply is the search criteria in the CRITERIA attribute.
11. Again, we use the `<CFIF>` statement to test the results of the search. If we find some records then we can display them. If not, the "sorry, no records" message will appear.
16-17. The rest of this application will display the results to the user. Again, we make use of `<CFTABLE>` and `<CFCOL>` to display this data. `<CFSEARCH>` allows you to report the score of search results back to the screen. The score is how well the results match the words you type as criteria. In the above example, we use the (*) operator as a wildcard search. This returns an exact match (as far as Verity is concerned) to what you typed, therefore it's ranked 100%. Since 'DNA' is only in part of the result, it's rated at 80%. (Please don't ask me to explain the rating system, as I am pretty sure nobody is supposed to know how it works. It just does so I will leave it at that.)
18-19. The KEY and TITLE fields in the collection coincide with the KEY and TITLE attributes in the `<CFINDEX>` tag used in Project II. The fields that were indexed in that operation are available to output to the user.
20-21. SUMMARY coincides with the BODY attribute of `<CFINDEX>`. This works the same way as the KEY and TITLE variables above.

NOTE

The wildcards in Verity searching are different from those of SQL. If you implement a Verity solution, be sure to inform your users how to search properly using wildcards. Failing to do so might not bring back the desired results. If you're doing e-commerce, that's not a good thing!

◆ Recap

Since searching websites is a big deal, it's nice to have a few options. Most sites can be well-fitted with the searching techniques used in Project II using SQL as the method of inquiry. This is an easy and powerful search you can implement very quickly. On that note, if your site is interactive with new data being published daily, you might consider using Verity collections. They take a bit more work, but will perform much better when searching large amounts of data. Either way, searching your site can be done easily with a little help from ColdFusion.

◆ Advanced Project

If you are looking for some ideas for advancing your site's search engine, think about using the Verity engine. SQL searches are fairly easy and quick to make, but more strength lies within Verity. You could use the Verity engine to control your e-commerce or document management needs. Using Verity as the full-text search engine for a document library is a great way to expand its usability. Verity will allow you to create collections of Microsoft Office documents and allow your users to find just what they need. This would be ideal for your intranet solution.

7 Knowing Who's Who

IN THIS CHAPTER

- Security Basics
- Project I: Protect Your Management Templates
- C is for Cookie
- Project II: Enhanced Functionality with <CFCOOKIE>
- New Functions
  - <CFCOOKIE>
- Recap
- Advanced Project

◆ Security Basics

Security with any dynamic web application is critical. As we have all heard, there are some people who would love to crash your website or, even worse, defame it in some way. This could not only cause some embarrassment, but lose potential customers and money to boot.

With ColdFusion, a simple and effective security system is easy to build around your application. With a little careful planning, you can integrate database interaction with your security system to allow multiple users into your administrative website.

Project I will take a look into setting up a security system built around the administrative templates you built in Chapter 4. Through the use of session variables and session management we can easily take the existing application and secure it.

◆ Project I: Protect Your Management Templates

In Chapter 4, you created some management templates for your online store at Shelley Biotechnologies. These templates would have to exist on the web server so they could be accessed by anybody knowing the name of the templates. Guessing the name of the files is not very likely, but it's better to be safe than sorry.

The security of this application can be summed up in two templates and a table addition to the *shelleyCatalog* database. First, we'll add the table and define what each field is used for. From there, we'll go into the code and create the security system.

Adding a Table to the shelleyCatalog *Database*

We need to create a user's table for the administrators of the website. This will allow us to check the table for authorized users. Below is a picture of the new table you'll need to add.

id	userName	password
1	Mike	mandm4ever
2	Micah	myPassword
(AutoNumber)		

FIGURE 7-1 AdminUsers table created in the *shelleyCatalog* database.

Now that we have a table to work with, let's get cracking! First comes the login screen for the administration homepage. Since we are working in the */shelleyAdmin/* directory, and want to protect all the files in this directory, we can use *login.cfm* for the file name of the login page.

Script 7-1
login.cfm

```
    <!DOCTYPE HTML PUBLIC "-//W3C//DTD HTML 4.0 Transitional//EN">
    <HTML>
    <HEAD>
        <TITLE>Shelley Administration Login</TITLE>
    </HEAD>
    <BODY>
1.  <CFIF IsDefined("URL.Login")>
2.      <CFQUERY NAME="getUser" DATASOURCE="shelleyCatalog">
3.          SELECT *
            FROM AdminUsers
4.          WHERE userName='#FORM.userName#' AND password=
5.          '#FORM.password#'
6.      </CFQUERY>
7.      <CFIF getUser.RecordCount GT 0>
8.          <CFSET SESSION.loggedIn="yes">
9.          <CFLOCATION URL="index.cfm">
10.     <CFELSE>
11.         <CFLOCATION URL="login.cfm?failed=yes">
12.     </CFIF>
13. </CFIF>
14. <CFIF IsDefined("URL.failed")>
15.     <CFSET errMsg="Login Failed, Please Try Again">
16. <CFELSEIF IsDefined("URL.notLoggedIn")>
17.     <CFSET errMsg="User Not Logged In">
18. <CFELSE>
19.     <CFSET errMsg="Please Login Below">
20. </CFIF>
    <CENTER>
    <BR><H3><B>Shelley Biotech Administration Website</B></H3><BR>
21. <H4><CFOUTPUT>#errMsg#</CFOUTPUT></H4><BR><BR>
22. <FORM ACTION="login.cfm?login=yes" METHOD="post">
23. UserName <INPUT TYPE="text" NAME="userName"><BR>
24. Password <INPUT TYPE="password" NAME="password"><BR>
25. <INPUT TYPE="submit" VALUE=" Login ">
    </FORM>
    </CENTER>
    </BODY>
    </HTML>
```

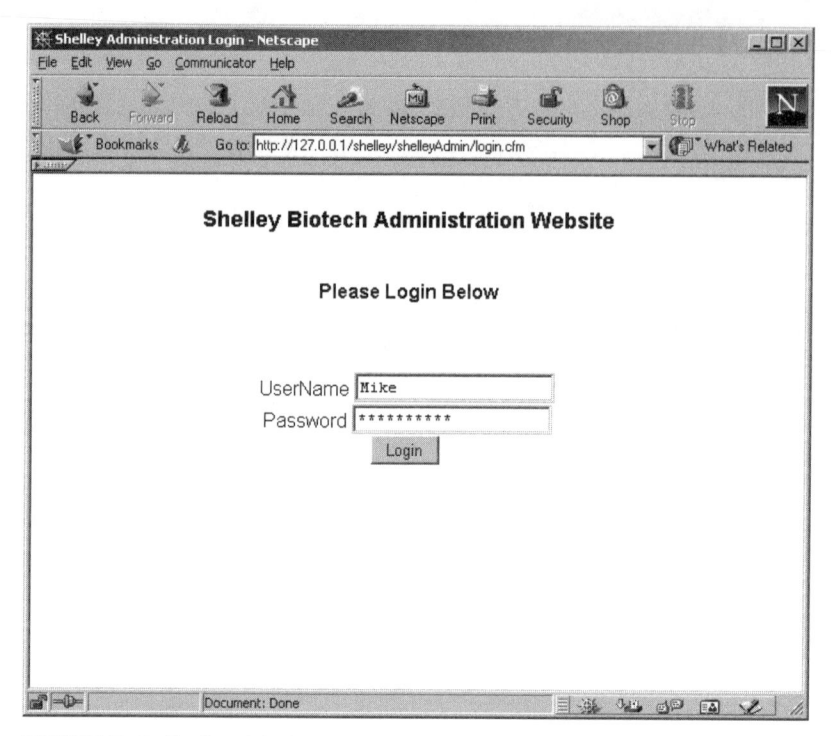

FIGURE 7-2 Shelley Administration Website Login Screen.

HOW THIS WORKS

1. This `<CFIF>` statement checks for the existence of the URL variable `login`. If it exists, the code in lines 2-13 will execute, logging the user into the system.
2-6. This query will select the user from the **AdminUsers** table. It checks that the `userName` AND `password` input from the form match the information in the table.
7. This `<CFIF>` statement evaluates the results of the above query. If the record count is greater then 0, a valid user is found and the code is executed. If the record count is not greater then 0, no user was found and the `<CFELSE>` code will be executed.
8. This sets the `loggedIn` variable to `"yes"` telling the system that the user has successfully logged in.
9. `<CFLOCATION>` will forward onto the Administration *index.cfm* since they have a valid `username` and `password`.

11. This `<CFLOCATION>` tag will forward the user back to the same page with a URL variable relaying that no match was found.

14-20. This series of `<CFIF>` statements sets the value of the status message. Depending on what URL variable is available, a message is sent to the `errMsg` variable for display.

21-25. The form element here captures the `userName` and `password` information from the user. They are submitted to the current file with a URL variable of `login` to signal ColdFusion to attempt a login of the administration website.

Now that we have our login page, we'll need to add an *application.cfm* file to the *admin* directory. Remember this is the file that gets executed every time someone requests a page from the *admin* directory.

Script 7-2
application.cfm

```
1. <CFAPPLICATION NAME="ShelleyAdmin" SESSIONMANAGEMENT="yes">
2. <CFIF #Right(SCRIPT_NAME,9)# NEQ "login.cfm">
3.     <CFIF NOT IsDefined("SESSION.loggedIn")>
4.         <CFLOCATION URL="login.cfm?notLoggedIn=yes">
   </CFIF>
</CFIF>
```

HOW THIS WORKS

1. Each *application.cfm* file must have a `<CFAPPLICATION>` tag in it if you are going to be doing any kind of application management. This application is named `"ShelleyAdmin"` and session management is enabled with the parameter supplied.

2. This page is executed every time a user requests an administration page. This statement checks to see which page is being requested using the `SCRIPT_NAME` CGI variable. This will return the path to the requested file. We test the right 9 characters and check to see if they are equal to *index.cfm*, which represents the login page.

3. If any page but the *index.cfm* page is requested, we'll test to see if the `loggedIn` variable is defined.

4. If the `loggedIn` variable is not defined we will send the user, via the `<CFLOCATION>` tag, to the login screen. How-

ever, if it is defined we will do nothing and display the requested page. Note that the only place the `loggedIn` variable can be set is where a user is validated. Therefore we can assume that a defined session variable will mean we have a valid user.

There you have it, a simple secured administration website! None of the other pages in the */shelleyAdmin/* directory can be accessed before the login.

Now we can start adding functionality with ColdFusion cookies!

◆ C Is for Cookie

```
<CFCOOKIE
    NAME="cookie name"                  Required
    VALUE="value of the cookie"         Optional
    EXPIRES="time"                      Optional
    SECURE="yes or no"                  Optional
    PATH="/pathname">                   Optional
    DOMAIN=".domain">                   Optional
```

TABLE 7–1 <CFCOOKIE> Attributes

Attribute	Description
NAME	Defines the name of the cookie.
VALUE	Defines the value of the cookie you wish to set.
EXPIRES	Can be a date, a number of days when the cookie expires, or NOW or NEVER. NOW will delete the cookie from the client's browser.
SECURE	Yes or No values. If SSL is available on the browser the cookie is transmitted securely.
PATH	Specifies the set of URLs that the cookie applies to. An example would be PATH="/admin"; this will apply the cookie to the *admin* directory only of the specified domain.
DOMAIN	Defines a domain to apply the cookie to. Example: DOMAIN=".polarisman.com". Note that the URL has to start with a "dot".

We're not talking about the kind the cookie monster likes to eat, but rather the ones that can identify unique users. Cookies are stored on the user's computer and can be retrieved by web browsers. They can aid a developer in many ways to uniquely identify a user and the profile that is associated with that user.

NOTE
Be aware that sometimes people turn cookies off. So if your application(s) will reply to them, be sure to warn your users that cookies must be turned on.

In the "old" days, you used to have to use JavaScript or VBScript to manipulate client side cookies. This wasn't a straightforward task at all as the syntax and amount of code needed to create and use cookies was just plain ugly. Once again, ColdFusion wraps the syntax behind creating cookies into the <CFCOOKIE> tag. Through a few simple parameters you can be setting and using cookies to your advantage.

◆ Project II: Enhanced Functionality with <CFCOOKIE>

Now that we have a secure environment to manage the website, we can use cookies to spice things up a bit. We will take the previous *login.cfm* file and make some additions to it, which will store the administration user's username as a cookie on their computer. Rewrite your *login.cfm* file to show the following:

Script 7-3
login.cfm

```
<!DOCTYPE HTML PUBLIC "-//W3C//DTD HTML 4.0 Transitional//EN">
<HTML>
<HEAD>
   <TITLE>Shelley Administration Login</TITLE>
</HEAD>
<BODY>
<CFIF IsDefined("URL.login")>
```

```
          <CFQUERY NAME="getUser" DATASOURCE="shelleyCatalog">
               SELECT *
               FROM AdminUsers
               WHERE userName='#FORM.userName#' AND
     password='#FORM.password#'
          </CFQUERY>
          <CFIF getUser.RecordCount GT 0>
               <CFSET SESSION.loggedIn="yes">
1.             <CFCOOKIE NAME="ShelleyAdmin" EXPIRES="NEVER"
               VALUE="#FORM.userName#">
2.        <META HTTP-EQUIV="refresh" CONTENT="5; URL=index.cfm">
          <CFELSE>
                    <CFLOCATION URL="login.cfm?failed=yes">
          </CFIF>
     </CFIF>
     <CFIF IsDefined("URL.failed")>
          <CFSET errMsg="Login Failed, Please Try Again">
     <CFELSEIF IsDefined("URL.notLoggedIn")>
          <CFSET errMsg="User Not Logged In">
     <CFELSE>
          <CFSET errMsg="Please Login Below">
     </CFIF>
     <CENTER>
     <BR><H3><B>Shelley Biotech Administration Website</B></H3><BR>
     <H4><CFOUTPUT>#errMsg#</CFOUTPUT></H4><BR><BR>
     <FORM ACTION="login.cfm?login=yes" METHOD="post">
3.   UserName <INPUT TYPE="text" NAME="userName"
          <CFIF IsDefined("COOKIE.ShelleyAdmin")> 4 VALUE="<CFOUTPUT>
          #COOKIE.ShelleyAdmin#</CFOUTPUT>"</CFIF>><BR>
     Password <INPUT TYPE="password" NAME="password"><BR>
     <INPUT TYPE="submit" VALUE=" Login ">
     </FORM>
     </CENTER>
     </BODY>
     </HTML>
```

> **NOTE**
> Since this is a modification to the code we explained earlier in the chapter, only the new information will be explained in detail.

HOW THIS WORKS

1. After a user has been logged in, we can set a cookie on their computer to identify the current user. Using the `<CFCOOKIE>` tag, we set the `"ShelleyAdmin"` cookie with the value of what was passed in the form variable `userName`. We also set this cookie to never expire using the `Expires` parameter.
2. We have a bit of change with this code. In the previous example we used `<CFLOCATION>` to redirect the user to the homepage after a successful login. When dealing with cookies, `<CFLOCATION>` cannot be used immediately after setting the cookie. Many tests (and hours) have revealed that the cookie is never set; rather, the user is redirected to the homepage. To combat this, use a META refresh tag, which will allow ColdFusion to set the cookie and will still get the user to the correct page.
3. The next time the user logs in, the username will be in place. We use a `<CFIF>` statement in conjunction with the `IsDefined` function to place the value of the cookie in the text box.

◆ Recap

Voila! You now have a lightweight security system and can focus your attention on developing the main applications. Cookies (both CF and conventional) are a really nice treat for a developer. They take much of the work out of identifying users or requiring them to log into your website to retrieve specific user data. As mentioned earlier, cookies can be refused by the user. By default, cookies are enabled on standard browsers but they can be disabled by a user. Just be sure to have a backup plan when building a website that uses cookies.

◆ Advanced Project

Since users can be identified by using cookies you can use this to personalize your website for your users. Take the *News* section of the main Shelly Biotechnologies website and make this a secure area. Remember to add a feature to allow users to create an account to access this area. You will need to build a new table (call it **NewsUsers**) into your database to accommodate these new users.

8 Using Custom Tags

IN THIS CHAPTER

- Introduction to Custom Tags
- The Ins and Outs of Custom Tags
- Where Can I Use Custom Tags?
- Project I: Counting Your Hits
- Project II: Creating a Random Product Custom Tag
- Other Functions Used in This Project
- New Functions
  - ListLen
  - ListAppend
  - ListGetAt
  - RandRange
- Recap
- Advanced Project

◆ Introduction to Custom Tags

In a nutshell, custom tags are custom functions that a developer can create to streamline an application. A custom tag can perform one specific function or it can be an entire application. Custom tags can be developed using the CFML language or C/C++. There are many benefits to using custom tags within your application:

- Flexible code—If you write all your code in one template and need to change the way it works, you can quickly remove one custom tag and replace it with another.
- Reuse of your code—If you have a function that is used numerous times throughout your website you can reuse the custom tag in all these areas. This will eliminate the need to maintain a series of pages if the function were to change.
- Code readability—Moving your code into custom tags will allow you to make your base code more readable. Sometimes complex and messy logic is required. Custom tags can make it much easier to read and maintain.
- Custom tags work like HTML tags. A tag has attributes which have acceptable values. It's these values that alter something's appearance.

◆ The Ins and Outs of Custom Tags

A custom tag is created by building a ColdFusion page just like any other on your website. Let's suppose we have a file called *sayIt.cfm*. In that file we have a simple statement.

Script 8-1
sayit.cfm

```
<FONT COLOR="red">Welcome! </FONT>
```

Pretty simple, huh? If you wish to call this custom tag you would use the following syntax:

```
<CF_sayIt>
```

Again, it's a no brainer. What you'll get is the word "Welcome!" in red text on your page. Note that the name of the file we are using is called in the custom tag call (sayIt). This tells Cold-

Fusion to look for a file called *sayIt.cfm* and execute it. If it doesn't find it, an error will occur.

Now let's expand on the tag to make it a bit more useful and explore how we can use variables within the custom tag.

Let's say we call the tag:

```
<CF_sayIt name="Mike">
```

Using the name as a parameter gives the custom tag a value that it can use during processing.

```
<CFOUTPUT>
    <FONT COLOR="red">Welcome #Attributes.name# !</FONT>
</CFOUTPUT>
```

This code would yield "Welcome Mike!" in red text on your page. The attribute's preface, you'll remember from earlier chapters, defines a custom tag scope variable. It's used to identify variables that are passed in through custom tag calls.

Consider the following modification to the *sayit.cfm* file.

```
<CFOUTPUT>
    <FONT COLOR="red">Welcome #Attributes.name# !</FONT>
    <CFSET Caller.Response = Attributes.name & " is cool">
</CFOUTPUT>
```

The `<CFSET>` statement above sets a new type of variable. The caller prefix allows the calling template (the one with the custom tag call on it) to use "response" in its processing. Response would have the string "Mike is cool" in it and you could now display it on your page.

◆ Where Can I Use Custom Tags?

The short answer is anywhere! ColdFusion tags can be used anywhere within your applications but there are some rules on how you store them on your web server. Improper reference to custom tags will result in many errors and will most definitely frustrate you. Follow the rules and everything will be just fine.

Consider the following directory structure.

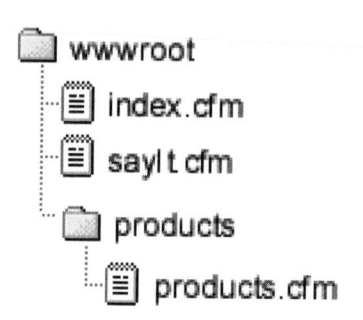

```
wwwroot
├── index.cfm
├── sayIt.cfm
└── products
    └── products.cfm
```

FIGURE 8-1 Directory structure for custom tags.

Here we have a root directory with a products directory within the root. An *index.cfm* file exists in the root while a *products.cfm* file exists in the products directory. Note that the *sayIt.cfm* file only exists in the root.

If we were to call the <CF_sayIt> tag from the *index.cfm* file, life would be good and we would get the expected results. However, if we used it on the *products.cfm* file we would get an error. ColdFusion looks for custom tags in two places:

- In the same directory the "calling" template exists; in this case it would be the root
- In the <install drive>/CFUSION/CustomTags directory

You can place all your custom tags in the above-mentioned directory on your web server and they will be accessible by all ColdFusion applications. However, if you don't own the servers on which you host your site, you may not be able to access this directory. Or even worse, you may be charged to have access to this directory. You can place all the custom tags in the root directory, but you'll have to reference them through the <CFMODULE> tag.

```
<CFMODULE TEMPLATE="../SayIt.cfm" NAME="Mike">
```

This tag will start at the root directory and trace up through the directory path. This will allow you to reference a directory within your control and gain the advantages of storing all your custom tags in one place.

◆ Project I: Counting Your Hits

One of the most common things you would want to know about your website is how many hits you are receiving. This can be an easy process for you using custom tags. We'll use the code below to track hits on any of your web pages. First, we'll have to add a table and explain a new variable you'll be using in this script.

SCRIPT_NAME Variable

The CGI (Common Gateway Interface) variable SCRIPT_NAME will return a relative path of the script that is being requested.

EXAMPLE 8-1

Let's suppose this is the URL you are calling:

```
http://www.polarisman.com/mail/getmail.cfm
```

with the following code on it:

```
<CFSET Page=SCRIPT_NAME>
```

The page would result with "\mail\getmail.cfm".

Adding the Hits Table to the shelleyCatalog Database

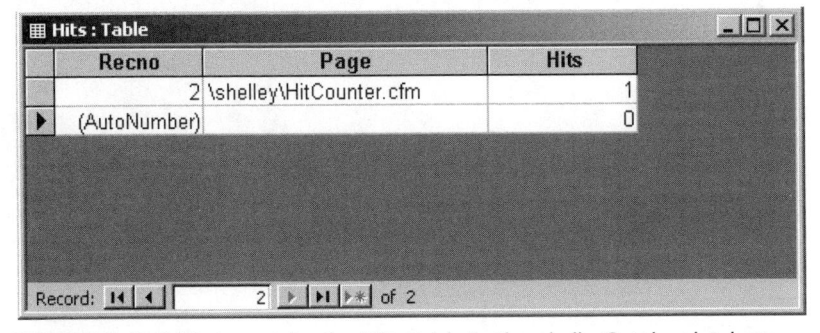

Recno	Page	Hits
2	\shelley\HitCounter.cfm	1
(AutoNumber)		0

FIGURE 8-2 Table layout for the **Hits** table in the *shelleyCatalog* database.

By now you should be fairly familiar with Microsoft's Access interface. Above is the layout of the **Hits** table we'll be using in the following project. If you're not familiar, then this is even more great practice.

Script 8-2
hitCounter.cfm

```
1.  <CFSET Page=SCRIPT_NAME>
2.  <CFQUERY DATASOURCE="shelleyCatalog" NAME="getPage">
3.  SELECT *
    FROM Hits
4.      WHERE page='#page#'
5.  </CFQUERY>
6.  <CFIF getPage.RecordCount EQ 0>
7.  <CFQUERY DATASOURCE="shelleyCatalog" NAME="addPage">
8.      INSERT INTO Hits (page,hits)
9.      VALUES ('#page#',1)
10. </CFQUERY>
11. <CFSET Caller.hitCount=1>
12. <CFELSE>
13. <CFQUERY DATASOURCE="shelleyCatalog" NAME="ppdatePage">
14.     UPDATE Hits
15.     SET hits=#getPage.hits# + 1
16.     WHERE Page='#getPage.page#'
17. </CFQUERY>
18. <CFSET Caller.hitCount=Evaluate(getPage.hits + 1)>
19. </CFIF>
```

HOW THIS WORKS

1. This `<CFSET>` statement sets the variable page to the value of the CGI variable named `SCRIPT_NAME`. This variable returns the relative path including the filename. In my example it would be \shelley\hitCounter.cfm. This is how we will keep track of each unique page.

2-5. `<CFQUERY>` will look in the **Hits** table to see if it can find the record that matches the current page.

6. This `<CFIF>` statement tests the `RecordCount` property of the `getPage` query. Two choices are used here; either it returns 0 or it doesn't, so it's easier to use a `<CFIF><CFELSE></CFIF>` combination versus `<CFSWITCH>` statement we have used in previous chapters.

7-10. If there are no records found, we must add a record for this page. Using the `<CFQUERY>` tag and an `INSERT` query we can add the record.

11. This line sets the variable `hitCount` within the caller scope. This means that we can now refer to the variable `hitCount` and use its value on the calling page.

12. `<CFELSE>` marks the spot where to execute code in the event that the `RecordCount` property of `getPage` is not equal to zero.

13-17. `<CFQUERY>` will allow us to update the record in the **Hits** table that matches the current page. This will increment the hit count by `1`.

18. This is the same operation as executed in line 11. The new count of hits is set to the `hitCount` variable, which will be available for use in the calling template.

Now that you have that code in place all you have to do is call it. To track hits all you have to do is include the code on every page within your application. In the case of the Shelley Biotechnologies website, the best place to put it would be in the *header.cfm* file since it will be used across the site. Simply add `<CF_hitCounter>` in the file and you'll start immediately tracking hits to your website.

◆ Project II: Creating a Random Product Custom Tag

The boss wants every page on the site to have a featured product. There is a section on the website that will display a product from the catalog along with its description and price. The trick is that the boss wants the featured product to change every time a user refreshes a page. To do this, we'll need the use of some new list manipulation functions in ColdFusion. Once we get those defined we can jump right into the application.

ListLen Function

The `ListLen` function will report back how many elements are in a delimited list.

For Example:

```
<CFSET myList="1,2,3">
<CFSET LengthOfList=ListLen(myList)
```

The value of `LengthOfList` is now `3`.

ListAppend Function

`ListAppend` will add any string to the end of a list.

For Example:

```
<CFSET AuthorList="Micah">
<CFSET AuthorList=ListAppend(AuthorList,"Mike")
```

The `ListAppend` function will add "Mike" to the AuthorList. Now the value of `AuthorList` is "Micah,Mike".

ListGetAt Function

`ListGetAt` will retrieve the value occupying a certain position in a list.

For Example:

```
<CFSET AuthorList="Micah,Mike">
<CFSET GetAuthor=ListGetAt(AuthorList,1)
```

`GetAuthor` now would contain the string "Micah" since it was retrieving the first element in the list.

♦ Other Functions Used in this Project

RandRange Function

`RandRange` will give you a random number between the supplied parameters. You can use ColdFusion variables or constants as the parameters.

For Example:

```
<CFSET RandomNumber=RandRange(1,1000)
```

`RandomNumber` would be equal to a number between 1 and 1000.

Now we're all set to create the custom tag. Place the following code into the *randomProduct.cfm* file and away you'll go!

Script 8-3
randomProduct.cfm

```
1.  <CFSET productList="">

2.  <CFQUERY NAME="getAllProducts"
3.  DATASOURCE="shelleyCatalog">
4.  SELECT *
    FROM Products
5.  </CFQUERY>

6.  <CFOUTPUT QUERY="getAllProducts">
7.  <CFSET productList=ListAppend(productList,#SKU#)>
8.  </CFOUTPUT>

9.  <CFSET RandomRange=RandRange(1,ListLen(productList))>
10. <CFSET randomSKU=ListGetAt(productList,RandomRange)>

11. <CFQUERY NAME="getRandomProduct"
12. DATASOURCE="shelleyCatalog">
13. SELECT *
    FROM Products
14. WHERE SKU=#randomSKU#
15. </CFQUERY>

16. <CFOUTPUT QUERY="getRandomProduct">
17. <CFSET productName=#name#>
18. <CFSET productPrice=#DollarFormat(price)#>
19. <CFSET productDescription=#description#>
20. </CFOUTPUT>
```

HOW THIS WORKS

1. The `<CFSET>` statement sets the value of the list to blank at the start of the application.
2-5. `<CFQUERY>` creates the recordset you want to work with. In this case it selects all products in the **Products** table.
6-8. The `<CFOUTPUT>` tag has the name of the query attached to it in the `QUERY` parameter. This allows us to loop through each of the records in the recordset. Using the `ListAppend` function, we will add the SKU of each product to the list. `ListAppend` will add the value passed in the second parameter to the list specified in the first parameter.
9. The `randomRange` variable that is set on this line makes use of the `RandRange` function. This function will return a random number from one to the total length of the list.

The `ListLen` function will report how many elements are in the list.

10. Once we have a random number, we can apply that number with the use of the `ListGetAt` function. The first parameter is the name of the list you want to retrieve a value from. The second parameter is the position you want to get the value from. In this case, it will be a random position each time you load a page. The value is now placed in the `randomSKU` variable, which can be used in a query.

11-15. This query will use the `randomSKU` variable to retrieve the random product we had generated in the code above.

16-20. Finally, the `<CFOUTPUT>` query sets the value of the query so you display your random products on your page.

Great, you say. I'm sure you're wondering what you do now. Since the boss wants this on every page in your application you have a couple of options.

Option 1—Code Every Page

I'm sure by now you have figured out that we are lazy and don't want to do anything that costs more development time. However, one long way to accomplish this is to put the custom tag on every page in your application. This will retrieve the data from the database and set the `productName`, `productPrice`, and `productDescription` variables to be used anywhere on that page.

```
<CF_randomProduct>
```

Option 2—Make Use of the Developer's Friend, the application.cfm File

Since this has to run for every page, why not just put the custom tag in the application file? That's the ticket! This is the easiest and quickest solution. The variables will be set and ready for use just as they were in option 1. However, be very careful if you use this method. Even though the boss wants a product on each page there may be instances where you won't need that information. If that's the case your performance may suffer on those pages since the query to get the random products is always executed.

◆ Recap

Easy, right? Using custom tags can save your sanity, and that's always a good practice to begin while you're learning a new language. Once you get the hang of how to use custom tags you can elevate your programming skills to the next level. The talk of the town these days is the reusability of the code. By breaking things into specific, logical functions you can share code with many different people and applications.

◆ Advanced Project

I've seen applications that were completely custom tags. This may sound strange but some of the commercial applications that are for sale allow you to simply place a custom tag call on your *index.cfm* file and you have a whole application. Your challenge would be to do the same. You could take the second project from chapter 4 (uploading a file) and create a generic tag you can call to upload any files to your server. Now this might not be the most logical application to do that with, but when you try to fit a round peg in a square hole you do learn a thing or two.

chapter 9
ColdFusion and Wireless

IN THIS CHAPTER

- What Is WAP and How Is It Useful?
- MIME Types
- Project I: WAP-Enabled Product List
- Wireless Palm™ Series of Handhelds
- Project II: Palm™-Enabled Product List
- Building and Installing the Palm™ Query Application
- New Functions
  - <CFCONTENT>
- Recap
- Advanced Project

◆ What Is WAP and How Is It Useful?

Being able to access data through a wireless device is something people have been looking forward to for years. Enter WAP! The Wireless Application Protocol (WAP) is a specification developed by the WAP Forum which is made up of several of the industry giants such as Ericsson, Nokia, and Motorola, to name a few. WAP-enabled cell phones have been very popular in Europe and have recently started popping up all over the United States. Many of the newer cell phones coming out on the United States market are now WAP-enabled but make sure before you buy one. Not all of them are.

The language used to write WAP is called Wireless Markup Language (WML) which is a tag-based language much like HTML. WML is a subset of Extensible Markup Language (XML).

Wireless Markup Language Script (WMLS) is also used to write code for WAP but will not be covered here. You're probably thinking by now, "Great, yet another language I have to learn." Yes and no. You can easily write some very functional applications in a short time using straight ColdFusion with a little WML wrapped around it.

Limitations

At first you can probably imagine all the advantages of these WAP phones but there are some limitations:

- Limited processing power and memory. The phones can't handle the same highly intensive applications that your computer can.
- Limited bandwidth and slower connections.
- Limited size screen. Phones come in an assortment of screen sizes. Some can handle 15 lines while some can only handle 3 or 4. Screen width is also a consideration to take into account. Some can handle 12 characters width while others might be able to handle 20 characters.
- Time. While you can enter data into a form through a WAP-enabled phone you don't want to require your customers to enter their entire address if it's not needed since entering text on a phone can be quite time-consuming.

Although WML has limitations, think about all the advantages it has over your desktop. You can check stock quotes, sports scores, local and world news, and yes, even order a book from Amazon.com through your WAP phone while relaxing at the park or on the road. If you're on the road and doing this, hopefully you're a passenger or you have pulled off to the side of the road!

If you currently do not have a phone that supports WAP you can go to www.phone.com and download their UP.SDK emulator, which will allow you to test your applications.

It also has several different phone types which you can add on to emulate a wide variety of phones.

You might want to think about joining their developers' program to share ideas with a large community of WAP developers.

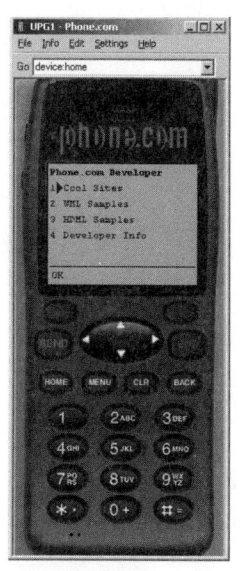

FIGURE 9-1
Phone.com's UP.Simulator
Image of UP.SDK courtesy of Phone.com

Each WML page is called a ***deck*** and can contain several cards (think of as each card being a page). When a user connects to this deck all the cards within it are loaded on the phone. When a choice is made to go to another card on that deck the page is loaded instantly since the card is already loaded as part of that deck. You can have several decks (pages) within an application so don't feel you have to load your entire application within the one deck. In fact, you should keep your file size down to 1.4 KB within a deck so all phones can handle it. Some phones can handle up to 8 KB, but unless you're developing specifically for those, it's best to play it safe by keeping the deck small.

◆ MIME Types

In order for your web server to understand the type of content to deliver you need to specify what MIME types to recognize.

Chapter 9 • ColdFusion and Wireless

TABLE 9–1 MIME Types

Add Type	MIME Type
wml	text/vnd.wap.wml
wmls	text/vnd.wap.wmlscript
wbmp	image/vnd.wap.wbmp
wmlc	application/vnd.wap.wmlc
wmlsc	application/vnd.wap.wmlscriptc

Internet Information Server 4 and 5

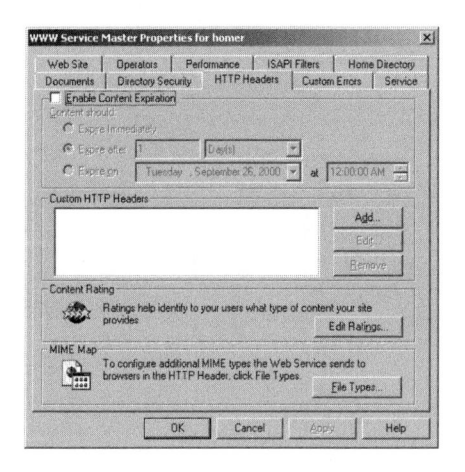

FIGURE 9–2 To add MIME types to IIS 4 and IIS 5, go to the properties settings of your website and select the HTTP HEADERS tab. Under MIME types select FILES TYPES.

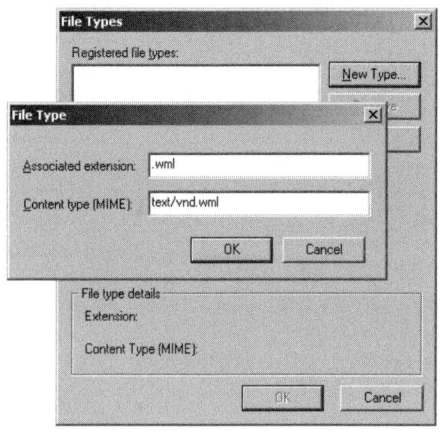

FIGURE 9–3 Here you can register new file types. Select NEW TYPE and add the associated MIME types.

MIME Types   169

Personal Web Site (PWS)

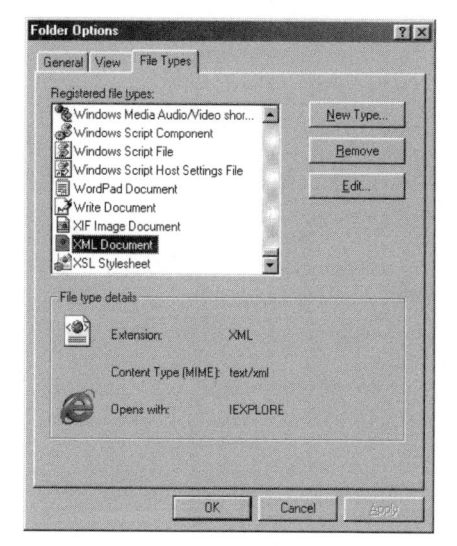

FIGURE 9-4 From the START menu, go up to SETTINGS and choose the FOLDER OPTIONS. Choose the FILE TYPES tab and select NEW TYPE.

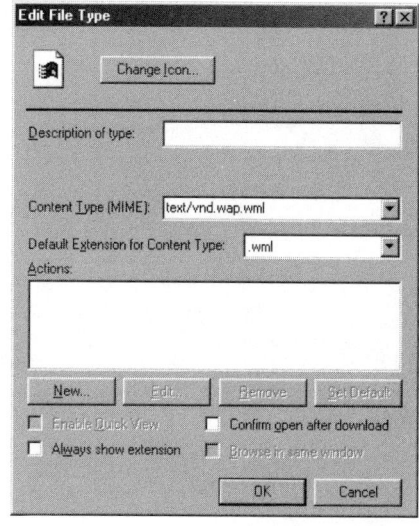

FIGURE 9-5 Here you can register new file types by adding the MIME Content Type and the Extension Content Type for the associated MIME types from Figure 9-1.

<CFCONTENT>

```
<CFCONTENT
    TYPE="MIME type"           Required
    FILE="File name"           Optional
    DELETEFILE>                Optional
```

TABLE 9-2 <CFCONTENT> Attributes

Attribute	Description
TYPE	Defines the MIME type to use.
FILE	Defines the directory path of the file to include.
DELETEFILE	Defines if the file should be deleted once sent. Leave as just DELETEFILE without a value.

WML has very strict rules when it comes to its tags which HTML doesn't. HTML in itself is pretty forgiving when it comes to case sensitivity or tags not always requiring ending tags, such as the `<LI>` tag. You can get away with not using `</LI>` to close the tag.

The basic components for building a deck are:

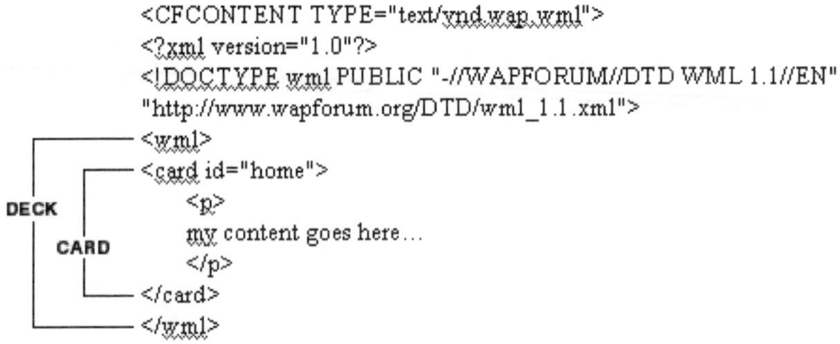

```
<CFCONTENT TYPE="text/vnd.wap.wml">
<?xml version="1.0"?>
<!DOCTYPE wml PUBLIC "-//WAPFORUM//DTD WML 1.1//EN"
 "http://www.wapforum.org/DTD/wml_1.1.xml">
         <wml>
            <card id="home">
DECK          <p>
     CARD        my content goes here...
               </p>
            </card>
         </wml>
```

FIGURE 9-6 Building a deck.

Notice how all the tags are in lower case and all have their associated ending tags. The `<wml>` tag starts off the deck where you can have several cards. Cards are defined by the `<card>` tag and must be enclosed within the `<p>` `</p>` tags. Finally you need to close the deck with the `</wml>` tag.

◆ Project 1: WAP-Enabled Product List

This project requires three separate files. The first file, or deck, builds a simple list of site features to navigate through the site:

- About us
- News
- Products

Script 9-1
indexWAP.cfm

1. `<CFCONTENT TYPE="text/vnd.wap.wml">`
2. `<?xml version="1.0"?>`
3. `<!DOCTYPE wml PUBLIC "-//WAPFORUM//DTD WML 1.1//EN" "http://www.wapforum.org/DTD/wml_1.1.xml">`

```
4.   <wml>
5.   <card id="home">
6.       <p>
7.       Shelley Biotechnologies<br/>
         <cfoutput>
         #DateFormat(Now(), "mmmm dd, yyyy")#</cfoutput><br/>
8.       <a href="#about">About us</a><br/>
         <a href="#news">News</a><br/>
9.       <a href="productsWAP.cfm">Products</a><br/>
10.      </p>
11.  </card>

12.  <card id="about">
         <p>
         ABOUT US<br/>
         We offer the finest scientific equipment for all of your
     bio-medical needs.
         </p>
13.  </card>

     <card id="news">
         <p>
         SHELLEY NEWS<br/>
         Shelley Biotechnologies has recently won the coveted
         NONLEAK award for the lowest amount of leakage from our
         containers than any other manufacturer.
         </p>
     </card>
14.  </wml>
```

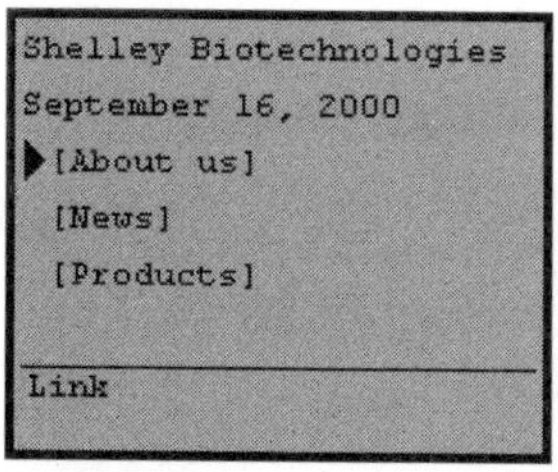

FIGURE 9-7 Home ID. 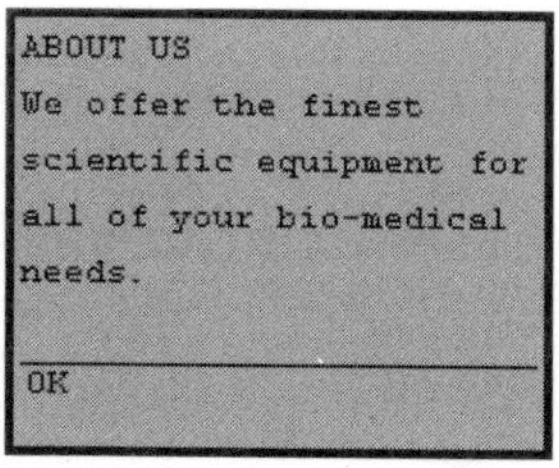   **FIGURE 9-8** About us. 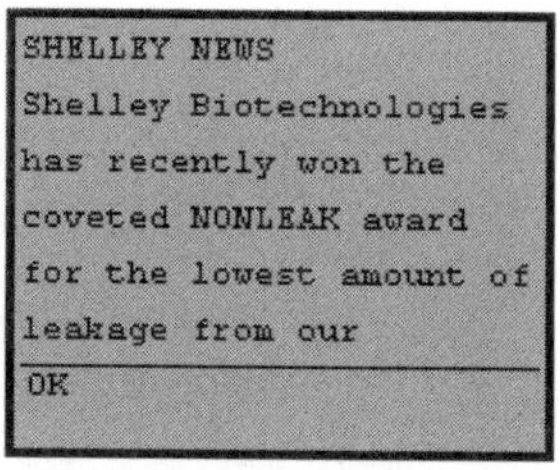   **FIGURE 9-9** Shelley news.

HOW THIS WORKS

1. Sets up the CONTENT TYPE so when this page is loaded by the web server, it knows how to deliver it.
2. Since WML is a subset of XML we need to give it this header.

3. WML requires a different Data Type Definition (DTD) than regular HTML. We just point to the DTD located in the WAP Forum.
4. The `<wml>` starts off the beginning of the deck.
5. The `<card>` tag defines the beginning of the tag. Since you are going to be having several cards in this deck you need to define each with its own `id=""` attribute. Even if you are going to have just one card on a page it's a good idea to have an `id=""` attribute in there anyway.
6. Before you begin the content you need to define the `<p>` tag.
7. Break lines can be used in WML but are tagged slightly differently. `<br/>` is the proper way.
8. `<a href="#about">` will pull up the card with the `id="about"`.
9. `<a href="productsWAP.cfm">` will go to the next deck, which will be introduced in **Script 9-2**.
10. When you are finished with the content for this card, close it off with the `</p>` tag.
11. When you are finished with the card itself, be sure to close it off as well with the `</card>` tag.
12. `<card id="about">` begins the next card. Even though this is loaded into the memory of the WAP phone, it is not viewed until the card is pulled up by someone hitting the **About Us** link. When it is selected, the contents of this card are then viewed.
13. Close the card when done.
14. Close the deck.

If the **Products** link is selected we will load the next deck **productsWAP.cfm** where we will run a query on the **Products** table in the *shelleyCatalog*. If the contents were going to be minimal, we might be able to have just the query run in another card on the same deck. But over time more and more contents will most likely be added to the **Products** table and we might get too much information back and the page won't be able to load properly into the phone as a result. A way to solve this is to limit the number of rows to return from the database using the MAXROWS attribute on the `<CFQUERY>`.

Script 9-2
productsWAP.cfm

```
<CFCONTENT TYPE="text/vnd.wap.wml">
<?xml version="1.0"?>
<!DOCTYPE wml PUBLIC "-//WAPFORUM//DTD WML 1.1//EN" "http://
www.wapforum.org/DTD/wml_1.1.xml">
<wml>
<card id="Home">
   <p>
   <cfquery name="listItems" datasource="shelleyCatalog"
dbtype="ODBC">
   SELECT    sku, name
   FROM      Products
   </cfquery>
   Our Products<br/>
   <cfoutput query="listItems">
   <a href="productsDescWAP.cfm?sku=#sku#">#listItems.name#</a><br/>
   </cfoutput>
   </p>
</card>
</wml>
```

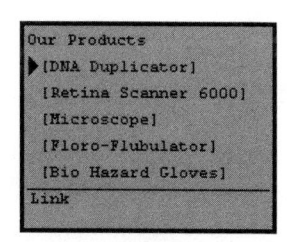

FIGURE 9–10 Our products.

All of this should be familiar to you by now. We are simply pulling up a recordset of all the products in the database and using a `<a href>` to link them to yet another deck (**Script 9-3**) where the products are displayed in more detail.

Script 9-3
productsDescWAP.cfm

```
<CFCONTENT TYPE="text/vnd.wap.wml">
<?xml version="1.0"?>
<!DOCTYPE wml PUBLIC "-//WAPFORUM//DTD WML 1.1//EN" "http://
www.wapforum.org/DTD/wml_1.1.xml">
```

```
<wml>
<card id="Home">
   <p>
   <cfquery name="itemDescription" datasource="shelleyCatalog" dbtype="ODBC">
   SELECT sku, name, price, description
   FROM    Products
   WHERE sku = #sku#
   </cfquery>
   <cfoutput query="itemDescription">
   #itemDescription.name#<br/>
   $#DollarFormat(itemDescription.price)#<br/>
   #itemDescription.description#<br/>
   </cfoutput>
   </p>
</card>
</wml>
```

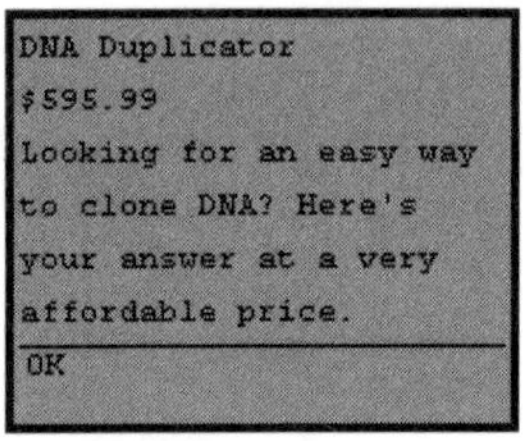

```
DNA Duplicator
$595.99
Looking for an easy way
to clone DNA? Here's
your answer at a very
affordable price.
OK
```

FIGURE 9-11 One product.

Another thing to keep in mind if you are passing more than one URL variable is that WML will choke on ampersands (&). So you will have to use & in its place:

```
productsDescWAP.cfm?sku=#sku#&amp;name=#name#
```

◆ Wireless Palm™ Series of Handhelds

Another growing trend in wireless application development is the Palm™ handheld and a protocol know as *web-clipping*. Web-clipping is basically a simplified version of HTML 3.2. If you already know HTML (chances are if you bought this book) then you can easily start developing web-clipping applications.

While the Palm™ handheld computers do have larger screens to view the information and customer input through forms is fairly easy and straightforward compared to the WAP devices, there are some limitations.

Limitations

- Limited bandwidth and slow connections
- Limited screen size. The screen area only allows 153 pixels in width
- Cannot use JavaScript, cookies, frames, or nested tables
- Graphics are limited to 1- or 2-bit: black, white, silver, and gray

With these limitations there is still plenty you can accomplish when writing a web-clipping application. You can even use Secure Sockets Layer (SSL) for encryption and authentication.

Palm Query Application

In order to get your application loaded onto your Palm™ or your customer's Palm™ series of handhelds, you will need to create a single application called a PQA. This is a compressed file that consists of a single file or set of files and images that sits on the Palm Pilot. To build this you use the *Palm Query Application* that you can either download from www.palm.net or it should be located on the CD that came with your Palm Pilot. Once the *.pqa* is compiled you will load it onto your Palm Pilot during the HotSync operation.

◆ Project II: Palm™-Enabled Product List

Now we will build the same type of application to be viewed from the wireless Palm™ Pilots or any web-clipping device. This project requires six separate files. The first file (index.html) builds a simple list of site features to navigate through the site:

- Index page (index.html)
- Image (shelleyLogo.gif)
- About us (about.html)
- News (news.html)
- Product search page (products.html)
- Product results (productResults.cfm)

When designing a web-clipping application there are a few things to keep in mind. First is that people using the wireless

Palm™ VII series handheld generally subscribe to a service plan that limits the amount of data they can transfer until they have paid extra. With this in mind you will want to keep all static data and images that never change in the *.pqa* on the local device. Data that gets updated regularly, such as news and events, stock quotes, or items in a database that need to be served dynamically will reside on your web server and be served to the Palm™ device wirelessly. If you need to update the data that is compiled into the *.pqa* then you will need to have your customers download and install the application again. So keep this in mind during design time.

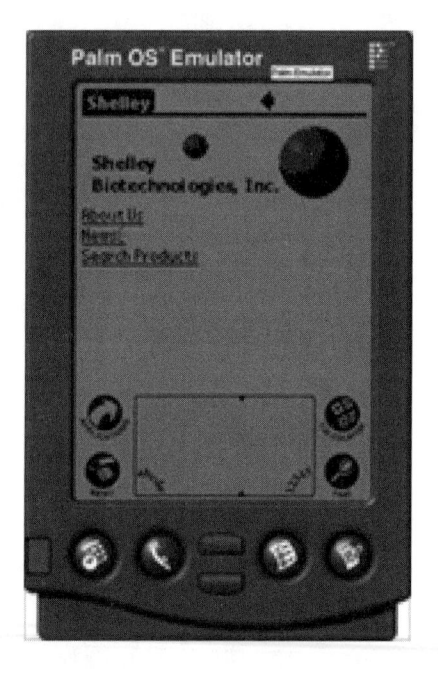

FIGURE 9-12 Shelley Biotechnologies' web-clipping application homepage.

For our application we will have all but the *news.html* and the *productResults.cfm* files compiled into the PQA. Since the company news will most likely be updated on a regular basis and the *productResults.cfm* page does the querying against the database, we will need to have these located on the server.

META Tags

All web-clipping pages should have Palm specific META tags included which let the device know these pages were authored for the Palm™ VII handheld.

PalmComputingPlatform

```
<META NAME="PalmComputingPlatform" CONTENT="true">
```

This lets the device know that the page was authored for the Palm OS® software. You should have this on every page.

HistoryListText

```
<META NAME="HistoryListText" CONTENT="page name">
```

Builds a history box on the Palm™ handheld with the time the pages in the application were accessed. This is optional.

Pages without the *PalmComputingPlatform* META tag will still work but be truncated to 1 KB by the proxy server.

Script 9-4
index.html

```
1.  <META NAME="PalmComputingPlatform" CONTENT="true">
    <!DOCTYPE HTML PUBLIC "-//W3C//DTD HTML 4.0 Transitional//EN">
    <HTML>
    <HEAD>
        <TITLE>Shelley</TITLE>
    </HEAD>
    <BODY>
    <TABLE WIDTH="153" BORDER="0" CELLPADDING="0" CELLSPACING="0">
    <TR>
        <TD VALIGN="top">
        <IMG SRC="shelleyLogo.gif">
        </TD>
    </TR>
    <TR>
        <TD VALIGN="top">
2.      <A HREF="about.html">About Us</A><BR>
3.      <A HREF="http://127.0.0.1/shelley/palm/news.html">News</A>
        <BR>
        <A HREF="products.html">Search Products</A>
        </TD>
    </TR>
    </TABLE>
    </BODY>
    </HTML>
```

HOW THIS WORKS

1. Sets the *PalmComputingPlatform* META TAG so the device knows this page is fine to run on the Palm OS and won't truncate the file.
2. Sets a local tag to the *about.html* page which was compiled as part of the *Shelley* PQA.
3. Sets a remote tag for the Palm™ handheld to find this page.

Script 9-5
about.html

```
<META NAME="PalmComputingPlatform" CONTENT="true">
<!DOCTYPE HTML PUBLIC "-//W3C//DTD HTML 4.0 Transitional//EN">
<HTML>
<HEAD>
    <TITLE>Shelley</TITLE>
</HEAD>
<BODY>
<TABLE WIDTH="153" BORDER="0" CELLPADDING="0" CELLSPACING="0">
<TR>
    <TD VALIGN="top">
    <IMG SRC="shelleyLogo.gif">
    </TD>
</TR>
<TR>
    <TD VALIGN="top">
    <H3>ABOUT US</H3>
    We offer the finest scientific equipment for all of your
bio-medical needs.
    </TD>
</TR>
<TR>
    <TD VALIGN="top">
    <FONT SIZE="1">
    <A HREF="index.html" BUTTON>HOME</A>
    </FONT>
    </TD>
</TR>
</TABLE>
</BODY>
</HTML>
```

1.

HOW THIS WORKS

1. This is a local tag back to the Index page. Setting an attribute called BUTTON we can turn this link into a button instead of an ordinary text link.

Script 9-6
news.html

```
<META NAME="PalmComputingPlatform" CONTENT="true">
<META NAME="HistoryListText" CONTENT="Shelley News">
<!DOCTYPE HTML PUBLIC "-//W3C//DTD HTML 4.0 Transitional//EN">
<HTML>
<HEAD>
    <TITLE>Shelley</TITLE>
</HEAD>
<BODY>
<TABLE WIDTH="153" BORDER="0" CELLPADDING="0" CELLSPACING="0">
<TR>
    <TD VALIGN="top">
```
1.
```
    <IMG SRC="file:Shelley.pqa/shelleyLogo.gif">
    </TD>
</TR>
<TR>
    <TD VALIGN="top">
    <H3>SHELLEY NEWS</H3>
    Shelley Biotechnologies has recently won the coveted
NONLEAK award for the lowest amount of leakage from our
containers than any other manufacturer.
    </TD>
</TR>
<TR>
    <TD VALIGN="top">
    <FONT SIZE="1">
```
2.
```
    <A HREF="file:Shelley.pqa/index.html" BUTTON>HOME</A>
    </FONT>
    </TD>
</TR>
</TABLE>
</BODY>
</HTML>
```

HOW THIS WORKS

1. Since this page is not local to the Palm device we want to use the image file that is already on the device instead of transferring a duplicate and wasting data transfer. We reference this with *file:Shelley.pqa/shelleyLogo.gif* which tells the device the image file already exists in the *Shelley.pqa* file and to load it from there.

2. We need to reference a link back to the *index.html* page on the Palm device so we reference it the same way as the image by telling the device to load the *index.html* file located in the *Shelley.pqa* file.

> **NOTE**
> Be sure when you are referencing a file on the Palm Pilot that you use the same case, as this is case-sensitive, or the link will result in an error.

Script 9-7
products.html

```
<META NAME="PalmComputingPlatform" CONTENT="true">
<META NAME="HistoryListText" CONTENT="Shelley Search">
<!DOCTYPE HTML PUBLIC "-//W3C//DTD HTML 4.0 Transitional//EN">
<HTML>
<HEAD>
   <TITLE>Shelley</TITLE>
</HEAD>
<BODY>
<TABLE WIDTH="153" BORDER="0" CELLPADDING="0" CELLSPACING="0">
<TR>
   <TD VALIGN="top">
   <IMG SRC="shelleyLogo.gif">
   </TD>
</TR>
<TR>
   <TD VALIGN="top">
   <H3>SEARCH</H3>
   Enter search criteria:
   </TD>
</TR>
<TR>
   <TD VALIGN="top">
   <FORM ACTION=
"http://127.0.0.1/shelley/palm/productResults.cfm"
METHOD="post">
   <INPUT TYPE="text" SIZE="15" NAME="name"><BR>
   <INPUT TYPE="hidden" NAME="method" VALUE="searchName">
   <INPUT TYPE="submit" VALUE=" Search "> <EM>OR</EM>
   </FORM>
   </TD>
</TR>
<TR>
   <TD>
   <FORM ACTION=
   "http://127.0.0.1/shelley/palm/productResults.cfm"
METHOD="post">
```

```
      <INPUT TYPE="hidden" NAME="method" VALUE="searchAll">
      <INPUT TYPE="submit" VALUE=" Display All">
      </FORM>
      </TD>
</TR>
<TR>
      <TD VALIGN="top">
      <FONT SIZE="1">
      <A HREF="index.html" BUTTON>HOME</A>
      </FONT>
      </TD>
</TR>
</TABLE>
</BODY>
</HTML>
```

HOW THIS WORKS

This form lets you choose two ways to pull data wirelessly from the remote page. You can either perform a search, or display the entire list of products to the screen.

Script 9-8
productResults.cfm

```
<META NAME="PalmComputingPlatform" CONTENT="true">
<META NAME="HistoryListText" CONTENT="Shelley Search">

<CFIF method EQ "searchName">
    <CFQUERY NAME="searchName" DATASOURCE="shelleyCatalog">
    SELECT*
    FROM    Products
    WHERE name LIKE '#FORM.name#%'
    </CFQUERY>
<CFELSEIF method EQ "searchAll">
    <CFQUERY NAME="searchAll" DATASOURCE="shelleyCatalog">
    SELECT *
    FROM    Products
    </CFQUERY>
</CFIF>

<!DOCTYPE HTML PUBLIC "-//W3C//DTD HTML 4.0 Transitional//EN">
<HTML>
<HEAD>
    <TITLE>Shelley</TITLE>
</HEAD>
<BODY>
<TABLE WIDTH="153" BORDER="0" CELLPADDING="0" CELLSPACING="0">
```

```
<TR>
    <TD VALIGN="top">
    <IMG SRC="file:Shelley.pqa/shelleyLogo.gif">
    </TD>
</TR>
<TR>
    <TD VALIGN="top">
    <H3>RESULTS</H3>
    </TD>
</TR>
<TR>
    <TD VALIGN="top">
    <CFIF method EQ "searchName">
        <CFOUTPUT QUERY="searchName">
        <B>#name#</B><BR>
        #description#<BR>
        <BR>
        </CFOUTPUT>
    <CFELSEIF method EQ "searchAll">
    <UL>
        <CFOUTPUT QUERY="searchAll">
        <LI>#name#</LI>
        </CFOUTPUT>
    </UL>
    </CFIF>
    </TD>
</TR>
<TR>
    <TD VALIGN="top">
    <FONT SIZE="1">
    <A HREF="file:Shelley.pqa/index.html" BUTTON>HOME</A>
    </FONT>
    </TD>
</TR>
</TABLE>
</BODY>
</HTML>
```

HOW THIS WORKS

The final script simply tests the `method` parameter to see what type of search the user performed and displays the data accordingly.

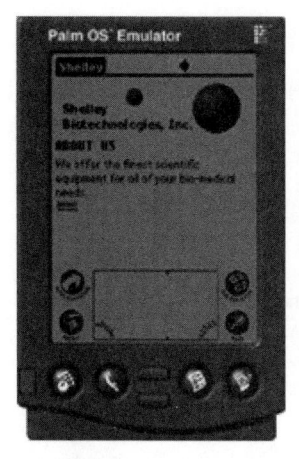

FIGURE 9-13 About us page (local).

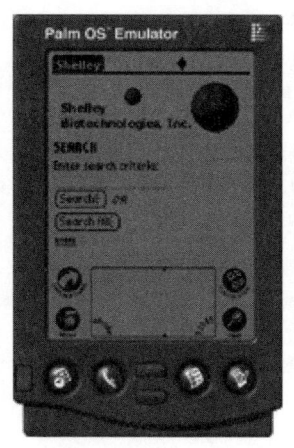

FIGURE 9-14 Search page (local).

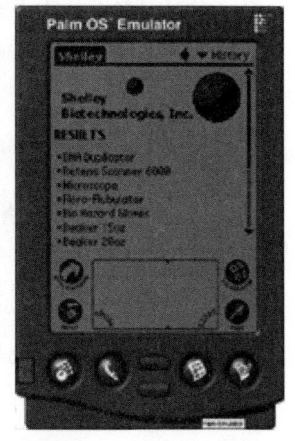

FIGURE 9-15 Results of search provided remotely from the server-side.

◆ Building and Installing the Palm™ Query Application

Now that you have all the files built you need to build the initial *.pqa* file to install on your Palm™ device.

Open the *index.html* File

1. Drag over or open (File => Open Index) the *index.html* file and the PQA will load all files associated with it in the window. It does this by scanning through the HTML and determining which files it uses.

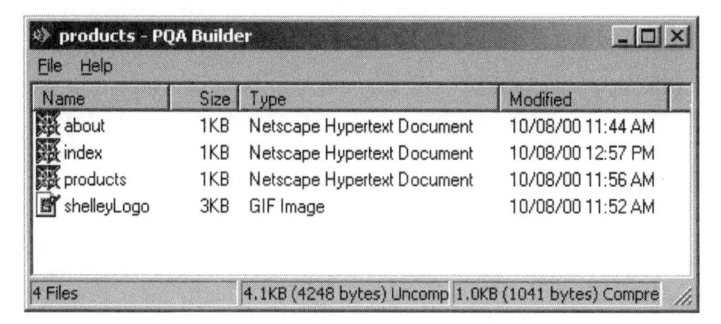

FIGURE 9-16 Files getting ready to be compiled into a *.pqa* file that will be loaded onto the Palm™ handheld.

Build the *pqa* File

1. Choose *Select File* and *Build PQA*.
2. Choose the File Name to save as. For this application call it Shelley.
3. Finally, select the Build button and the application is built for you. Load this file onto your Palm™ handheld and you're ready to go.

NOTE
When testing this on a live device you will need to replace the appropriate IP address and path name of the *news.html* and *productResults.cfm* files or you will get an error.

◆ Recap

The world of wireless is really starting to take off and there seems to be no end in sight for the possibilities. Although wireless isn't quite as fast as we would like at this time, the technology is in demand. And as we all know, when technology is in demand the growth rate at which it is developed is enormous.

◆ Advanced Project

Using your newfound wireless expertise, create a login function to the Shelley Biotechnology Palm OS® application. Set up the application so that it requires a login for the *News* section using the same logins from the **AdminUsers** table already in the *shelleyCatalog* database.

Appendix A: An Introduction to Forms

One of the most powerful parts of a web page, besides the fact that you can display information to your users, is that you can get information from them as well. This is where forms come into play, and in this appendix you will learn how to use the different types of forms to make your own forms.

When using forms, you always need to enclose the entire contents of the form within the `<FORM>` `</FORM>` tags so the browser treats the contents as form elements. If you do not do this, the forms will not work properly.

Within the beginning `<FORM>` tag you need to tell this particular form what template you will be using to process the input. This is done with the ACTION tag.

```
<FORM ACTION="process.cfm">
```

Next, you need to include the METHOD of how to use the information your HTML forms are going to pass to your script. There are two types of METHODS that you can pass: GET and POST. By default, ColdFusion will use GET as the METHOD type.

GET

The GET method will append the query to the end of the URL you are passing preceded with a question mark.

```
http://127.0.0.1/form.cfm?firstName=Micah&lastName=Brown&id=200010
```

This is used to get information from the server based on the passed information.

POST

The POST method passes form fields along with the page and is called by the ACTION page using **FORM.variablename**.

```
<FORM ACTION="process.cfm " METHOD="POST">
```

There you have it! You now have your form all ready to go and pointed at the correct template, but before you get ahead of yourself you still need to build the page visually. You can use HTML along with your forms in here. The <FORM> </FORM> tags are merely wrapping around all the HTML content so it knows to use whatever form elements are between the tags and handles them with the script. You can have as many forms on a web page as you like. For example:

```
<HTML>
<HEAD>
<BODY BGCOLOR="#FFFFFF">
<FORM METHOD="POST" ACTION="process1.cfm">
<SMALL>(This is script 1)</SMALL><BR>
Enter your name:<BR>
<INPUT TYPE="text" NAME="name" SIZE="34"><BR>
<INPUT TYPE="submit" VALUE="Submit" NAME="submit">
<INPUT TYPE="reset" VALUE="Reset" NAME="submit">
</FORM>
<BR>
<FORM METHOD="POST" ACTION="process2.cfm">
<SMALL>(This is script 2)</SMALL><BR>
Enter your age:<BR>
<INPUT TYPE="text" NAME="name" SIZE="5"><BR>
<INPUT TYPE="submit" VALUE="Submit" NAME="submit">
<INPUT TYPE="reset" VALUE="Reset" NAME="reset">
</FORM>
</BODY>
</HEAD>
</HTML>
```

(This is script 1)
Enter your name:

[   ]

[Submit] [Reset]

(This is script 2)
Enter your age:

[ ]

[Submit] [Reset]

FORM A-1 Two separate forms with a separate text field for each. You can use one or several FORMs in an HTML page.

With this bit of HTML, we are actually using two forms. The first one is *process1.cfm*, which is used to get the user's name. The second, *process2.cfm*, is used to get the user's age. Of course you could use the same script for both; we are using two just for demonstration purposes. For now, don't worry if you don't understand what all the INPUT lines are about, they will be explained soon enough.

All form fields allow you to pass them *attributes*. Attributes are just a simple way of telling a form field how to behave, or to add extra functionality to the form field. Usually these are visual things like how wide or tall the particular piece will be, or if a check box or radio button has been checked or not.

The basic form elements lie within these six types of attributes:

- Submit buttons
- Single-line textbox
- Text blocks
- Menus
- Check boxes
- Radio buttons

◆ Buttons

You need a way to send the information the user has just entered, and this is what the Submit button is for. Without a Submit button, users might spend half an hour entering name, address, Social Security number, Swiss bank account number, and so on, before they realize that there is no way to send all this information they have just entered. This would probably prompt them to send you a nasty note thanking you for all the time they wasted.

Two Types of Buttons

- Submit
- Reset

```
INPUT TYPE=SUBMIT
INPUT TYPE=RESET
```

VALUE = The name that visually appears on the button.

NAME = This is the name that will be passed to the script.

THE SUBMIT BUTTON

```
<INPUT TYPE="SUBMIT" VALUE="Submit" NAME="submit">
```

A Submit button is used to transfer all input from the form fields to the template that was specified in the <FORM ACTION=" "> tag. This is a required button for every form you build; otherwise, as I mentioned earlier, users will be stuck there looking at all the valuable information they just spent hours typing in. Even worse, you won't receive any of that valuable information.

THE RESET BUTTON

```
<INPUT TYPE="RESET" VALUE="Reset" NAME="reset">
```

This is for when users want to clear all the fields they just completed before they submit the information. This is much quicker than going back and deleting every field individually. The Reset button is not required, but it is nice to have it available for the users.

◆ Single-Line Text Box

A single-line text box is exactly what its name implies: It allows you to enter a single line of text whether it is one character, one word, or an entire sentence. You can control the visible width of the text box as well as the maximum physical length of the content that will be entered.

Attributes for the single-line text box are:

INPUT TYPE = "text" This tells the browser this is a single-line text box.

NAME = The NAME you give to this field is a unique identifier for when it passes this information to the script.

SIZE = Sets the physical width of the box itself in characters.

MAXLENGTH = The maximum number of characters that can be entered into the text box.

VALUE = You can also set an initial value so that the text box will already have text in it. It is up to the users to delete it.

Example 1

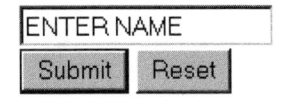

FORM A-2 Single-line text box with a VALUE filled in.

```
<INPUT TYPE="text" NAME="name" SIZE="20" MAXLENGTH="30"
VALUE="ENTER NAME"><BR>
<INPUT TYPE="submit" VALUE="Submit" NAME="submit">
<INPUT TYPE="reset" VALUE="Reset" NAME="reset">
```

Let's take a look at what is happening in Example 1:

1. The preceding code is the HTML that will make a single-line text box.
2. We assign the NAME attribute as "name."
3. The physical width of the box has been defined to 20 characters with the SIZE attribute.
4. The actual maximum amount of characters the user can type into this field is 30 as defined with MAXLENGTH.
5. An initial value is set as "ENTER NAME" with the VALUE attribute. If the VALUE tag is left out, then the box is displayed empty, as in Example 1.

Example 2

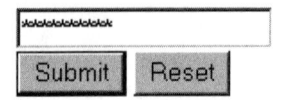

FORM A–3 Single-line text box with a VALUE filled in and the TYPE attribute set to PASSWORD instead of text. The password attribute will allow all content entered to be in asterisk format so wandering eyes can't read.

```
<INPUT TYPE="password" NAME="name" SIZE="20"
MAXLENGTH="30" VALUE="ENTER NAME"><BR>
<INPUT TYPE="submit" VALUE="Submit" NAME="submit">
<INPUT TYPE="reset" VALUE="Reset" NAME="reset">
```

Let's take a look at what is happening in Example 2.

1. The only difference in this example is that we're assigning the `type` to be `password` instead of `text`. Now everything the user types in will display only as asterisks.

◆ Scrolling Text Box

The scrolling text box is similar to the single-line text box except that with the scrolling text box, you can enter several lines of text instead of just a single line. As with the single-line text box, you can set the width of the scrolling text box, but you can set the height of the box as well.

Attributes for the scrolling text box are as follows:

`TEXTAREA` = This tells the browser that this is a scrolling text box. Unlike all the others that start off with `<INPUT TYPE=" ">`, this will start off with `<TEXTAREA>`.

`NAME` = The `NAME` you give to this field is a unique identifier for when it passes this information to the script.

`ROWS` = Defines the height of the box by the number of lines it will show before the box needs to scroll to hold additional lines.

`COLS` = Defines the visual width of the box by the amount of characters the box will hold. Unlike the single-line text box, you cannot set a `MAXLENGTH` for the scrolling text box.

WRAP = You can use this feature as WRAP="virtual" so your text doesn't continue to scroll to the right until the user clicks return. This will wrap the text, as the COLS limit is reached. Your users will really appreciate this.

Example 3

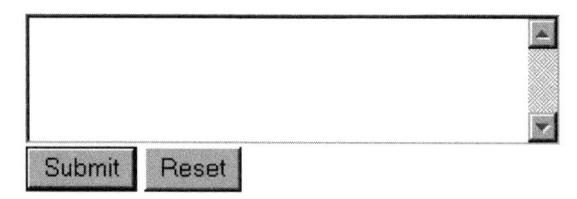

FORM A-4 Text area box, used for entering several lines.

```
<TEXTAREA NAME="information" ROWS="4" COLS="34"
WRAP="virtual"></TEXTAREA><BR>
<INPUT TYPE="submit" VALUE="Submit" NAME="submit">
<INPUT TYPE="reset" VALUE="Reset" NAME="reset">
```

Let's take a look at what is happening in Example 3.

1. The preceding code is the HTML that will make a scrolling text box.
2. We assign the NAME attribute as "information."
3. There will be four ROWS for height in this box.
4. The width of the box is defined with COLS as 34 characters.

As seen in the single-line text box in Example 2, there is a VALUE attribute where you can add predefined text to the box. You can also do this to the scrolling text box by simply adding the text between the <TEXTAREA> </TEXTAREA> tags.

Example 4

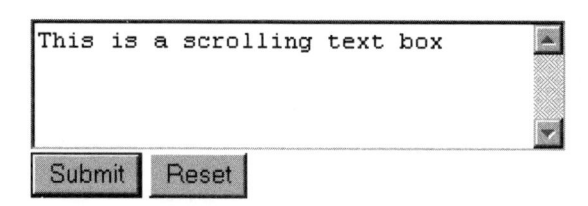

FORM A-5 Text area box with text already entered.

```
<TEXTAREA NAME="information" ROWS="4" COLS="34"
WRAP="virtual">This is a scrolling text box</
TEXTAREA><BR>
<INPUT TYPE="submit" VALUE="Submit" NAME="submit">
<INPUT TYPE="reset" VALUE="Reset" NAME="reset">
```

Let's take a look at what is happening in Example 4.

1. The preceding code is the HTML that will make a scrolling text box.
2. There will be four ROWS for height in this box.
3. We assign the NAME attribute as the value "information."
4. The width of the box is defined with COLS as 34 characters.
5. The WRAP="virtual" attribute will wrap the text as it is entered after the COLS limit is reached.
6. The content between the <TEXTAREA> and the </TEXTAREA> tags shows that there is an initial value that the user will view. The user can leave the initial value, add to it, or simply type over it.

◆ Menus

These are sometimes known as drop-down menus because they appear as a one-line field with a little arrow to the right of it. When you point and click on the arrow, a whole menu drops down and you are presented with many options. Sometimes you are presented with too many options.

Attributes for the menus are as follows:

SELECT NAME = The NAME you give to this field is a unique identifier for when it passes this information to the script.

SIZE = Sets the vertical SIZE or amount of lines to show.

MULTIPLE = Allows the user to select any amount of selections you have in the menu. This is optional.

SELECTED = Used if you would like to have an option made to be the default. This is optional.

OPTION VALUE = Where the actual selections are made. The VALUE is like the NAME that is a unique identifier that will be passed back to the script. Between <OPTION VALUE=" "> and </OPTION> is where you type in the actual text that will appear on the screen.

Example 5

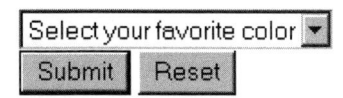

FORM A-6 The drop-down menu with just one selection showing.

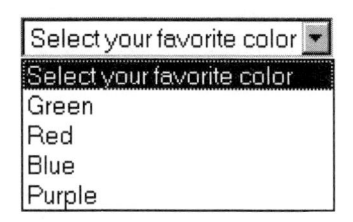

FORM A-7 The drop-down menu after the arrow has been selected to show all the possible choices the user can make.

```
<SELECT NAME="favoriteColor" SIZE="1">
<OPTION SELECTED VALUE="">Select your favorite color</OPTION>
<OPTION VALUE="Green">Green</OPTION>
<OPTION VALUE="Red">Red</OPTION>
<OPTION VALUE="Blue">Blue</OPTION>
<OPTION VALUE="Purple">Purple</OPTION>
</SELECT>
<BR>
<INPUT TYPE="submit" VALUE="Submit" NAME="submit">
<INPUT TYPE="reset" VALUE="Reset" NAME="reset">
```

Let's take a look at what is happening in Example 5.

1. SELECT tells the browser we want to draw a Menu box.
2. NAME assigns favoriteColor as the identifier for this menu as a whole.
3. SIZE tells that this will be showing only one line to start with.
4. OPTION is used for each individual choice you would like to put into this list.
5. VALUE assigns an identifier for the choice.

Example 6

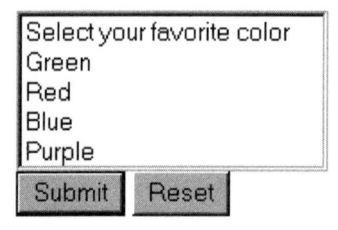

```
Select your favorite color
Green
Red
Blue
Purple
```
[Submit] [Reset]

FORM A-8 The drop-down menu with the SIZE set to 5 so all five selections of the box are visible at once.

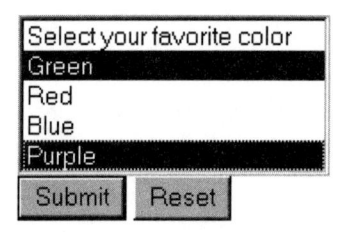

```
Select your favorite color
Green
Red
Blue
Purple
```
[Submit] [Reset]

FORM A-9 With the MULTIPLE attribute set, the user can select multiple choices.

```
<SELECT NAME="favoriteColor" SIZE="5" MULTIPLE>
   <OPTION VALUE="Select your favorite color">
   Select your favorite color</OPTION>
   <OPTION VALUE="green">Green</OPTION>
   <OPTION VALUE="red">Red</OPTION>
   <OPTION VALUE="blue">Blue</OPTION>
   <OPTION VALUE="purple">Purple</OPTION>
</SELECT>
<BR>
<INPUT TYPE="submit" VALUE="Submit" NAME="submit">
<INPUT TYPE="reset" VALUE="Reset" NAME="reset">
```

Let's take a look at what is happening in Example 6. This is pretty much the same as the previous example with a couple of changes to give it this particular look and feel.

1. SIZE has been changed to 5 to show all five choices in this menu. You actually could have used SIZE=3 and show only three lines and have a scroll bar that would scroll down to the other two choices.
2. MULTIPLE lets users select more than one choice.

◆ Check Boxes

Check boxes allow a user to select several options in a set of check boxes with the same name, such as types. The value is what will determine which check box is selected out of this types set. Suppose you want to ask users what type of music they like. Most people do not prefer just one type of music, so you want them to be able to select several types in that set of music. To allow for this, you would simply set the NAME on all of these check boxes to be music and set the value for each to a type of music. You will see this example defined in the example HTML at the end of this appendix.

Attributes for the check box are:

NAME = The NAME you give to this field is a unique identifier for when it passes this information to the script.

VALUE = This value is sent back to the script if this box is selected and will be the output for that selection.

CHECKED = If this is in the INPUT field, then this box will be CHECKED when it is drawn to the screen.

DISABLED = If this is in the INPUT field, then the box will appear but the user cannot select it.

Example 7

☐ Standard checkbox
☑ Checked checkbox
▨ Disabled checkbox

[Submit] [Reset]

FORM A-10 First, the normal CHECKBOX; second, with attribute CHECKED to have it selected; and, third, the DISABLED attribute to gray out the box and make it visible but inactive.

```
<INPUT TYPE="checkbox" NAME="checkbox_1" VALUE="ON">
Standard checkbox<BR>
<INPUT TYPE="checkbox" NAME="checkbox_2" VALUE="ON"
CHECKED>Checked checkbox<BR>
<INPUT TYPE="checkbox" NAME="checkbox_3" VALUE="ON"
DISABLED>Disabled checkbox
<BR>
```

```
<INPUT TYPE="submit" VALUE="Submit" NAME="submit">
<INPUT TYPE="reset" VALUE="Reset" NAME="reset">
```

Let's take a look at what is happening in Example 7.

1. This is a standard check box. If this is selected, then it will pass a value of ON to the variable `checkbox_1` when it is passed back to the script.
2. With the CHECKED attribute added in here, the check box will automatically have itself checked and pass a value of ON to the variable `checkbox_2` when it is passed back to the script.
3. This last example has the attribute DISABLED added, meaning that this is a dead box.

◆ Radio Buttons

Radio buttons are similar to check boxes in that you can have selections, but radio buttons will accept only one selection in a set. Each selection in that set will again have the same NAME and separate VALUES just like the check box.

Attributes for the radio button are:

NAME = The NAME you give to this field is a unique identifier for when it passes this information to the script.

VALUE = This value is sent back to the script if this button is selected, and will be the output for that selection.

CHECKED = If this is in the INPUT field, this button will be CHECKED when it is drawn to the screen.

DISABLED = If this is in the INPUT field, then the button will appear, but the user cannot select it.

Example 8

⦿ Checked radio button
○ Unchecked radio button
○ Disabled radio button

[Submit] [Reset]

FORM A-11 There are three choices: with the attribute CHECKED to have it selected; second, an unchecked radio button; and, third, with the DISABLED attribute to make the radio button visible but inactive.

```
<INPUT TYPE="radio" VALUE="false" NAME="question"
checked>Checked radio button<BR>
<INPUT TYPE="radio" VALUE="true" NAME="question">
Unchecked radio button<BR>
<INPUT TYPE="radio" VALUE="true" NAME="question"
DISABLED>Disabled radio button
<BR>
<INPUT TYPE="submit" VALUE="Submit" NAME="submit">
<INPUT TYPE="reset" VALUE="Reset" NAME="reset">
```

Let's take a look at what is happening in Example 8.

1. With the CHECKED attribute added in here the radio button will automatically have itself checked and pass a value of FALSE to the variable question when it is sent back to the script.
2. This is a standard radio button. If this is selected, then it will pass a value of TRUE to the variable question when it is passed back to the script.
3. This last example has the attribute DISABLED added, meaning that this is basically a dead radio button.

◆ Putting It All Together

Up to this point we have covered a great deal about forms and how they work. You can have one form or several forms together on a page. The following is an example of a form you could use to gather information from users. This information could then be saved to a database file, emailed back to you, or used as information to build personalized pages.

Appendix A • An Introduction to Forms

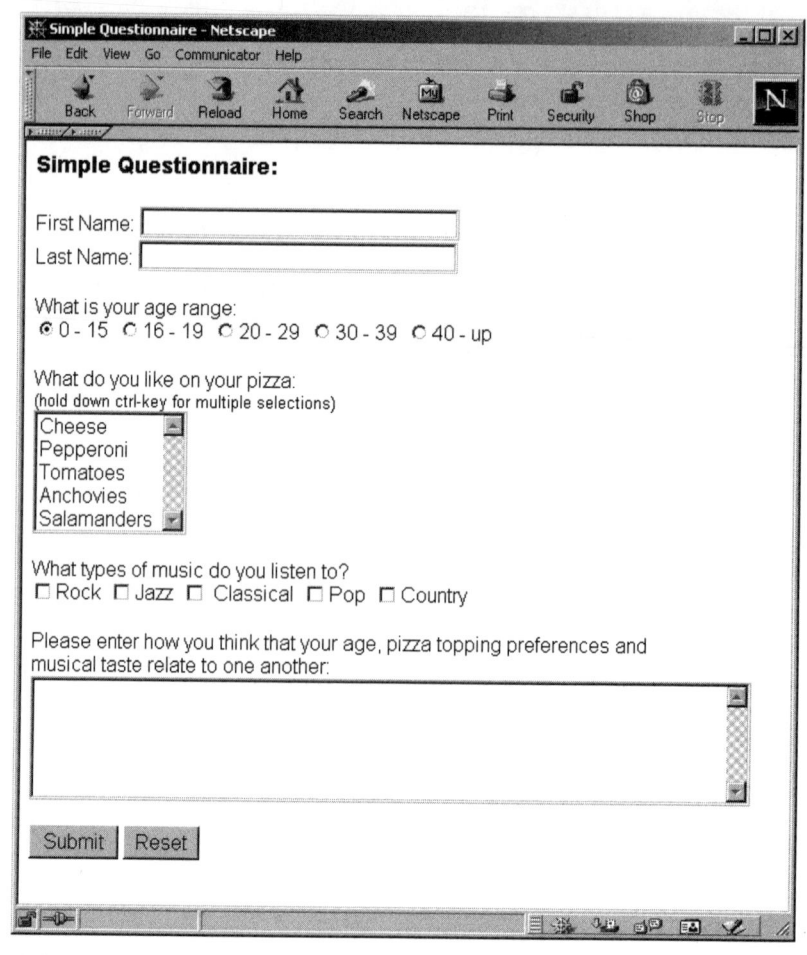

FORM A–12 This is what several of these FORM types look like all together on a page.

```
<HTML>
<HEAD>
<TITLE>Simple Questionnaire</TITLE>
</HEAD>
<BODY BGCOLOR="#FFFFFF">
<P><STRONG><BIG><FONT FACE="Arial">
Simple Questionnaire:</FONT></BIG></STRONG></P>
<FORM METHOD="POST" ACTION="process.cfm">
<P>
<FONT FACE="Arial">First Name:
<INPUT TYPE="text" NAME="firstName" SIZE="20" MAXLENGTH="25"><BR>
```

```
Last Name:
<INPUT TYPE="text" NAME="lastName" SIZE="20"></P>
<P>What is your age range:<BR>
<INPUT TYPE="radio" VALUE="0_15" NAME="age" CHECKED>0 - 15 
<INPUT TYPE="radio" VALUE="16_" NAME="age">16 - 19 
<INPUT TYPE="radio" VALUE="20_" NAME="age">20 - 29 
<INPUT TYPE="radio" VALUE="30_" NAME="age">30 - 39 
<INPUT TYPE="radio" VALUE="40_above" NAME="age">40 - up
</P>
<P>What do you like on your pizza:<BR>
<SMALL>(hold down ctrl-key for multiple selections)
</SMALL><BR>
<SELECT NAME="toppings" SIZE="5" MULTIPLE>
   <OPTION VALUE="Cheese">Cheese</OPTION>
   <OPTION VALUE="Pepperoni">Pepperoni</OPTION>
   <OPTION VALUE="Tomatoes">Tomatoes</OPTION>
   <OPTION VALUE="Anchovies">Anchovies</OPTION>
   <OPTION VALUE="Salamanders">Salamanders</OPTION>
</SELECT></P>
<P>What types of music do you listen to?<BR>
<INPUT TYPE="checkbox" NAME="music" VALUE="rock">Rock 
<INPUT TYPE="checkbox" NAME="music" VALUE="jazz">Jazz 
<INPUT TYPE="checkbox" NAME="music" VALUE="classical">
Classical 
<INPUT TYPE="checkbox" NAME="music" VALUE="pop">Pop 
<INPUT TYPE="checkbox" NAME="music" VALUE="ctry">Country
</p>
<P>Please enter how you think that your age, pizza topping
preferences and<BR>
musical taste relate to one another:<BR>
<TEXTAREA ROWS="5" NAME="comments" COLS="50" WRAP="virtual">
</TEXTAREA></P>
<P><INPUT TYPE="submit" VALUE="Submit" NAME="submit">
<INPUT TYPE="reset" VALUE="Reset" NAME="reset">
</FONT></P>
</FORM>
</BODY>
</HTML>
```

Appendix B: ColdFusion Reference

◆ ColdFusion Information and Discussion

Allaire—ColdFusion Support Forum

    http://forums.allaire.com/devconf/main.cfm

Here you will find several different types of forums covering ColdFusion server, Studio, and many other specialized areas in ColdFusion development. This list has thousands of users and is a great resource for asking questions (as well as giving advice to others).

Allaire—Developers' Exchange

    http://devex.allaire.com/developer/gallery

A repository of custom tags, applications, and more from ColdFusion users all over the world. Some of these will cost you but many are free. If you need some type of application to integrate with your ColdFusion site, chances are it exists here.

Allaire—Security Zone

    http://www.allaire.com/developer/securityzone/

Keep up to date with security patches for ColdFusion.

ColdFusion Developer's Journal

    http://www.sys-con.com/coldfusion

This is also available in print version.

CFVault.com	http://www.cfvault.com
Fusion Authority	http://www.fusionauthority.com
House of Fusion	http://www.houseoffusion.com
Cfnewbie?com	http://www.cfnewbie.com

◆ Wireless Development

Phone.com	http://developer.phone.com
Palm.com	http://www.palmos.com
WirelessAdvisor.com	http://www.wirelessadvisor.com
WAP Drive	http://www.wapdrive.com

◆ ColdFusion E-commerce Solutions

AbleCommerce	http://www.ablecommerce.com
CF Webstore	http://www.cfwebstore.com

◆ Hosting Companies

Whek-Web	http://www.whekweb.com

Index

A

about.html, 178
ACCEPT attribute, <CFFILE>, 77
Access (Microsoft), database file, creating, 8-10
ACTION attribute:
    <CFCOLLECTION>, 131
    <CFDIRECTORY>, 80
    <CFFILE>, 76
    <CFFORM>, 109
    <CFINDEX>, 132
    <CFPOP>, 117
Administration screen:
    building, 66-67
    setting up, 67
ALIGN attribute, <CFCOL>, 126
AND attribute, 6, 35-36
Append action, <CFFILE>, 75
application.cfm, 52, 57, 147
Application file, defining, 52-57
ApplicationTimeout attribute, <CFAPPLICATION>, 53
Application variables, 31
ASC attribute, 5
ASP, 2

ATTACHMENTPATH attribute, <CFPOP>, 117
Attributes, 30
ATTRIBUTES attribute, <CFFILE>, 77

B

BCC attribute, <CFMAIL>, 107
BETWEEN attribute, 6
BLOCKFACTOR attribute, <CFQUERY>, 19
BODY attribute, <CFINDEX>, 132
BORDER attribute, <CFTABLE>, 125
Buttons, 187-88
    Reset button, 188
    Submit button, 188

C

CACHEDAFTER attribute, <CFQUERY>, 19
CACHEDWITHIN attribute, <CFQUERY>, 19
CC attribute, <CFMAIL>, 107
<CFAPPLICATION>, 53-54
    attributes, 53-54

203

<CFCASE>, 111-12
<CFCOL>, 124-26
    attributes, 126
<CFCOLLECTION>, 130-31
    attribute, 131
<CFCONTENT>, 169-70
    attributes, 169
<CFCOOKIE>, 149-51
    attributes, 148
    enhanced functionality with, 149-51
<CFDEFAULTCASE>, 111-12
<CFDIRECTORY>, 79-82
    attributes, 80
cfDirectory.cfm, 81
<CFELSE>, 37-38
<CFELSEIF>, 39
<CFERROR>, 55-57
cferror.cfm, 55-57
<CFFILE>, 75-79
    actions, 75-76
    attributes, 76-77
cfFile.cfm, 77
<CFFORM>, 109-10
    attributes, 109
<CFIF> tag, 35
<CFINCLUDE>, 58-62
<CFINDEX>, 131-32
    attributes, 132
<CFINPUT>, 110-11
<CFINSERT>, 91-93
<CFLOOP>, 46-49
    attributes, 47
cfLoop.cfm, 48
<CFMAIL>, 106-9
    attributes, 107-8
    functions of, 108
<CFOUTPUT>, 16-17
<CFPARAM>, 27-28
<CFPOP>, 117-18
<CFQUERY>, 18
<CFSEARCH>, 138
cfsearch.cfm, 139
<CFSELECT>, 133
    attributes, 133
<CFSET>, 16
<CFSWITCH>, 111-12

<CFTABLE>, 124-25
<CFUPDATE>, 93-95
CGI variables, 31
CHECKED attribute, <CFINPUT>, 111
CHECKED = attribute:
    checkboxes, 195
    radio buttons, 196
ClientManagement attribute,
            <CFAPPLICATION>, 53
ClientStorage attribute,
            <CFAPPLICATION>, 53
Client variables, 31
ColdFusion:
    basics of, 25-50
    <CFLOOP>, 46-49
    comments, 26
    display days left until user defined
            date, 43-46
    e-commerce Solutions, 202
    information and discussion, 201-202
    passing variables, 28-45
    quotes, 26-28
    reference, 201-2
    scope, 31-32
    tags, custom, 153-63
    Verity, using with, 130-33
    and wireless, 165-84
ColdFusion Developer's Journal, 201
ColdFusion server administrator, 12-15
COLHEADERS attribute, <CFTABLE>, 125
COLLECTION attribute:
    <CFCOLLECTION>, 131
    <CFINDEX>, 132
    <CFLOOP>, 47
    <CFSEARCH>, 138
Collection management, 134-37
COLS = attribute, scrolling text box, 190
COLSPACING attribute, <CFTABLE>, 125
Comments, 26
Conditional logic, 36
CONDITION attribute, <CFLOOP>, 47
CONTAINS, DOES NOT CONTAIN
            operators, 35
Control panel, Windows, 10-12
Cookie variables, 30
Copy action, <CFFILE>, 75

Index   205

countdown.cfm, 44
CreateTimeSpan function, 54
CRITERIA attribute, <CFSEARCH>, 138
CurrentRow function, 70-71
CUSTOM1 attribute, <CFINDEX>, 132
CUSTOM2 attribute, <CFINDEX>, 132
Custom tags, 30, 153-63
    benefits to using, 154
    counting hits project, 157-59
    defined, 154
    ins/outs of, 154-55
    random product custom tag,
        creating, 159-60
    where to use, 155-56

D

Database:
    adding records to, 82-85
    editing an existing record in, 86-90
Database file, creating in Access, 8-10
DATASOURCE attribute:
    <CFINSERT>, 92
    <CFQUERY>, 18
    <CFUPDATE>, 91
Datatypes, relational databases, 3-4
DateDiff, 43
DBNAME attribute:
    <CFINSERT>, 92
    <CFQUERY>, 18
    <CFUPDATE>, 91
DBSERVER attribute:
    <CFINSERT>, 92
    <CFQUERY>, 18
    <CFUPDATE>, 91
DBTYPE attribute:
    <CFINSERT>, 92
    <CFQUERY>, 18
    <CFUPDATE>, 91
DEBUG attribute, <CFQUERY>, 19
Deck, 167
DE function, 72
Delete action, <CFFILE>, 75
DELETE attribute, 5
DELETEFILE attribute,
        <CFCONTENT>, 169
DELIMITERS attribute, <CFLOOP>, 47

DES attribute, 6
DESTINATION attribute, <CFFILE>, 76
DIRECTORY attribute,
        <CFDIRECTORY>, 80
DISABLED = attribute:
    checkboxes, 195
    radio buttons, 196
DISPLAY attribute, <CFSELECT>, 133
Display days left until user defined
        date, 43-46
    DateDiff, 43
    IsDefined, 43
DISTINCT attribute, 6
DollarFormat function, 69-70
DOMAIN attribute, <CFCOOKIE>, 148

E

Email, 105-21
    <CFMAIL>, 106-9
    retrieving from a POP server
        <CFPOP>, 117-18
emailList.cfm, 112-14
ENABLECAB attribute, <CFFORM>, 109
ENCTYPE attribute, <CFFORM>, 109
ENDROW attribute, <CFLOOP>, 47
Ericsson, 165
EXPIRES attribute, <CFCOOKIE>, 148
EXTENSIONS attribute, <CFINDEX>, 132
EXTERNAL attribute:
    <CFINDEX>, 132
    <CFSEARCH>, 138

F

FILE attribute, <CFCONTENT>, 169
FILEFIELD attribute, <CFFILE>, 76
FILTER attribute, <CFDIRECTORY>, 80
FirstQuery.cfm, 20
_footer.cfm, 60-61
<FORM> tag, 185
FORMFIELDS attribute:
    <CFINSERT>, 92
    <CFUPDATE>, 91
Forms, 185-99
    buttons, 187-88
        Reset button, 188
        Submit button, 188

checkboxes, 195-96
GET method, 185-86
menus, 192-94
POST method, 186-87
radio buttons, 196-97
scrolling text box, 190-92
single-line text box, 188-90
Form variables, 30
freegift.cfm, 116
FROM attribute:
<CFLOOP>, 47
<CFMAIL>, 107

G

GENERATEUNIQUEFILENAMES
attribute, <CFPOP>, 117
getMail.cfm, 118-19
GET method, 185-86
Global templates, 51-61
application file, defining, 52-57
<CFAPPLICATION>, 53-54
<CFERROR>, 55-57
Global values, setting for a site, 57-58
GREATER THAN (GT), LESS THAN (LT)
operators, 35
GREATER THAN OR EQUAL (GTE), LESS
THAN OR EQUAL (LTE)
operators, 35
GROUP attribute:
<CFMAIL>, 107
<CFOUTPUT>, 17
GROUPCASESENSITIVE attribute:
<CFMAIL>, 107
<CFOUTPUT>, 17

H

HEADER attribute, <CFCOL>, 126
_header.cfm, 59-60, 62
Header/footer files, defining, 58-62
HEADERLINES attribute, <CFTABLE>, 125
hitCounter.cfm, 158
Hosting companies, 202
HTMLTABLE attribute, <CFTABLE>, 125

I

IIP function, 72-73
IN attribute, 7
INDEX attribute, <CFLOOP>, 47
index.cfm, 61-62
index.html, 177
INSERT attribute, 5
IsDefined, 43
IS, EQUAL (EQ) operators, 35
IS NOT, NOT EQUAL (NEQ) operators, 35
ITEM attribute, <CFLOOP>, 47
itemManager.cfm, 83-84, 87-89
itemManagerProcess.cfm, 95-96

K

KEY attribute, <CFINDEX>, 132

L

LANGUAGE attribute:
<CFCOLLECTION>, 131
<CFINDEX>, 132
<CFSEARCH>, 138
LIKE attribute, 6
ListAppend function, 160
LIST attribute, <CFLOOP>, 47
listCategories query, 85
ListGetAt function, 160
ListLen function, 159
login.cfm, 145, 149-50

M

MAILERID attribute, <CFMAIL>, 107
MAXLENGTH attribute, <CFINPUT>, 110
MAXROWS attribute:
<CFMAIL>, 107
<CFOUTPUT>, 17
<CFPOP>, 117
<CFQUERY>, 19
<CFSEARCH>, 138
<CFTABLE>, 125
Menus, 192-94
MESSAGE attribute:
<CFINPUT>, 110
<CFSELECT>, 133

MESSAGENUMBER attribute,
    <CFPOP>, 117
META tags, Palm-specific, 177
METHOD attribute, <CFFORM>, 109
Microsoft Access, 2, 8
Microsoft SQL server, 8
MIMEATTACH attribute, <CFMAIL>, 107
MIME types, 167-70
MODE attribute:
    <CFDIRECTORY>, 80
    <CFFILE>, 77
MOD function, 71-72
Motorola, 165
Move action, <CFFILE>, 75
MULTIPLE attribute, <CFSELECT>, 133
MULTIPLE = attribute, menus, 192
myInfo2.cfm, 34, 35-36
myInfo.cfm, 32-33, 35

N

NAME attribute:
    <CFCOOKIE>, 148
    <CFDIRECTORY>, 80
    <CFFORM>, 109
    <CFINPUT>, 110
    <CFPOP>, 117
    <CFQUERY>, 18
    <CFSEARCH>, 138
    <CFSELECT>, 133
NAME = attribute:
    checkboxes, 195
    radio buttons, 196
    scrolling text box, 190
NAMECONFLICT attribute. <CFFILE>, 76
_navBar.cfm, 67
NEWDIRECTORY attribute,
    <CFDIRECTORY>, 80
news.html, 178
Nokia, 165
NOT, 35-36
Now() object, 39-40

O

ODBC connection:
    ColdFusion server administrator, 12-15
    setting up, 10-15
    Windows control panel, 10-12
ONERROR attribute:
    <CFINPUT>, 110
    <CFSELECT>, 133
Online catalog:
    adding hits gable to, 157-59
    adding a table to, 144
    administration screen:
        building, 66-67
        setting up, 67
    building, 65-103
    CurrentRow function, 70-71
    DollarFormat function, 69-70
    IIP function, 72-73
    MOD function, 71-72
    RecordCount function, 74
    viewing items in a database, 68
ONSUBMIT attribute, <CFFORM>, 109
ONVALIDATE attribute, <CFINPUT>, 110
OPTION VALUE = attribute, menus, 192
Oracle, 8
OR attribute, 6, 35-36
ORDER BY attribute, 6

P

Palm-enabled product list, 175-83
Palm Query Application (PQA), 175
    building/installing, 183-84
Palm series of handhelds, wireless, 174-75
Palm-specific META tags, 177
Passing variables, 28-31
    application variables, 31
    attributes, 30
    CGI variables, 31
    client variables, 31
    cookie variables, 30
    form variables, 30
    server variables, 31
    session variables, 31
    URL variables, 30
    variables, 29
PASSTHROUGH attribute:
    <CFFORM>, 109
    <CFINPUT>, 111
    <CFSELECT>, 133

PASSWORD attribute:
    <CFINSERT>, 92
    <CFPOP>, 117
    <CFQUERY>, 18
    <CFUPDATE>, 91
PATH attribute:
    <CFCOLLECTION>, 131
    <CFCOOKIE>, 148
PHP, 2
PORT attribute:
    <CFMAIL>, 107
    <CFPOP>, 117
POST method, 186-87
(pound sign), 17
PQA, *See* Palm Query Application (PQA)
Processing information, 90
productDescription.cfm, 100-102
productResults, cfm, 181-82
products.cfm, 96-97
productsDescWAP.cfm, 173-74
products.html, 180-81
productsWAP.cfm, 173
PROVIDER attribute:
    <CFINSERT>, 92
    <CFQUERY>, 19
    <CFUPDATE>, 91
PROVIDERDSN attribute:
    <CFINSERT>, 92
    <CFQUERY>, 19
    <CFUPDATE>, 91

Q

QUERY attribute:
    <CFLOOP>, 47
    <CFMAIL>, 107
    <CFOUTPUT>, 17
    <CFSELECT>, 133
    <CFTABLE>, 125
Quotes, 7, 26-28
    single, preserving, 124

R

Radio buttons, 196-97
randomProduct.cfm, 161
Random product custom tag:
    creating, 159-60

ListAppend function, 160
ListGetAt function, 160
ListLen function, 159
RandRange function, 160
RandRange function, 160
Read action, <CFFILE>, 75
RecordCount function, 74
Records:
    adding to database, 82-85
    deleting, 95
RECURSE attribute, <CFINDEX>, 132
Relational databases, 2-3
    common datatypes found in, 3-4
    defined, 2
REQUIRED attribute:
    <CFINPUT>, 110
    <CFSELECT>, 133
Reset button, 188
Retrieving data, 16-21
ROWS = attribute, scrolling text box, 190

S

SCRIPT_NAME variable, 157
Scrolling text box, 190-92
search.cfm, 126-28
SECURE attribute, <CFCOOKIE>, 148
Security, 143-44
    <CFCOOKIE>, 149-51
SELECT attribute, 5
SELECTED attribute, <CFSELECT>, 133
SELECTED = attribute, menus, 192
SELECT NAME = attribute, menus, 192
SERVER attribute:
    <CFMAIL>, 107
    <CFPOP>, 117
Server variables, 31
SessionManagement attribute,
    <CFAPPLICATION>, 53
SessionTimeout attribute,
    <CFAPPLICATION>, 54
Session variables, 31
SetClientCookies attribute,
    <CFAPPLICATION>, 54
Single-line text box, 188-90
Single quotes, preserving, 124
SIZE attribute, <CFINPUT>, 110

SIZE = attribute, menus, 192
SORT attribute, <CFDIRECTORY>, 80
SQL Builder, 21-22
SQL (Structured Query Language), 5
    attributes, 5-7
        AND, 6
        ASC, 5
        BETWEEN, 6
        DELETE, 5
        DES, 6
        DISTINCT, 6
        IN, 7
        INSERT, 5
        LIKE, 6
        OR, 6
        ORDER BY, 6
        SELECT, 5
        UPDATE, 5
        WHERE, 5
    basics, 5
STARTFROM attribute, <CFLOOP>, 47
STARTROW attribute:
    <CFMAIL>, 107
    <CFOUTPUT>, 17
    <CFPOP>, 117
    <CFSEARCH>, 138
    <CFTABLE>, 125
STEP attribute, <CFLOOP>, 47
Structured Query Language, *See* SQL
    (Structured Query
    Language)
SUBJECT attribute, <CFMAIL>, 107
Submit button, 188

T

Table, setting up, 8
TABLENAME attribute:
    <CFINSERT>, 92
    <CFUPDATE>, 91
TABLEOWNER attribute:
    <CFINSERT>, 92
    <CFUPDATE>, 91
TABLEQUALIFIER attribute,
    <CFINSERT>, 92
TARGET attribute, <CFFORM>, 109

TEXTAREA = attribute, scrolling text
    box, 190
TEXT attribute, <CFCOL>, 126
TIMEOUT attribute:
    <CFMAIL>, 107
    <CFPOP>, 117
    <CFQUERY>, 19
TITLE attribute, <CFINDEX>, 132
TO attribute:
    <CFLOOP>, 47
    <CFMAIL>, 107
TYPE attribute:
    <CFCONTENT>, 169
    <CFINDEX>, 132
    <CFINPUT>, 110
    <CFMAIL>, 107
    <CFSEARCH>, 138

U

UPDATE attribute, 5
uploadImage.cfm, 78
Uploading files to a site, 75-82
    <CFFILE>, 75-79
        actions, 75-76
        attributes, 76-77
URLPATH attribute, <CFINDEX>, 132
URL variables, 30
USERNAME attribute:
    <CFINSERT>, 92
    <CFPOP>, 117
    <CFQUERY>, 18
    <CFUPDATE>, 91
User pages, 96-102

V

VALIDATE attribute, <CFINPUT>, 111
VALUE attribute:
    <CFCOOKIE>, 148
    <CFINPUT>, 110
    <CFSELECT>, 133
VALUE = attribute:
    checkboxes, 195
    radio buttons, 196
Verity:
    searching with, 137-51
    using with ColdFusion, 130-33

verityControlPanel.cfm, 134-35
viewItems.cfm, 72-73

W

Web-clipping, 174-77
WHERE attribute, 5
WIDTH attribute, <CFCOL>, 126
Windows control panel, 10-12
Wireless, and ColdFusion, 165-84
Wireless Application Protocol (WAP), 165-67
   defined, 165-66
   limitations of, 166-67
   WAP-enabled product list, 170-74
Wireless development, 202
Wireless Palm series of handhelds, 174-75
   limitations of, 175
   Palm Query Application (PQA), 175
WRAP = attribute, scrolling text box, 191

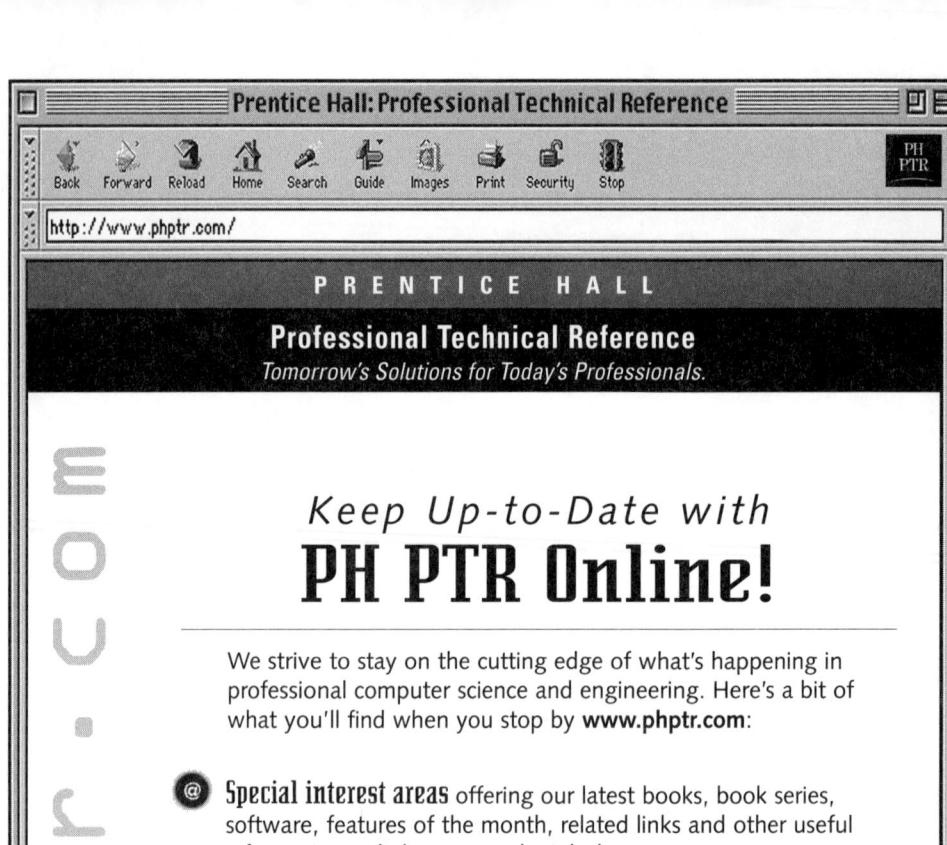

PRENTICE HALL
Professional Technical Reference
Tomorrow's Solutions for Today's Professionals.

Keep Up-to-Date with PH PTR Online!

We strive to stay on the cutting edge of what's happening in professional computer science and engineering. Here's a bit of what you'll find when you stop by **www.phptr.com**:

@ Special interest areas offering our latest books, book series, software, features of the month, related links and other useful information to help you get the job done.

Deals, deals, deals! Come to our promotions section for the latest bargains offered to you exclusively from our retailers.

$ Need to find a bookstore? Chances are, there's a bookseller near you that carries a broad selection of PTR titles. Locate a Magnet bookstore near you at www.phptr.com.

What's new at PH PTR? We don't just publish books for the professional community, we're a part of it. Check out our convention schedule, join an author chat, get the latest reviews and press releases on topics of interest to you.

✉ Subscribe today! Join PH PTR's monthly email newsletter!

Want to be kept up-to-date on your area of interest? Choose a targeted category on our website, and we'll keep you informed of the latest PH PTR products, author events, reviews and conferences in your interest area.

Visit our mailroom to subscribe today! **http://www.phptr.com/mail_lists**

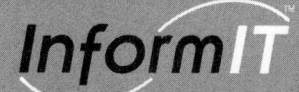

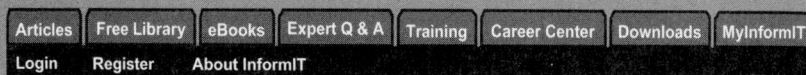

RELY ON
Essential Guides for ALL the Web Skills You Need!

Everything a working professional needs to get up and running on today's hot Web tools and technologies.

**ESSENTIAL DESIGN
FOR WEB PROFESSIONALS**
BY CHARLES J. LYONS

© 2001, Paper, 262 pp., 0-13-032161-3

**ESSENTIAL PHP
FOR WEB PROFESSIONALS**
BY CHRISTOPHER COSENTINO

© 2001, Paper, 188 pp., 0-13-088903-2

**ESSENTIAL ASP
FOR WEB PROFESSIONALS**
BY ELIJAH LOVEJOY

© 2001, Paper, 300 pp., 0-13-030499-9

**ESSENTIAL FLASH 5
FOR WEB PROFESSIONALS**
BY LYNN KYLE

© 2001, Paper, 261 pp., 0-13-091390-1

**ESSENTIAL GIMP
FOR WEB PROFESSIONALS**
BY MICHAEL J. HAMMEL

© 2001, Paper, 352 pp., 0-13-019114-0

**ESSENTIAL COLDFUSION 4.5
FOR WEB PROFESSIONALS**
BY MICAH BROWN & MICHAEL FREDRICK

© 2001, Paper, 250 pp., 0-13-040646-5

Also Available:

**ESSENTIAL JAVASCRIPT
FOR WEB PROFESSIONALS**
BY BARRETT, LIVINGSTON, & BROWN
© 2000, Paper, 208 pp., 0-13-013056-7

**ESSENTIAL PERL 5
FOR WEB PROFESSIONALS**
BY BROWN, BELLEW, & LIVINGSTON
© 2000, Paper, 208 pp., 0-13-012653-5

**ESSENTIAL CSS & DHTML
FOR WEB PROFESSIONALS**
BY LIVINGSTON & BROWN
© 2000, Paper, 208 pp., 0-13-012760-4

**ESSENTIAL PHOTOSHOP 5
FOR WEB PROFESSIONALS**
BY EIGEN, LIVINGSTON, & BROWN
© 2000, Paper, 304 pp., 0-13-012833-3

Prentice Hall PTR
WWW.PHPTR.COM/ESSENTIAL

ORDERING INFORMATION:

SINGLE COPY SALES
Visa, Master Card, American Express, Checks, or Money Orders only
Tel: 515-284-6761 / Fax: 515-284-2607
Toll-Free: 800-811-0912

GOVERNMENT AGENCIES
Pearson Education Customer Service
(#GS-02F-8023A), Toll-Free: 800-922-0579

COLLEGE PROFESSORS
Desk or Review Copies—Toll-Free: 800-526-0485

CORPORATE ACCOUNTS
Quantity, Bulk Orders totaling 10 or more books. Purchase orders only — No credit cards.
Toll-Free: 800-382-3419

INTERNATIONAL ORDERING:

CANADA
PEARSON EDUCATION CANADA
Ms. Michelle Bish — Tel: 416 386 3613
Email: Michelle.Bish@pearsoned.com

UNITED KINGDOM — Europe, Middle East & the Continent of Africa
PEARSON EDUCATION EUROPE
Mr. Jonathan Hardy — Tel: (44) 20 7 447 2149
Email: Jonathan.Hardy@pearsoned-ema.com

NETHERLANDS
PEARSON EDUCATION
Mr. Fred Cremers — Tel: 31206142912
Email: Fred.Cremers@pearsoned-ema.com

GERMANY & AUSTRIA
MARKT & TECHNIK
Ms. Denniss Brunnotte — Tel: (49) 89 46003 262
Email: DBrunotte@pearson.de

SWITZERLAND
MARKT & TECHNIK VERTRIEBS AG
Mr. Patrick Frei — Tel: 041 747 47 47
Email: Patrick.Frei@pearson.ch

FRANCE
CAMPUS PRESS
Mr. Patrick Ussunet — Tel: 33 (1) 44-54-51-10
Email: Patrick.Ussunet@pearson.fr

SPAIN
PEARSON EDUCATION ESPANA
Mr. Daniel Heredero
Email: Daniel.Heredero@pearsoned-ema.com

AUSTRALIA
PEARSON EDUCATION AUSTRALIA
Ms. Bridget Holland — Tel: (61) 2 9454 2327
Email: Bridget.Holland@pearson.com.au

**ASIA & PACIFIC RIM COUNTRIES
(Excluding Japan, China, Hong Kong)**
PEARSON EDUCATION ASIA PTE. LTD.
Mr. Steven Lim — Tel: (65) 378 0226
Email: Steven.Lim@pearson.com.sg

HONG KONG, CHINA
PEARSON EDUCATION NORTH ASIA LTD.
Ms. Cheran Leung — Tel: (852) 2960 2707
Email: CheranL@pearsoned.com.hk

TAIWAN
PEARSON EDUCATION TAIWAN
Ms. Amy Cheng — Tel: 886-2-27365155
Email: AmyC@pearsoned.com.hk

JAPAN
PEARSON EDUCATION JAPAN
Mr. Toshiyuku Mizutani — Tel: (81) 3 3365 9079
Email: Toshiyku.Mizutani@pearson.com.jp

MEXICO, CENTRAL AMERICA & CARIBBEAN
PEARSON EDUCACION LATIN AMERICA
Ms. Nora Valencia — Tel: (525) 387 0877
Email: Nora.Valencia@pearsoned.com